The gloves are off...

PADDY KENNY

WITH DANNY HALL

verticaleditions.com

Front cover image: Richard Markham Photography
Back cover image: Tony O'Brien/EMPICS Sport

First published in the United Kingdom in 2020 by Vertical
Editions, Unit 41 Regency Court, Sheffield, S35 9ZQ

VERTICAL
editions
www.verticaleditions.com

Follow us on Twitter:
@VerticalEds
@PaddyKenny17

ISBN 978-1908847188

A CIP catalogue record for this book is
available from the British Library

Printed and bound by Jellyfish Print
Solutions, Swanmore, Hants

To Beth, Jonjo,
Kaelin and Ashlin.
You are my world.

CONTENTS

I first became aware of Paddy Kenny when I was in charge of Bury and a friend telephoned me to say he had seen this kid playing for Bradford Park Avenue and that he would recommend him to me. I went to see Paddy in action and we signed him straightaway. That was back in 1998 and I kept signing him until 2016 after that! My friend said that Paddy was a little overweight, but I could kick him into being a top-class goalkeeper and I liked what I saw immediately, especially when I met him for the first time. What struck me was that Paddy was hungry and determined to change his life, but also very humble.

I wanted to give him some experience in a man's league, so I sent him up to Whitby Town for two months on loan. A couple of weeks later I remember vividly a phone call from Paddy one evening. "Gaffer, I've never known anywhere as cold as this," he said. I told him that it was all part of making him a man and that he should keep warm by running across his 18-yard box when the ball was at the other end of the pitch!

I remember telling my assistant, Mick Jones, about that conversation and the both of us laughed our heads off at the thought of Paddy freezing on the coast. In fairness Whitby made him grow up a lot and, when he returned to us at Bury, he soon got his opportunity in goal. I consequently signed Paddy a further four times and had some of the best times in my career with him – and a few hair-raising moments, too!

I'll never forget the feeling of pride I had, having picked him up from Park Avenue and nurturing him for all those years, to then see him represent his country. I can still picture the moment I told him, after getting the notification that he had been called up to the Republic of Ireland squad for the first time while he was at Sheffield United. The smile on his face just seemed to go on and on. It made me realise how much hard work he'd put in, to reach the point when he was good enough to play for his country – which, deep down, is what every player really wants to achieve.

We were promoted together with United and Queens Park Rangers, and Paddy was instrumental in both. So, what makes a good goalkeeper? I always say they're the ones who make the least mistakes. And I could count the number Paddy made while playing for me on my hands. Off the pitch, Paddy was such a likeable lad in the dressing-room and I loved having him around. I could not begin to tell you all my stories regarding Paddy – and I look forward to seeing if he mentions all our escapades in this book!

During our time at QPR, Paddy won both the players' player of the year and supporters' player of the year awards in one season. The awards night sticks in my head because, halfway through the night, Adel Ta-arabt walked out and later texted me, saying he could not believe that he hadn't won the awards. "Don't worry, son," I told him. "I've just won the Championship with you lot, and I won't win manager of the year either!" And I didn't!

Paddy certainly deserved his awards that season. The players' player of the year is always the one any footballer wants to win, because to have your fellow teammates voting for you is the biggest accolade they can receive. All the lads at QPR knew that Paddy was always nine out of 10 on a match day, come rain or shine, and that gave that team a feeling that we were invincible. Other teams knew they had to play well just to get through our lads, but then they had to beat the best goalkeeper in the league – a difficult feat to achieve, as his number of clean sheets that season proved.

The nicest thing I can say about Paddy – apart from what a quality goalkeeper he was – is that, when I saw him, he always made me smile. And my days always passed quicker when he was around. He is a colossus of a man, but just a big soft kid underneath.

- Neil Warnock, 2020

PROLOGUE

Wembley. It's the home of football, where dreams are made. One of my most vivid early Wembley memories is of Wimbledon beating Liverpool in the 1988 FA Cup final, with Dave Beasant saving a penalty under the famous Twin Towers. I played *Wembley* as a kid in Halifax, the game where you shoot at one net and go through to the next round if you score. I always dreamed of appearing there one day.

But not like this.

I had actually made my Wembley debut a few months earlier. It was the summer of 2009 and I had played for Sheffield United in the play-off final to Burnley. We lost 1-0 – my second play-off final defeat, in six years – and I had gone away to lick my wounds when I got a call to tell me I had failed a drugs test. My first instinct was to laugh, but it turned out to be no joke and a few weeks later, I was back at Wembley. This time, I was in a suit, sitting nervously in a hospitality box rather than running out onto that famous hallowed turf. And now, there was more than promotion on the line. It was my career. My livelihood. My life.

Eighty thousand people had watched me at Wembley on my last visit, but this time my audience was three strangers in suits, sitting behind a table. I told them what had happened, that I had taken six ChestEze tablets over three nights to help me to sleep before our semi-final against Preston. It turned out that the tablets contained ephedrine, a banned substance. I didn't even know what ephedrine was and, even if I did, I would have needed to take 50 or 60 of these tablets, just kick off, just to get a 20-minute buzz. As a goalkeeper, that wouldn't have been any use to me anyway and when one of the suits said that the panel accepted I hadn't taken ChestEze to enhance my performance, I thought to myself: *No shit.*

Under the table, my QC kicked me and pushed a piece of paper across the table in front of me. "No ban," it read. My heart raced.

But then the suit spoke again. They were doing me for negligence. I got nine months.

Nine. Months. Banned.

I could see and hear him speaking, but I couldn't take it in.

Before long my name was all over the 'papers and TV. *"Sheffield United goalkeeper Paddy Kenny given nine-month ban for failing drug test"* was the headline in the *Daily Telegraph*. It was similar in papers like the *Daily Mirror* and the *Daily Mail*. I was big news now, it seemed, and it suddenly felt a world away from my early days in Halifax, kicking a ball around without a care in the world. Maybe I thought about those times when I drove back north after leaving Wembley. Maybe I thought about my family. Maybe I thought about the future. I honestly couldn't tell you. It was just a blur.

Then the questions began in my head. How had I got to this point? Was my career over?

And, most vividly... *Where the fuck do I go from here?*

1

A CLOSE CALL

One eighth of an inch. Three millimetres, give or take. It sounds like nothing, doesn't it? But that is how close I came to having a very different life entirely. I came within three millimetres of not playing professional football, full stop, let alone featuring on some of the game's greatest stages and against some of its greatest names. Those international caps on my wall would belong to someone else and I would have been sat at home, watching Premier League games on TV rather than being right there and in the middle of the action. Just an eighth of an inch more and all that I achieved in my career would have been someone else's dream. It's crazy how life can pan out sometimes; how the smallest thing can almost change everything.

It happened back in my hometown of Halifax. I was born and raised in a small corner of the West Yorkshire town and one of the best things about life in Pellon was the golf course that sat a decent tee shot from my front door, called West End. I liked a bit of golf when I was younger – although really, by that, I mean I liked nicking golf balls from the greens at West End. There was one favourite hole in particular – a long par five up a really steep hill. Me and a few mates would sit up in the trees and wait for the sound of the golfers teeing off. If they connected well, the ball would fly up that hill and we would pounce. Out of the tree, onto the course, ball in pocket. Job done. The golfers probably knew what was coming, but there was no way that they were getting up that hill in time to do anything about it. It was the perfect crime.

Then one day, it wasn't. I knew the routine like clockwork by that point and waited, as usual, for the *thwack* of club on ball before jumping out of the tree. The grass on my side of the wall was long and unkempt, but I knew every inch of it like the back of my hand. Or I usually did. This time there was a problem – in the shape of a broken bottle hiding in the long grass. I fell straight onto it and the glass sliced straight through my skin. My knee was absolutely gaping. The glass had cut me wide open and the damage was so deep that I needed three layers of stitches to connect the muscle and skin and whatever else is under there back together again. Despite all that, I had still been fortunate. A doctor told me later that I was one eighth of an inch away from losing the feeling in my left leg. Forever.

I was 10 years old.

That fateful day had significance in the Kenny family anyway. It was my late grandma's birthday and my mum was at the cemetery when I was rushed to A&E by a neighbour because my dad didn't drive. My mum remembers sitting by the grave, daydreaming and wishing her mum a happy birthday, when her peace and quiet was shattered by the sound of someone breathlessly shouting her name and telling her that her Patrick had hurt himself and she needed to go straight to the hospital. I am a parent now and I can only imagine how terrifying it must have been to hear those words, and what worries must have been running through her head as she rushed to A&E.

I ended up in the operating theatre for three hours and I will never forget that experience for as long as I live. They first had to clean all the glass and other crap out of my knee before they even thought about stitching me up and I was awake throughout the whole thing. I could feel everything. I screamed my little lungs out in agony while 37 stitches were put in and to this day, I can't feel anything in that small area of my knee. I can still picture my mum and dad with me in that room, holding my hands and trying to distract me while the surgeon got to work. They tried everything to calm me down and, looking back, it's a little bit ironic that the only thing that worked was the promise of a present when we left hospital. Golf clubs!

Maybe they thought I would get in less trouble if I was actually on the course when I was meant to be, rather than running on there to nick balls? About a fortnight later I slipped on the snow on my crutches and could feel a weird, dripping sensation in my knee. My mum had to take the top bandages off every single night, to change and tighten them, and this time the bandage underneath was absolutely caked in blood. The wound had split straight back open again and the surgeons couldn't agree whether it was worth stitching again. The alternative was letting it scab over and heal for about three months but thankfully, the surgeon decided to restitch it. He put me to sleep this time, which saved me a lot of pain and spared my parents from having to buy me any more sports equipment, and also made sure I got a splint the second time around. It worked – within a few weeks, my dad had me back out and playing football again.

We couldn't afford the luxury of knee pads or anything like that to cushion the wound, so he improvised with a few leftover lengths of carpet and the stuffing out of an old cushion. He stitched the carpet together on three sides, filled it and sellotaped it to my knee. I played football for six months like that! All because we didn't have any spare money for proper bandages. When it came to pulling the tape off, I was in absolute agony every time. But I had no-one to blame but myself and the scar is still there today, in the shape of a number seven. Maybe it *was* my lucky number.

I loved football so much, though, that I am sure I would have found a way of continuing to play, *somehow,* even if the worst had happened with my leg. I was absolutely football-mad as a kid. As far back as I can remember, I was a goalkeeper and my entire life pretty much revolved around either kicking a ball around or trying to stop one. When I wasn't playing football, I was at an adventure playground called Ling Bob, which was about five minutes from my house. The people who ran it would take us on bike rides or trips away, or we would go camping. Me and my mates would leave home at 10 in the morning and we wouldn't come back until it was dark, but our parents knew that we were safe and being looked after. When I look back now, my upbringing was unbelievable – and I mean that in a good way. The world has changed so much since I came into it on May 17th, 1978.

I think it was a far simpler time. Kids now seem to have games consoles and mobile phones from a young age. Such luxuries didn't really exist when I was a kid and, even if they did, we would never have dreamed of affording them. There were no texts or phone calls from mum – we would be out and playing football for 10 hours straight and she knew exactly where I was. The only issue was coming home and facing her when I had ripped my tracksuit bottoms, diving to stop a shot from my mates. You know how people say that no-one ever *actually wants* to be a goalkeeper? That's absolute bollocks. I always did! Being right in the middle of the action, when the ball is bouncing around and the boots are flying and you can be the hero and maybe the difference between winning a game and losing? *Bring it on*, I thought.

The sense of freedom we had as kids was brilliant, but there's no dressing it up – Pellon was rough. I always thought it was strange that I could go wherever I wanted to play football all day but, if I was out on my bike, I wasn't allowed off our street! Whether my mum and dad didn't trust me on the bike or thought someone might nick it off me, I never found out. But I have an idea. There were a lot of kids who just wanted to cause trouble all the time: kids that did drugs and drank, kids that just hung around and sniffed glue all day. My group of friends were never into any of that shit. We just wanted to play football – that, rather than sticking stuff up our nose or going out thieving, was our idea of fun.

At the same time Pellon also had a sense of community that you only seem to get among working-class people. It was a typical council estate and everyone knew each other somehow. I'm friends on Facebook now with people that I was shit-scared of when we were kids and I have a laugh with them, telling them I used to go home a different way from school to avoid them! But I would not change a thing about the way I was brought up and one of the fondest early memories is of the Ling Bob playground, and the bloke who ran it. Graham Bedford treated us all like his own kids and proper looked after us. I spent a lot of time with him growing up, but sadly the place has shut down now. I think that's a shame because anything that keeps kids off the streets and away from trouble has to be a positive in my book. I'll never forget the day I turned 15 and I found out that I was too old to go to Ling Bob. It honestly felt like someone had taken both my legs off!

I soon found something to fill the void, though. By that point I had actually been working for three years after picking up a milk round when I was 12 from Mick Galvin, who played a big part in my life. It was damn hard work, getting up at four in the morning, but to earn £25 a week at that age felt incredible. My mum drilled it into me from when I was young that I had to pay my way and a tenner of my wages went to her for board. But the rest of it was all mine. Fifteen quid a week. I felt like Rockefeller – although I bet he didn't stink of milk all the time.

Mum and Dad never really had much. My dad's name is actually William, but everyone knows him as Paddy. When he was younger, his brothers and sisters couldn't say William for some reason. Paddy was easier to say, so it stuck all his life! Him and my mum Mary always worked, and worked damn hard, to make sure their kids never went without, but there were never really any luxuries in our lives. Nowadays I'm lucky enough to be able to take my kids out for food all the time but, with my mum and dad, having fish and chips at the end of a week was a real treat! There was no silver spoon in our mouths, that's for sure. We had one of those TVs that needed 50p in the back to work and I remember the gasman knocking on the door because of our dodgy meter. But I wouldn't change a minute of it for the world because of the things that an upbringing like that teaches you; respect, humility and, probably above all, the value of working bloody hard.

Once, I got up to do my milk round and was so tired that I didn't realise we'd been burgled overnight. Our house didn't have double glazing, so someone just smashed one of the windows, put a hand through and opened it from the inside. They took the TV, the video recorder and whatever else they thought was valuable. I woke up at 4am for my milk round, walked through the living-room like a zombie and didn't even notice. There was a big space where the TV should have been and glass all over the floor. I don't know how I didn't notice the TV had gone. It was one of those big-backed ones. Absolutely huge. I'm not even sure how they managed to lift it, never mind get it out through the window!

Those early starts became part of my early-life routine. From being 12 years old I worked from half-four in the morning until 7.30am before running home and trying furiously to scrub the smell of milk off me before school. I got that out of the way and then it was time to get to Ling Bob, or in the summer play football until it went dark, before getting home, going to bed and then doing it all again the following day. Nowadays, asking a kid to work before school would probably be seen as child cruelty or something, but back then I knew no different – and didn't mind anyway.

I had seen how hard my mum and dad worked to provide for their kids and some of that probably rubbed off on me. Although we didn't have much left over, they worked their arses off for us. Everything we owned seemed to be out of a catalogue and paid for weekly – "on the tick," it used to be called – and everyone on the estate was in the same boat. Dad worked for the water board and later repaired the roads, leaving for work at six in the morning and getting home at six at night. Mum was mostly a cleaner with a spell as a dinner lady thrown in somewhere along the way. We went to Blackpool every year for our holidays and they had to break a leg to afford that. It suited me just fine, though. I loved Blackpool; the seaside, the 2p machines and, most of all, the bingo.

Me and my brother, Sean, used to go to Pat's Bingo religiously. We were pretty much inseparable all through our childhoods. We lived in a three-bedroomed house, so there was a spare room, but we always wanted to share. Like all kids we had fallings-out about stupid stuff, but since growing up, we've never had a cross word with each other. Sean was born four years after me, but we were still unbelievably close and we always wanted to be together as kids. It probably helped that despite the age difference, we were on the same intelligence level! He was miles cleverer than me and we spent hours hanging about with a next-door neighbour called Lee Hand and his younger sister. Jessica was a really pretty girl and Sean was really close to her. Then one day she died suddenly, at about 10 years old, and it hit him really hard.

Despite all my efforts I could never get Sean to share my love of football and, although he did occasionally kick a ball at me in the back garden, I could tell his heart was never quite fully in it. One Christmas my mum and dad bought us a mountain bike, out of the catalogue, and they had to leave us on Christmas morning while they sorted out the mess from Christmas Eve at a club she worked at. Whatever we did, she told us, we weren't allowed to get up until they got back. The door had hardly shut and me and Sean were downstairs, rooting through our presents. They'll never know, we thought. Of course they were a step ahead of us – courtesy of some paper they'd put on the back of the door so they knew it had been opened!

The bike was an absolute beauty. A mate of mine had got one as well for Christmas so we were out on Christmas Day, messing about and jamming on the brakes so whoever was behind had to stop suddenly. But eventually, we tried that trick one too many times. I didn't see the brake lights and flew at full speed straight into the back of my mate. My front wheel buckled and the brand new bike, just a few hours old, was completely knackered. I wheeled it all the way back home and insisted that I had no idea what had happened to it. My mum ended up sending it back and saying it had arrived like that! Can you imagine them falling for that nowadays? I can't. But the catalogue took it back and sent out another one for us. I'm not going to say which company it was, though… I might have to pay the cost of the bike back!

Life as a kid in Pellon was fairly normal for the time, but I was never sure how many other people on that Halifax council estate had a little tub of holy water hanging off the wall and shamrocks all over the house. My upbringing was very Irish – my dad is from Longford – and everything in our house was Irish-focused. We had to bless ourselves before we went upstairs and, although I don't follow religion too closely as an adult, we went to church every Saturday without fail. Mum still has the holy water at home to this day.

As a kid I supported Ireland in major sporting events and the green and gold was a big part of my life, even in our little corner of West Yorkshire. Both my mum's parents were Irish and my dad's family moved to England when he was still very young. Both his parents had died by the time he was 10 years old and he was brought up by his brothers and sisters. What I've never been too sure about is why they ended up settling in Halifax when they could have quite literally gone anywhere in England. Imagine that conversation? "Let's go to Halifax! It rains every day, it's cold…"

I'm just glad they did. It does seem to rain every day and it is cold. But it's also home, and I wouldn't have swapped it for anywhere on earth.

2

A LOVE OF THE GAME

The Shay, Halifax Town's home ground, was a strange old place. Back in the day the main stand was probably only 20 rows deep and there was a big speedway track all the way around the pitch. One of the other stands was basically a tarmacked hill and, if people couldn't afford to pay the money to get into the ground, they used to climb up the slope and watch the game from the bus station that overlooked the pitch. Halifax's first team wasn't in much better shape than their ground at the time but, to me, my hometown club still represented my biggest and best chance of being taken on as a YTS and getting a foot on the lowest rung of the football ladder.

I had caught someone's eye at Halifax through playing for a combination of my school, my Sunday League team and for the West Yorkshire representative side. An invitation to train with Halifax followed and although we didn't play any actual matches, I thought I had done enough to be taken on their Youth Training Scheme. I had trained well, progressing through the levels at school and with West Yorkshire and winning everything. Then me, my mum and dad were called into a meeting with a bloke called George Mulhall in a poky office at the Shay and we were told that they didn't think I was tall enough to be a goalkeeper.

Fuck, that was tough to hear. The irony was that a few months later I had a growth spurt and shot up to about six foot. But by then it was too late and the next time I returned to the Shay, it was on the wrong side of the touchline as far as I was concerned. I was with my mates, standing on the tarmacked area opposite the main stand, convinced that my football journey was over.

To be fair to Halifax, I think they knew that I had something, ability-wise. But genetics were against me, simple as that. Mum and Dad aren't the tallest and I wasn't either. By this point I was 15 years old and Halifax probably presumed I wasn't going to get any bigger. Then, within six months, I had shot up. What can you do? I can't blame George for that, if it was even his decision in the first place. He was actually a really nice bloke. He had played for Aberdeen in his native Scotland before moving to Sunderland and had two spells as manager of Halifax, almost 25 years apart. But at the time he was in charge of the kids, with his bald head and wisps of silver hair down the side, and he was the one who had to deliver the bad news. "You bastard," I thought.

I had shuffled into his office with my mum and dad and stared at the ground nervously until I heard the words, in that Scottish drawl, tumble out of his mouth. "Unfortunately, we're not giving Patrick a YTS," Mulhall said. "He's too small. We don't think he'll ever make a goalkeeper." I remember being in total shock and my dad reacting, in his own way. He stood up, booted a chair over and leaned over George's desk, pointing in his face. "I will prove you wrong, you Scotch cunt," he said. Those were his exact words. "Mary, we're going," he added, before marching out of the room with me and my mum in tow.

The journey home seemed to last a lifetime and Dad had still not calmed down when we made it through the front door. "Get your gloves and boots," he said to me. "We're off down Ling Bob with the dog." That was our training routine – we'd go to the local park to walk our dog while my dad pelted balls at me, with his steel toe-cap boots on. I loved it, diving around in the mud. But not that day. Mulhall's words were still ringing around my head. *We don't think he'll ever make a goalkeeper.*

"I don't want to go," I told my dad.

"Get your boots and gloves," he said. "We're going down with the dog."

I just wasn't in the mood. "Dad," I repeated. "I don't want to go." I could hear his voice get a little sharper, the volume raising a few notches.

"Get your *fucking* boots and..."

Now I knew he meant business, so did as I was told. We went through our usual routine – Dad toe-pegging balls at me while the dog ran around in the park – but I did not want to be there one bit. With all the respect in the world to Halifax, if they didn't think I was good enough, who else would? They were slowly slipping out of the Football League and were on the verge of starting what ended up being a long spell in the Conference. I thought my chance was gone: in that situation, who wouldn't?

I wasn't very good at schoolwork and didn't get the best results when I left, so real-world opportunities were hardly coming at me from left, right and centre. But I knew I had to do something. My attitude was very much: "Right, come on… life goes on. You've got to get on with it. Go and get a job." My dad had taken the "I'll prove you wrong approach" with Mulhall, but the same thoughts never entered my head. I just think it was his way of dealing with the bad news. Dad was always the stricter of my parents and, when he was mad, we used to get the slipper or a flip-flop across the arse. Sometimes he'd switch it up and throw it. You maybe can't imagine that hurting, but I can assure you it did!

Dad was a dirty bastard on a football pitch, but from what I understand, he could play as well. Both him and my uncle Jimmy, another 'keeper in the family, played at the top level in Halifax and Dad had the chance to go for trials at professional clubs when he was younger. But he loved his ale too much and would rather go on the piss. He was always more ruthless when it came to my football career because he always knew I had *something,* and at that crucial point in my career it was him who really pushed me rather than me actually wanting to do it. I don't know if he knew that he had missed his opportunity to do something and didn't want me to miss out in the same way, but it was *ruthless* at times. I would come off the pitch after a game and Mum would be like mums are: "Well done, love!" But if I hadn't played well, Dad wouldn't hold back. "You're shit!" he would say to me. "Did you have your boots on the wrong feet or something?"

If that happened in the present day, Dad probably would have got reported for bullying me or something. But I had so much respect for him – and fear as well. I had to do what he said or I would get that slipper thrown at me again! But I realise now that he was doing it out of love for me and I wouldn't have achieved anything in the game if he hadn't pushed me like he did. I could very easily have fallen out of love with football completely – and God knows what would have happened in my life then.

Dad became a goalkeeper towards the back end of his career, but even then couldn't always stay on the pitch for the full 90 minutes. Some of the stories I have heard about him are frightening. Back then players were banned for months if they were sent off and so a red card meant you would miss huge chunks of the season. Even that didn't stop him. Once, one of Dad's teammates broke his leg while wearing a brand-new pair of boots. The game was stopped until the ambulance arrived and, as the lad was loaded onto the stretcher, my dad sprinted over and nicked his boots off his feet! "You won't be needing these for a while, will you?" he asked.

I watched him play a lot and remember one game at Denholme, on a pitch with a real slope. The ball was at the other end of the pitch, so Dad came around the back of his net to have a kickabout with me. The other team won the ball back, broke quickly and scored into the empty net. Understandably his teammates weren't too happy, but Dad wasn't having any of it. He told them where to go and threw his gloves down on the grass. "My son comes first," he said and with the game still going on, he stormed off for a shower before buggering off home. He had, as we say in Yorkshire, the right face on!

Watching him taught me so much, as did later playing alongside him and most of my other family members in open-age men's football. I was getting smashed every week by big, bruising centre-forwards and learned far more on those parks pitches than any YTS deal could have taught me. Six or seven of my old mates from Halifax got taken on and, while I was out learning the game, they were cleaning boots and sweeping the changing-room. Only one of those lads, Noel Horner, signed a professional deal and by the time I came through at Bury, he was more or less out of the game.

It really can be a minefield. Kids do grow at different stages and different abilities come out at different times. But who knows what would have happened if I'd have been taken on at Halifax? I could have been there for two years and then, *boom*. That could have been me, done and dusted, spat out into the real world. Instead I had time to learn a new career and play men's football, rediscovering a love of the game that I had first felt playing as a kid for a team called Boothtown. What a team we had there, by the way. In some games we would be about 25-0 up and I'd come out of goal for the last 10 minutes and play upfront. I'd end up with 10 goals at the end of some seasons, just from doing that!

But it was always the thrill of stopping goals that appealed to me most, rather than scoring them. When I was a baby, Mum would put me in one of those round play-pen things when she wanted to do something else and there must have been 20 footballs in there. Whenever anyone asked what I wanted for Christmas, the answer was always the same: gloves, boots and a football. Mum probably didn't appreciate my love of diving about when I went out to play football all day and came home with rips in my clothes and covered in mud, but nothing could stop me.

Thinking back now, I can't really put my finger on when or why my love of goalkeeping began. I loved diving about, but then I got to a point where I realised I was actually all right at it. Others started to notice as well and our little group who used to play together after school were picked for West Yorkshire. Our school won the Halifax Cup to qualify for the West Yorkshire Cup and in the first round we were 5-0 down at half-time. We came back to draw 6-6, and won the replay 1-0 on the way to lifting that trophy as well. That got us into the Yorkshire Cup, playing schools from all over the county, and we pissed that. That's how good we were. There were some brilliant players in that group and I was the only one who didn't get taken on at Halifax.

For as long as I live, I will never forget being in that room at the Shay. In fairness to Halifax I was fairly short at the time, but it is still a big statement to tell a 15-year-old kid that he will never make a goalkeeper. I hadn't finished growing. I was always a stocky, little kid with big, curly hair, but I was never fat or anything. I had freckles and a big core flick. "Give me a chance," I thought.

I am by no means the first to have been rejected and make it back, though, and, although I think attitudes have improved on that front with young players, I wasn't the last either. Jamie Vardy is the stand-out example after being released by Sheffield Wednesday. He played for £30 at Stocksbridge Park Steels, but later won the Premier League and played for England. Ian Wright earned the same amount playing for Greenwich Borough, also in non-league, and he didn't do badly either!

Stories like that show that there is no right or wrong way to 'make it' in professional football and I don't think that going down the academy route necessarily means that a career in the game is any more of a certainty. There is obviously a benefit to being in that environment from a young age, but at the same time you don't know anything else except life at that club. My mates who were on the YTS at Halifax were basically slaves of the club, earning their keep, but that doesn't happen nowadays. Some clubs mollycoddle their young players and, when reality hits and these lads are released, they have no choice but to start working. A lot of them simply don't know how because they've never had to do it. I think that's a big problem nowadays – what do these kids do if and when that bad news arrives?

I would challenge anyone to prove that they had a better football education than the one I received on the pitches of the Halifax league. Instead of training with and playing against kids of my own age, I was working Monday to Friday and then playing open-age at the weekends. Then after the games I was out drinking with them as a 15-year-old with my fake ID. And those nights out definitely taught me a few things off the field as well!

On Saturdays I played on Ling Bob fields for St Columba's – they were managed by Mick Galvin, my old milk-round boss – and on Sundays I went in goal for Pellon Social Club. My dad was in charge of the team and that was tougher than you might imagine it would be. My first job early on a Sunday morning was to round up all the players who were still pissed, or out, from the night before. Then after I had put sawdust on the pitch, put the wooden goalposts up and whatever else, the game started and I got absolutely smashed all over. Every single week, without exaggeration. But it toughened me up so much and brought me on, as a player and a person. Suddenly teams from higher up the divisions in Halifax were asking me to join them.

The answer was always the same: "He's staying with his friends and family." My cousin, Paul Kenny, played at right back and my cousin, Tim Enright, and my brother, Tony Clarke, were also at centre-half, so I had them looking after me. I was still small, but I always had something about me. And I was a right cheeky little twat as well. I wasn't very good at kicking, so Tony used to take my goal-kicks for me. When the referee turned his back, he just used to kick it out of his hands! The other team would be going mental, but the ref hadn't seen it happen and just waved play on.

Tony did that for weeks and weeks until one day, being a clever bastard, I told him I wanted to give it a go. So when the ref's back was turned, I picked the ball up and booted it out of my hands – not knowing that the league had cottoned on and sent three officials to the game. It was the only time I'd tried it and I got caught and banned! We had some tough, tough players – a few of them were bouncers in town – and everyone knew not to mess with St Columba's on a Saturday.

It was similar on a Sunday, although a little bit more relaxed; nine times out of 10, the lads were still pissed from the Saturday night when they turned up in the morning, and another of my Sunday-morning jobs was to go around the local pubs and pick up their kit where they had left it the night before to go straight out. Lads who had been out together the night before would then kick the shit out of each other for 90 minutes on the park, and go for a few more beers after. In winter, when it was frosty and games got called off, there were queues outside a café in Halifax called the Beefeater. Everyone in Halifax went straight there for a full English breakfast if a match had been called off, while they waited for the pubs to open.

Before long I was joining my teammates on the piss, with the help of my fake ID and the lads in our team who worked as bouncers. I was 15 and going out with lads who were at least five or six years older than I was, so I was absolutely blind-drunk in no time. One of my teammates, Phil Lodge, lived on the same street as us and we became a running joke among the lads. "Get ready, Paddy and Lodgie are going to sneak off for the Nightrider tonight!" Before I knew it, Lodgie was tapping me on the shoulder. "I think you've had enough, Patrick… Come on, let's get something to eat and get off." I probably needed the help getting myself home most weeks… but the tight twat always made me pay his bus fare!

By the time I was almost old enough to get my own, real ID and drink legally, I began to graduate through the leagues in Halifax. I joined Stump Cross, who were in the top division, before signing for Ovenden in the West Riding League, which was an even better standard. In my first year at Stump Cross I think we finished second in the league and won two cups. Both finals went to penalties and I scored the winning spot-kick in one of them! Experiences like that and playing open-age football were some of the best things that ever happened to me. It wasn't the "conventional" route, but it toughened me up physically and helped me so much mentally as well. With every step up I felt increasingly confident that I could hold my own.

I was suddenly a long way away from the sights of Sunday League, watching the lads finish a fag and down a can of lager before kick-off. I was now playing teams further afield in places like Huddersfield and Leeds and little things, like grounds having barriers around the pitch, showed how much more professional the standard was. In the last game of the season we were top of the league and had to win our game to seal the title. We were 1-0 up with five minutes to go when I came to catch a long throw and the ball went straight through my hands. I thought I had literally let the title slip through my fingers. But their striker, who was about five yards out and facing an open goal, hit the top of the bar and we were champions. That was some celebration that night, too!

People who played with me at the time knew I had something about me, but it's a little bit ironic that I was originally told I was too small to be a goalkeeper. Then, throughout my career I was told in no uncertain terms that I was too big to be a goalkeeper! The truth, I like to think, is somewhere in the middle. And yes, Dad... we did prove him wrong in the end, didn't we?

3

THE REAL WORLD

As much as I loved travelling to every corner of Yorkshire, chucking myself around in goal and inevitably ending the weekend in some boozer or another, that did not pay the bills at the end of the month. The big, wide world beckoned. I had started full-time work as soon as I left school, loading and unloading lorries in a packing factory, until a neighbour called Mick Bagnall mentioned that Dixons of Halifax were looking for a toolmaker. Mick got me in there and I became a qualified engineer. I wouldn't have a clue what to do if you put me back in there now, but back then I was a fully-fledged toolmaker. Nowadays everything is made by CNC machines, but this was proper, hand-made stuff, using lathes and millers and grinders. Our factory made wire drainers for pots and the wire frames that go in car seats, things like that. It was hands-on stuff.

The factory had 50 or 60 machines with each one making a certain part. When they broke – which they did, all the time – our job was to take them apart, see which part had broken and then go and remake it to get the machine back up and running as soon as possible. Being honest, I absolutely loved it – although it was damn hard work – and at the time I thought that was where my life was going.

At the same time I had moved up the football levels again – to the dizzy heights of the UniBond League Division One, with Bradford Park Avenue. Locally they simply call themselves Avenue and I had been invited to train with them by Bobby Barr, who was from Halifax and their assistant manager at the time. The manager was a bloke called Trevor Storton, who played for Liverpool under Bill Shankly and won the UEFA Cup in the 1970s. I accepted Bobby's invitation and before I knew it, I was in the first team.

The only real downside from my point of view was having to give up playing for Pellon on Sundays, even if I couldn't let go completely. I used to run the line instead and I'm surprised I didn't get shot with some of the decisions that went in Pellon's favour. The difference between Sunday League and semi-pro level was absolutely huge, and life was hectic. I worked at Dixons from half-seven until half-five every day and trained with Avenue after work on Tuesday and Thursday nights before playing at the weekend. I would sometimes have to finish early if we had a midweek game and luckily my boss liked his football so always cut me a little slack.

Juggling both sides of my life was proving difficult, but that balancing act was something else that gave me an invaluable sense of perspective later in my life when I eventually got my football break. I had seen what life was like on the other side, working hard through the week to earn a living and basically playing football as a hobby.

Then I became a professional and towards the end of my career, played alongside people who didn't appreciate it at all. They would moan if training got moved forward and say it was too early. I sat there thinking: "Do you have any idea what it's like in the real world?" We were in training for an hour-and-a-half, maybe two hours at a push. I used to do that on the back of a 10-hour shift in a factory!

Life at Avenue was a definite eye-opener. There were a lot of ex-pros there, getting paid, at the time and everything was again a lot more professional than anything I had experienced before. The social side wasn't as good – I used to head back to Halifax to go out with my mates rather than my teammates – but after only three or four games Avenue gave me a contract. I was earning about £50 a game before, but the contract meant that I would get paid every week, whether I played or not. They clearly saw something in those few games that they liked because the decision wasn't for my benefit!

They were quite open about it – now I had a contract, they would get some money if someone else wanted to sign me. As far as I could see, it was a win-win scenario. The club were happy to protect their investment and I knew I was going to be paid every week no matter what. I earned £150 working through the week and then got that much again at the weekend from playing football. Remember when I thought I was Rockefeller with my £15 a week from the milk round? I was suddenly earning 20 times that amount and felt like I had won the lottery.

Trevor knew the score as an ex-player and tried to help me out, steering me in the right direction. I think he was another who saw something in me and was another big influence on my career early on. Sadly he passed away with cancer back in 2011, aged just 61. Under his valuable guidance, people began to talk about me.

"Why did he get binned off by Halifax again?" they would ask. I was 18 and playing well but technically, I wasn't very good at all. Any technique I had later in my career came much further down the line, when I eventually got to work with a goalkeeping coach. What I did have was a knack of making saves and keeping the ball out of the net, which is pretty handy for a goalkeeper. I see it now in my son, Jonjo. He's a goalkeeper and reminds me of me at his age. Technically, he's rubbish. I am completely honest with him about that. But when he pulls on the gloves and crosses that white line, he makes saves. I did the same thing and for a goalkeeper, that's what it's got to be all about.

That knack soon began to attract interest from elsewhere and things began to get really serious when I was invited down to the Midlands for a trial with Birmingham City. They were in Division One at the time and had just paid a million quid - a decent amount in 1998 - for Dele Adebola, so clearly meant business. Trevor put a good word in for me with someone he knew down there, but I found the whole experience horrible. Trevor Francis was their manager at the time and he was okay with me, but I didn't like it at all. I was in the same hotel as Adebola and away from home for five days, which I hated. I couldn't wait to go home on the weekend. And I had to use holiday days from Dixons to book the time off, too! But despite my homesickness, I must have impressed them and while they ummed and aahed about offering me a contract, another club made their move.

Legend has it that their manager came to watch an opposition striker and was impressed by the tubby lad in goal for Avenue. He says that he actually received a tip-off about me from an old pal. Either way I had a shit-hot game in front of a certain Neil Warnock and my life was about to change forever as a result.

4

HUMBLE BEGINNINGS

I watched him on a filthy night and he was out of condition, a porky young lad, but I just liked the look of him. And when we met I liked the way he was, he was a likeable rogue. I signed him, but we had Dean Kiely in goal so I sent him on loan to Whitby Town to get games. He rang me one night to say, 'Gaffer, it's that cold if we are attacking I can't feel me fingers'. I said to him, 'it will make Bury seem like Saint-Tropez when you come back.'
- Neil Warnock, The Independent, April 2011

Warnock wasn't kidding about Whitby, either. It was absolutely freezing. But it was his idea of toughening me up and, although I maybe didn't appreciate it at the time, it did the job. I thawed out, went back to the glorious warmth of Bury and soon became their No. 1 goalkeeper, after Dean Kiely was sold. I had no idea that it would be the start of a long and successful association with Warnock when he spent a few quid to sign me from Bradford Park Avenue in 1998 after being tipped off by Avenue boss Trevor Storton. Warnock came to watch me in a game, I played well and Bury invited me over for pre-season in the summer of 1998.

I figured that I had nothing to lose, so I accepted. In those days Bury played a little pre-season competition against their neighbours, Oldham and Rochdale, and both of our games against them finished in a draw and went to penalties. I saved two spot-kicks in both shoot-outs, which probably cemented any hunch that Warnock had about me, and I was offered a contract soon after. It wasn't long after I had become a qualified engineer with Dixons, which meant my wages doubled there, and on top of my earnings from Avenue, the offer from Bury was effectively a pay cut. Welcome to professional football!

I'm not sure if Birmingham suddenly got wind of Bury's interest, but all of a sudden there was an offer on the table from them as well after my trial there a few months earlier. There was no doubt that Birmingham were a bigger club than Bury – three years later they won the League Cup and qualified for Europe – but at the time both clubs were in Division One. Birmingham had a couple of experienced goalkeepers on their books, Ian Bennett and Kevin Poole, and Trevor and his assistant Bobby Barr took me to one side.

"If we were you, we'd choose Bury," they advised me. "You have more chance of playing there than at Birmingham." Deep down I knew they were right and followed their advice to sign at Gigg Lane. I had been a professional footballer for a grand total of two weeks when Dean was called up to the Republic of Ireland squad. Who do you reckon we had to play that weekend, with Dean missing and me as the only goalkeeper left at the club? Yep. Birmingham!

I was still unbelievably raw and when I trained on the Monday before the game, I was absolutely horrendous. Then the following day, Bruce Grobbelaar rocked up at the training ground! He was about 900 years old by this point and still had his trademark moustache. He also played in the game against Birmingham and, being honest, I was relieved. I was nowhere near ready to be chucked into league football.

I watched Bruce make his one and only Bury appearance in a 1-0 defeat – with my former hotel mate Dele Adebola scoring the winner – and he played two more games that season for Lincoln City before dropping down into the Conference with Northwich Victoria. I wonder if he remembers those days as fondly as his six league titles, three FA Cups and one European Cup!

Bruce was as funny as hell to be around in training. He was actually 41 at the time and obviously just still loved football because he certainly wouldn't have been at Bury at that time for the money. At one point Bruce played more than 300 consecutive games for that great Liverpool side of the '80s and is probably best remembered for his "jelly legs" performance in the 1984 European Cup final against Roma. I didn't see the wobbly legs when I trained with him, but Bruce was definitely a showman and, even when we were doing something as simple as volleying and catching the ball, he couldn't just throw it back to me.

He had to do something different, like chucking it behind his head or spinning it on his finger or whatever. To be fair, he could still play as well. But as soon as Dean came back from Ireland duty, Bruce was on his way and I was back in the reserves.

As Dean's career shows, he was an unbelievable goalkeeper and so, as a kid fresh out of non-league, I couldn't really have too many complaints. But I had gone from playing week in, week out at Avenue to being stuck in the reserves at Bury and it wasn't doing me too much good. So Warnock sent me to the coast for the last few months of that season. Whitby were in the UniBond Premier, a league higher than Avenue, and I remember us beating Lancaster City 1-0 on my debut. Apart from the frostbite my spell there was a brilliant experience and, by the time I returned to Gigg Lane, Bury were a Division Two club after being cruelly relegated.

For one year only the Football League changed their rules; instead of goal difference separating clubs on the same number of points in the table, "goals scored" was used instead. Bury finished on 47 points, level with Port Vale. Our goal difference was -25, five goals better than Vale's. In any other year we would have survived. But that season Vale scored 10 more goals than us, so they survived and we were down. To this day I have no idea why the rule was changed. Maybe it was to encourage more attacking play or something. I do know that it was immediately switched back and never revisited since, which probably shows how good an idea it was in the first place.

Relegation was heartbreaking, especially in that manner, but it also paved the way for me to get the chance I had been desperate for. The drop in division forced Bury to sell five players for decent money – including Chris Lucketti, Lenny Johnrose and Dean – and Dean was on the verge of a £1m move to Charlton when Warnock told me that I had five games to impress him, or he was bringing another goalkeeper in. *No pressure there then!* As it turned out, I ended up playing 53 times in both the 1999/2000 and 2000/2001 seasons, so the first five games obviously went well. Of course, there was the odd hiccup here and there. On my debut I was knocked clean out after five minutes!

I dropped every ball in the warm-up because I was so nervous and the day didn't get much better from there. I rushed out of my goal to get to a through ball and smashed straight into Gillingham's Nicky Southall, who had gone for the ball with his foot up. I was knocked unconscious and my face absolutely ballooned. Nowadays I would have been ruled out for about two or three weeks, but there was no such thing as "concussion protocol" in Division Two in the late 1990s. I woke up, got up and finished the game. We won 2-1 and it was only after the final whistle that someone suggested getting me checked out at hospital because the medical lads thought I had fractured my cheekbone. Warnock's five-game warning was going around in my head on the way to hospital and I remember thinking that it would be just my luck to be ruled out for ages. Luckily my face was fine and I played every game for the rest of the season.

Coming off the pitch wasn't an option. I had been brought up on the parks pitches of Halifax in the tough school of men's football, so being battered around wasn't exactly a new experience for me. I must admit I wasn't exactly used to getting knocked clean out, but it's part and parcel of being a goalkeeper, isn't it? Come round, pick yourself up and get on with the game. I think the fans there respected me for the way that I went about the game, but, even after establishing myself as Bury's No. 1 and winning the player-of-the-year award, I was still unbelievably shy and unsure of myself.

I had come into the professional game a lot later than many of my teammates and, while they had been in the set-up for years by that point and knew the score, I didn't have a clue about how it all worked. Even when I got into my mid-20s, I was still quiet and timid and it was only after I had played about 300 professional games that I finally came out of my shell. Later in my career I was seen as a big character in the dressing-room. But the thick skin that I have now was certainly not always there.

I had to learn with stuff that was chucked my way and it was something that came with experience. It wasn't anywhere near as bad in the early days, though, and Bury fans used to make me laugh on the pitch with their chants about me looking like Tyrone from *Coronation Street*. I didn't know who should have been more offended by that, me or him! There was the odd comment from the stands that was a little less flattering, but overall I loved the experience and learned so much. Like a lot of the lads, I couldn't afford to drive to training every day in my own car, so a few of us Yorkshire-based lads used to meet up in Huddersfield and travel in together on the M62 to save the petrol money.

There was no food laid on for the players, as some clubs do now, so we would stop off at a service station on the way back from training and pick up a meal deal. We would scoff the lot in the back of the car like pigs, sending bits of sandwich and crisps and pop flying everywhere. Can you imagine a group of professional footballers doing that now, eating at a motorway services every day after training? Forget the healthy eating problems – they would also be bankrupt in no time!

Unlike a few lads who were coming to the end of their careers and had experienced life at other clubs, I didn't know any different and, looking back, there was something brilliantly old school about Bury at that time. After games there would be crates of beer on the team bus for us and we would stop off for fish and chips on the way home from away matches. Terry Robinson, the chairman and chief executive, would sit at the front of the coach smoking while the players – on the way to a game, remember – would be at the back, coughing away as the smoke wafted down.

It was a brilliant time, but we couldn't mount a challenge for promotion back to Division One and, after Warnock had left in December 1999 to take over at his boyhood club, Sheffield United, we finished 15th that season – well clear of relegation, but also miles off the play-offs. One of the highlights of the season was beating our neighbours Blackpool 5-0 at their place and, shortly after he had left, Warnock called my mobile again.

"Keep doing what you're doing," he told me. "You never know... I might sign you one day." And that was it. Andy Preece had replaced Warnock as player-manager, but we were relegated in 2001/02 and I was preparing myself for a new challenge in Division Three when he pulled me into his office. There was a bid on the table for me from United. Bury, I heard later, owed the taxman just over 40 grand and were struggling to find the cash. By that point Terry had joined Warnock at Bramall Lane and a deal was struck, with Bury using the money they got for me to settle the tax bill. I was suddenly on my way to Bramall Lane, and a First Division club.

I was absolutely shitting myself.

5

BECOMING A BLADE

Described somewhat cruelly as looking like a pub footballer but playing like a Premiership goalkeeper, Paddy Kenny has been as vital a plank of Sheffield United's remarkable cup runs this season as the pace and midfield assurance of the two Michaels, Brown and Tonge.
- David Conn, The Independent, March 2003

The story didn't add exactly who had described me in those terms, but I think there is a compliment in there somewhere! I'm not sure if I was *quite* performing like a Premiership player, but I was certainly proud of my efforts at Bury. The amount of games I had played suggested they were quite happy with how I was doing as well and, although we were relegated to Division Three in 2001/02, that was as much down to the financial situation of the club as anything we were doing on the pitch. The club's money struggles eventually caught up with them 20 years down the line but even at the turn of the millennium, Bury had major financial worries.

The club was backed by a former stockbroker who lost about £20m on the market and, after he had quit, the bank also pulled their own financial support and the ground was remortgaged. Two men who were part of a takeover bid were later discovered to be convicted fraudsters and Bury went into liquidation, owing nearly £5m. But football rallied to help the club out and money was pledged from all over the world. Gordon Sorfleet, who was officially our Press officer, but was one of many working at the club who seemed to have 100 other jobs, ended up being named fan of the year by UEFA for his fundraising efforts and Bury were saved.

That time at least.

Even back then, the idea that Bury could go out of business was big news. It was a proud old club, winners of the FA Cup twice in three seasons in the early days, and suddenly journalists who wrote about finance were as interested in the club as those who covered football. It was obvious that the club would again have to cash in on their prized assets, but unlike the last time there weren't a lot of lads there who would command decent money. I know some people at Bradford Park Avenue were a bit pissed off that I went to United for such a small fee: they had read reports linking me with million-quid moves and were rubbing their hands together at the prospect of a few quid coming their way courtesy of the sell-on clause they had. I think they ended up with a couple of grand.

I didn't know a thing about the negotiation process, as many players don't. The first I heard about a move was when Andy Preece pulled me into his office and told me to get myself off to United. My agent at the time even agreed everything with my contract, without even asking me about money or anything like that. He just called me and told me to meet him at Bramall Lane. In fairness to him, I later found out that United were tripling the wage I had been on at Bury, to £1,200 - which seemed an incredible sum of money to me, and was far more than I would have dared ask for! Even before I heard about the wages, though, I knew this was an opportunity I couldn't turn down. I had loved my time at Bury, but this was a different level entirely – moving to the top end of Division One and to a club the size of Sheffield United. As I pulled into the Bramall Lane car-park for the first time, I was absolutely terrified.

Maybe Warnock sensed it because he did his best to reassure me. "It's the biggest club you will be at in your life," he said. "Just enjoy yourself and do what you can do – what I know you can do. No-one is up your arse. I'll just let you be. There is no pressure on you whatsoever." I can't lie, though – it felt as if there was. On the day I signed we played a friendly at Baslow and there were thousands of fans there. For a friendly. I had played in front of lower crowds at Bury for league games. *Oh wow, I thought to myself. What have I come to here?* All these years later, when I drive through Baslow to get to Bakewell and go past that tiny pitch, next to a kids' playground, I have a little smile to myself at the memory.

United were level on points with third-bottom Walsall when Warnock was appointed in 1999 and had won just four of their 21 league games. Warnock steadied the ship and guided them to 16th in the table that season, finishing 10th and 13th in the two campaigns that followed.

In the summer before I joined he made some big changes, shipping out lads like Lee Sandford and Bobby Ford and bringing some experienced pros in. The most experienced of them all was Stuart McCall, who was about 50 when he signed, but was still frighteningly good.

Warnock knew exactly what he would get from a player like Macca and he loved that. The same with lads like big Wayne Allison. You knew full well that he wasn't going to run any channels or beat anyone running with the ball, but the Chief would get battered by his centre-half for 89 minutes and, come the 90th, he would still be winning those headers.

Macca was a legend of the game after winning trophies galore at Rangers and I had watched players like Simon Tracey on TV before I signed. All of a sudden, I was in the same dressing room. Not that some of them would have even noticed, I bet. Rob Page told me later that a few lads thought I was actually called Kenny Paddy – no-one had a clue who I was and I was really too shy to make them aware. I'm not sure if it was someone's attempt to bring me out of my shell, but we went down to Warnock's part of the world, Cornwall, for my first pre-season and I was told that I was sharing a room with a shy and retiring full-back by the name of Rob Kozluk.

Kozzy's character is well-known throughout the game, but for anyone who has not come across him before, I am trying to think of the best way to describe him. The man is a fucking crackpot. On our first night away in these chalet-style things in Cornwall, Kozzy was bored – which was dangerous for him and, more importantly, for everyone else. "Come on," he said to me, beckoning me down to reception where he nicked a newspaper. He slid the 'paper under the doors of the other lads' rooms and poked their keys out of the doors and onto the 'paper before sliding it slid back out. The next morning my new teammates were having to climb out of windows and down trees to get out of their rooms. They knew exactly where to look – and I was an accomplice!

On the same trip we had an afternoon off and went for a game of golf – Kozzy and Michael Brown against me and Nick Montgomery. "Watch these two," Monty warned me. "They're proper cheats." Brownie was in the bunker, which must have been as deep as a house, and got a driver out before hitting his ball out of the bunker and about 200 yards onto the green. Now Brownie was an unbelievable player and sportsman, but that was a special shot, even for him. "How the fuck's he done that?"

I thought. Then a few seconds later we saw a tee spinning in the air. "You've hit it off the tee!" Monty shouted. Brownie still denied it and it ended up almost being one of the last things he ever did when our buggy toppled over and fell on top of him on the next hole. I don't know how he wasn't killed. We just tipped it back over and carried on the game. Killing the star player and Warnock's favourite... What a welcome to the club that would have been!

Kozzy wasn't scared of the classic pranks, either. He glued Brownie's brand-new Prada shoes to the dressing-room floor on a match day and once stole the false leg of our chairman Derek Dooley, God rest his soul. Kozzy was also a big part in the decision to put Colin Cryan's bed on the middle of a golf course, with Colin still asleep in it. As a player Kozzy was underrated, but he was priceless as a person around the changing-room. I remember a manager once saying that he was worth signing just to have among the players, even if he didn't play.

Every squad I have had any success with in my career has been full of good players, but more importantly good people, and that United dressing-room was one of those. Macca was class and still had it; Peter Ndlovu was a great player and Paul Peschisolido, our little Canadian, seemed to come off the bench in every game and nick us a goal. Brownie was a great character as well as a superb player and the likes of Monty, Phil Jagielka and Michael Tonge were just starting to come through the academy. There's a lot of talk about "team spirit" in football and I don't think you can overestimate how important it really is. You spend more time with your teammates off the pitch than you do on it, in hotels or on coaches or whatever, and you have to be able to chill out around training and games when the serious head is on. A squad of 25 lads cannot be serious 24/7, so that ability to take the focus off football, even for a small period of time, is so important. And in Kozluk we had one of the finest around.

Besides dealing with Kozzy and trying to avoid becoming the next name on his hit list, moving to United also introduced me to another novelty – my first proper goalkeeping coach. I was 24 years old. Even then Andy Leaning came in only part-time. Andy had a decent career in the game that was actually not too dissimilar to my own, at least in its early days. After he was released by York City, Andy played for York Railway Institute and Rowntree Mackintosh in the Northern Counties East League while working for British Rail. He played for United in the late '80s – his son, Jack, later became a professional cricketer with Yorkshire and Kent – and after hanging up his gloves and moving into coaching, Andy came in two days a week to work with me and the other United 'keepers at the time on a Tuesday and Thursday afternoon.

His help and guidance really improved my technique for the first time and after we had a bit of success in my first season at United, Andy became the first full-time goalkeeping coach I had worked with in my career. And he was one of the best around, too. Andy spotted straightaway that my arm got stuck under my body when I dived for the ball, so I couldn't use it if I had to react quickly and stop any follow-up shot. The problem was that I had been doing it for so many years, without being told, that it had become ingrained in my technique. In every session from then – day after day, week after week, month after month – Andy was on my case. "Your arm, your arm!" he would yell at me. Then at the end of one week, we had suddenly cracked it. "I haven't told you once about your arm," he smiled.

I had eight years at Bramall Lane with Andy – we later worked together again at Leeds under Warnock – and he did so much for my career. He knew how and when to work me hard, but he also knew when to ease off. He knew if I needed beasting and also when I needed leaving alone completely. We had such a good relationship and I had so much respect for him. He never shouted at me because he knew that doing that would just make me either switch off or push back. He pushed my buttons and got the best out of me. If I'd had a bad game or let in a soft goal, he knew that I didn't need telling – not straightaway anyway.

He'd leave it until our next training session and talk about it constructively. Most of the time I knew what I had done wrong, but he taught me so much as well and I still speak to him a lot even now, long after I have hung up my gloves. He was someone I would call for advice towards the back end of my career when we weren't working together: his biggest skill was knowing that you simply cannot treat every person the same way.

Andy used to insist that I told him if I'd been on the piss the night before. "At least then I know where I stand," he said. "If you've had a skinful, tell me. Otherwise, if you're a bag of shit in training, I won't know why." He made me a better goalkeeper and I would like to think that Andy takes some pride in what I achieved in the game because he played a big part in making it happen. We had some amazing nights together and also went through some really rough times when I was at my lowest. He was by my side through the good and the bad and at the end of it, is just a genuine bloke who was always honest and didn't blow smoke up my arse when it wasn't warranted. A lot of people talk about Warnock's man-management, and rightly so, but Andy had the same knack. I have no doubt that he treated me differently from the other goalkeepers he coached, but for me that is what good management is all about.

It wasn't all plain sailing with Andy, though, and he did stitch me up properly on one occasion. It was the week before my little one's christening on the Sunday and I told Andy that I planned to have a few beers. He told me not to worry. "Listen, just come with me on Monday. The reserves have got a game, so it'll just be the first team in and you won't have to do much after the game on Saturday. We'll make it look as if we're busy, have a game of two-touch and start again properly on Tuesday." Brilliant, I thought. I came in on Monday, rough as anything, and we had a game of two-touch as planned. Then I heard the shout from one of the lads. "Let me do some shooting, Paddy."

I looked around and felt a horrible sinking feeling in my stomach, which wasn't from the beers at the christening. I was the only 'keeper there. So for an hour, with me hanging out of my arse, I was peppered with shots from the strikers. I told Andy that he had stitched me right up. He denied all responsibility, of course, but over the years I certainly repaid him – and then some. One year at United we went to Puerto Banús in Marbella and my wife at the time told Pagey that it was my birthday while we were over there, so he was ready to get me absolutely paralytic with all sorts of daft drinks.

Andy's birthday is the day after mine and he came up to me quietly to wish me many happy returns, suggesting I should probably keep it quiet. We had a really good day drinking around the pool, before going to the Sinatra Bar at night. We were stood outside boozing when, 15 minutes before midnight, Pagey remembered it was my birthday. *Bastard,* I thought. I thought I had got away with it! The next thing I knew, I was passed this drink. It was completely clear – fuck knows what was in it – and it was set it on fire too, to make it even worse. I had to neck it and it was the most revolting thing I have ever tasted in my life. I was nearly sick in the port.

Andy nudged me and asked me not to say anything about it being his birthday next. "Will I 'eck?" I said to him. "I'm not that sort of guy." At a quarter past 12 I shouted out: "Just to let you all know, lads... it's Andy's birthday today!" The same drink came out and he handled it even worse than I had. He was calling me all the names under the sun that night! He used to shit himself whenever me and Phil Barnes, a goalkeeper and big Blades fan we had signed from Blackpool, got going. Me and Barney were like Dumb and Dumber whenever we had a few beers in us. "You two are going to get me sacked!" he used to say.

Ironically, I believe it was his loyalty to me that eventually did get Andy the boot from United. But I will always be grateful for everything he did for me – as a coach and more importantly as a bloke.

6

IRELAND'S CALL

When I close my eyes now, I can still picture the goal. USA 1994, the Republic of Ireland against Italy. Four years after losing to them in the quarter-finals of Italia '90, revenge from the left boot of Ray Houghton. A poor header out from Franco Baresi, a sweet volley from Houghton, some pretty average goalkeeping from Gianluca Pagliuca. We – and, because of my Irish upbringing and heritage, it was "we" – were ahead against the mighty Italians; Maldini, Baggio and all the rest. We were knocked out in the round of 16 by another ridiculously strong team in Holland, but that victory over the mighty Italians means that June 18, 1994, is fixed in my memory as one of Ireland's greatest-ever sporting dates.

I watched the game back home in Halifax, a wide-eyed 16-year-old glued to our fat-back rented TV. Irish blood ran through me from both my mum and dad's side of the family and you can only imagine how bizarre it felt just 10 years later when I was called up to the Ireland squad and Packie Bonner, who was in goal for that World Cup game, greeted me as my goalkeeping coach. I used to love him when he was a player and here he was, giving me the benefit of his wisdom. It was surreal.

For some players it seems like playing for Ireland is a second-best choice if they don't get picked for England, but that was never the case with me. I always considered myself Irish, despite being born and bred in Yorkshire, and pulling on that Irish jersey was always an ambition of mine – even when the chance to do so felt a million miles away. Some of the greatest players in Irish football history, like Paul McGrath, have qualified through their ancestry and when I eventually got that first taste of international football with Ireland, there was not a prouder man in the whole world – regardless of where I was born.

Joining United at the top end of the Championship showed that I was capable of handling myself at that level and at one point I was apparently the highest-ranked Irish player in England who hadn't been capped at senior level by Ireland. Ironically the international retirement of my old Bury clubmate, Dean Kiely, opened the door a little bit for me, but I owe a lot of my Irish adventure to the intervention of David Kelly. We called him "Ned" – he didn't mind being christened after the infamous outlaw Ned Kelly and even had NED on his training kit instead of his initials when he later moved into coaching – and, despite coming from Birmingham, he was another member of that remarkable Ireland squad I watched at the 1994 World Cup. He also travelled to Italia '90 after scoring a hat-trick on his senior Ireland debut, so was some player in his prime.

He was at the back end of his career when he came to United as a player and later returned to Bramall Lane as Warnock's assistant. I'm not even entirely sure if the FAI knew that I had Irish descent, but Ned either informed or reminded them of my family background and pushed for me to get a senior call-up. I didn't want to get my hopes up too much, but whatever Ned said evidently did the trick. Warnock broke the news to me of my first call-up and, before I could really get my head around it, I was on the bench, with an Ireland badge on my chest, at a packed Lansdowne Road. To make it even more surreal, we were only playing fucking Brazil! A little more than 18 months earlier they had won the World Cup and although the game was "only" a friendly, the team they put out showed how seriously they took it... Dida, Cafu, Lucio, Roque Junior, Carlos, Kleberson (Julio Baptista, 45), Ronaldinho, Silva (Edmilson, 14), Kaka, Ze Roberto, Ronaldo.

Not bad, eh? I must have had 50 people ring me up after the squad had been announced and my name was in it. "Can you get me this signed by Ronaldo?" "If I get you this, can you get Ronaldinho to sign it for me?" I had to tell them I didn't have a clue how it all worked. It was an international game, not a day out, and I didn't want to turn up looking like a competition winner – although, thinking back, I can't remember anything about Ronaldinho from that game, so he can't have done much! Stephen Carr and Robbie Keane had some good chances for us and big Aiden O'Brien stopped Ronaldo right at the death to seal us a creditable 0-0 draw against the samba stars. The real "What the fuck?" moment for me came a while later when we played in front of almost 79,000 at the

Stade de France in a World Cup qualifier and held France to a credible 0-0 draw. I was on the bench next to Gary Doherty, watching Thierry Henry flying up and down the wing in front of us. He was frightening. I tapped Doch on the arm and just said: "Wow." Henry looked as if he wasn't even touching the grass. Shit, I thought to myself silently. I hope I don't have to come on here... how am I going to be able to cope with that?

My Ireland debut was an eight-minute cameo against the Czech Republic, replacing another legend of Irish football in Shay Given off the bench. It might not have been on the same level as facing Brazil or France, but it didn't matter a bit to me – I was an international footballer and no-one could take that away from me. The Czechs were no mugs, either. Petr Čech had just agreed a move to Chelsea, where he went on to win pretty much everything, and another future Champions' League winner Milan Baroš was upfront. Oh, Pavel Nedved was in midfield for them that day. He was officially the best player on the planet as the holder of the Ballon d'Or and here was me, ambling past him to take my place in goal. Just over two years earlier I had been playing in Division Two with Bury. I don't feature in the short highlights video of the game on YouTube, but it does show Robbie Keane scoring a last-minute goal to get my Ireland career up and running on a winning note.

Robbie was a brilliant footballer, one of a few we had in the Ireland squad at the time. Damien Duff had earned a huge-money move to Chelsea on the back of his performances for Blackburn and we had tons of Premier League experience with the likes of Shay, Ian Harte and Matt Holland. Then there was Roy Keane, who had come back into the Ireland squad after falling out with Mick McCarthy at the 2002 World Cup. I was lucky enough to be named in a few squads alongside him after his recall and I always found him a good, decent bloke. As a player, you don't need me to tell you that he was fiery, but that wasn't just something he switched on for games. He was just as bad in training. Once, we were playing a five-a-side at Lansdowne Road before a game and Keane was on my team. He wanted the ball, but I didn't give it to him. He started moaning, so I told him to shut the fuck up.

He flashed me that stare of his and I thought: "Oh, no. What have I done here?" I was rooming with Alan Quinn at the time because he was one of the few lads I knew from United and he told me later that

Keane had looked for him after that training session. As my teammate at United, Quinny thought he was in for some kind of backlash. "Your 'keeper..." Keane began. "I fucking love him. He's had a right go at me today. I love all that shit." He walked off laughing while Quinny breathed a sigh of relief. I did, too, when Quinny told me the story later that day. I wish I could say I wasn't shit-scared after having a go at Roy Keane, but I was. In the moment I just thought I would go for it. And here I am today to tell the tale!

Keane did also give me one of my biggest lessons after making the step up from club to international football. In one of the games he came short for the ball and asked, or demanded, for it to be played into him. It happened two or three times in the first half and each time I had taken a touch and cleared it long. He had bitten his tongue before ripping into me at half-time. "Listen," he snarled at me. "The next time I come short, you give me the fucking ball. You're not playing for Sheff United now. I don't care if there's a man up my arse. Give me the ball and I'll deal with it. If I lose it and we concede, I'll take the blame." *Jesus*, I thought. This is the difference now. I simply wasn't allowed to do that at United. War-nock would have absolutely hammered me. I loved Nick Montgomery, who was in midfield for United at the time, to bits, and still do. But I couldn't give him the ball short and watch him trip over his own feet, could I?

It happened once with Quinny at United. I had broken my habit and rolled the ball to him because he had ages to turn with it. But an opposition player had closed him down and the ball ricocheted between them both, before Quinny got away and passed it wide. We ended the move with a shot on target but from the touchline I could hear Warnock having a go at me for giving the ball to Quinny. "Hold up?" I thought. "We almost scored from it." But Warnock was not happy and carried on ranting at me in the dressing-room after the game. That was how much he hated me rolling the ball out – it didn't matter that we had nearly scored from it! The best moment was when he threatened to substitute me if I did it again. We didn't have a sub goalkeeper on the bench.

Overall the whole early Ireland experience was a brilliant one and to win my first cap was a massively proud moment for me and my family, who came to every game I was involved in, whether I played or not. But after an eight-minute taste of international football against the Czechs, I was desperate for more and my first start came later that summer when Ireland were invited to take part in something called the Unity Cup. We played Nigeria and Jamaica at Charlton's ground of all places and after we lost 3-0 to Nigeria, I was given the No. 1 shirt for the game against Jamaica on June 2nd.

There were only just over 6,000 fans there, but a lot of Jamaican supporters had congregated behind one goal in what is normally the away end at The Valley. Honestly all I could smell for the entirety of the second half was weed drifting through the air. There I was, making my first start for my country, and I felt like I was off my tits! It was ridiculous. I remember laughing all the way through the half. Luckily I didn't have too much else to contend with in a 1-0 win and my international career was shaping up nicely – played two, won two. Goals conceded: none – although that would soon change later into my Irish adventure.

I had a lot of time for Brian Kerr, who took over when Mick resigned, and not just because he was the man who gave me my first caps. He was just a really good bloke. He was easy to like, and I thought he did well in his time in charge. Managing Ireland is always going to bring its own challenges because of the sheer size of the island and the difficulties that brings in terms of the pool of players available. He was a well-regarded and well-liked youth coach and took over in really difficult circumstances after Mick's exit. He was also on the ball one evening to thwart a night out the players had planned before we were due to fly to the Faroe Islands for a game. We were cooped up in the hotel and planned our exit strategy with military precision, even getting the hotel security on our side so they could help us out.

The plan was simple enough – we'd sneak out of the fire exit, leg it across the golf course and jump into pre-booked taxis which would be waiting for us across the other side. I don't know how we ever thought we would get away with it, but the entire squad was in on it, led by chief planners Shay and John O'Shea. I was still new to everything at the time, so was sucked in easily enough. "You're coming," they told me. "All right, I'm in!" Everything was planned to the letter – until Doch wandered out of his room, fully dressed in shoes and a suit jacket and covered in aftershave. We had the hotel floor to ourselves with security at either end and Brian caught Gary red-handed – and red-faced. "Hello, Doch," Brian said calmly. "Where are you off to?"

Doch looked a bit flustered and tried to come up with something: "Err, err, err... I'm just trying on my gear in case we get a night out when we go away." Brian wasn't having any of it. "We're coming straight back after the game," he said. Doch, to be fair, looked a million dollars, but it wouldn't have taken Columbo to figure that something was going on when he should have been in his training gear and flip-flops. The lads were gutted – but, as it happened, we ended up getting our night out after all. We flew out to the Faroe Islands and won the game 2-0 with Harte and Kevin Kilbane getting our goals. But Brian's plan to fly straight back after the game was ruined by fog around their airport, which meant our flight was cancelled. What else were we supposed to do? We were out.

The only issue was that none of us had brought any gear to change into, so ironically, we ended up in this nightclub, absolutely blind-drunk, in our Ireland tracksuits. We would have killed for Doch's jeans at that point! We didn't look particularly smart, but come the end of the night our bar bill certainly was. I had to look at it a few times and, when I realised that I wasn't seeing double and the bill actually was almost seven grand, I sobered up pretty quickly.

"Jesus," I thought to myself. "I can't afford this." At the time I was on relative pennies at United and there were players in that Ireland squad who were on 60 and 70 grand a week, ordering bottles and bottles of all sorts. It had never crossed my mind that it would need paying for. I was starting to panic when Stephen Carr handed over his credit card, as casually as if he was buying a round in his local. "I'll get this, lads," he said, without batting an eyelid. The bill was about two months' wages for me.

I don't want to give off the impression that being called up for the Ireland squad was an excuse for us to get pissed up or an equivalent of a lads' holiday abroad. That wasn't the case at all. We worked really hard for our country during the international breaks and the experience, learning from other players and how they went about their business, was massively beneficial for me in making me a better footballer and a better goalkeeper. I had one of the legends of Irish football in Shay with me and I couldn't help but learn from him. But the trips did also give us a chance to blow off some steam at the right time and sometimes we did pay for it – not just in the wallet either.

Once, Quinny and I were late in joining up with the Ireland boys because we were playing for United, away at QPR. It was just before the international break and me and Quinny had arranged to stay down in London after the game and fly over to Dublin the following morning. We won the game 1-0 and Quinny and me were absolutely buzzing our tits off when we got back to the hotel, so we went to the bar for a few beers to calm us down. On the way we told the receptionist that we were being picked up at half-five the next morning and asked if an alarm could be set for us for 5am. The next thing I remember was the same receptionist tapping me on the shoulder: "Er, lads, do you know your taxi is here?" It was half-five in the morning and we were still in the bar, pissed as farts. I couldn't believe it.

"Oh fuck," I said to Quinny. "We've got training today!" He tried his best to reassure me. "We'll be fine," he said. "We had a game last night... We'll probably have a massage and train tomorrow." It made me feel a little better even if I wasn't exactly a million dollars after 45 minutes of sleep on the plane journey over. We checked in at training and I found out Shay had a little niggle. I looked around and it dawned on me that me and Nick Colgan were the only other 'keepers. "Paddy, you're going to have to train," one of the coaching staff told me. "We need two 'keepers. Quinny, go and have a massage and chill out."

Honestly, I felt sick. I tried to plead my case, saying I'd played the night before, but wasn't getting any joy. "Yeah, but you didn't have to run about, did you? I'm sure you can go and stand in goal for a bit." I had no choice but to suck it up. I didn't have the relationship with Packie that I had with Andy Leaning at United. I would have just been honest with Andy. "Andy, I've had no kip... We ended up getting a bit giddy last night, didn't we? Me and Quinny ended up drinking and talking shit for five or six hours and I've had 45 minutes of sleep." I don't know what Packie would have made of that if I had been honest with him... but, to be fair, I bet there were a few pints of Guinness sunk by the Ireland squad after that win over Italy!

7

TRIPLE ASSAULT

I t seems a little strange to say this – because ultimately nothing came out of it in the end – but the 2002/03 season was an absolute dream. I had started it fresh out of Bury, who used to get about 2,500 fans through the gates, and finished it playing in the play-off final in Cardiff in front of 70,000. I played 59 games that season, at places like Anfield, Old Trafford and the Millennium Stadium, and it was some introduction to life as a Sheffield United player. Being honest, it was absolutely crazy and, when I look back now, I realise how easy it could all have been so, so different.

My league debut for United was away at Coventry, who had Gary McAllister as their player-manager. I had grown up watching players like McAllister playing on TV and suddenly we were on the same pitch. My first game at Bramall Lane was against Portsmouth, who had Paul Merson in midfield. I remember lining up before the game and thinking to myself: "I'm actually playing against Paul Merson." Pompey had spent some serious cash that summer, but we drew 1-1 despite me nearly dropping a corner at the Kop end.

It was a routine catch, but I spilled it completely. A Pompey player – I don't even know who it was because it happened so quickly – volleyed the loose ball goalwards and, completely instinctively, I just stuck out my hand and deflected the ball over the bar. Andy Leaning, my part-time goalkeeping coach at the time, pulled me after the game. "Imagine if that had gone in," he said. "It would have broken you." I didn't realise it at the time, but he was probably right. I still remember that save now because it was such a big point in my career; further down the line I saw fellow goalkeepers make mistakes early on and never recover.

A club legend in Simon Tracey was recovering from a knee operation when I arrived at Bramall Lane and the other 'keeper was a Dutch lad called Wilko de Vogt, who struggled to concentrate in training because he talked about porn all the time. Later in the season Tracey retired and we signed Gary Kelly, the brother of another United goalkeeping legend in Alan. Gary's first game of that season was in the Conference for Northwich Victoria and three months later he was on the bench for the play-off final. I remember thinking my own journey was a crazy one – Gary's was on a different planet!

Having Kelly among the substitutes in Cardiff was a bit of a novelty in itself because Neil Warnock very rarely bothered putting a 'keeper on the bench. We never really discussed why and the closest we got was when he gave me some advice: "Don't get sent off and don't get injured." But his thinking was obvious – by not having a goalkeeper on the bench, it freed up another spot for a striker. Warnock loved strikers and used to collect them like little kids collect football stickers. And to be fair I bet it worked successfully more times than it cost us. If you look through an entire season, the odds on your goalkeeper being sent off or getting injured would be quite low. But in 2002/03 the amount of times we came back to draw or win games late on was ridiculous. We were a fit team and had Michael Brown scoring goals from all over the pitch, which helped. But more often than not it was probably because we had about nine strikers on the pitch.

United had finished 13th the season before I signed and Warnock was never shy of dipping into the transfer market. Patrick Suffo and Georgos Santos both went after being sent off in the infamous "Battle of Bramall Lane" game and Warnock signed me, a legend of the game in Stuart McCall and about 50 more strikers. The Gaffer also thought that season would be his last. He used to talk about retiring every year, especially later in life. But at the end of 2002/03, he would be 55 and his tractor in Cornwall was calling him. Before he went, he fancied a good crack at a cup competition. He used to think that the teams he was managing would never win the FA Cup or League Cup in a million years, so what was the point? But at the start of 2002/03, something changed. He thought: 'Why not?' And the result was one of the most remarkable seasons in the club's long history.

One game that sticks in my mind most, though, was one that I didn't even play in. We drew Ipswich in the fourth round of the FA Cup and

I was given a rare day off. It was unreal viewing. Wilko took the gloves and probably thought he would have one of the easiest games of his career as we went 3-0 up. Brownie scored two, naturally from outside the box, and a young lad called Phil Jagielka got the other. Brownie's second, a stunning volley at the Kop end, sparked Ipswich into life and they scored three times in four minutes to make it 3-3. Poor Wilko didn't know what had hit him. But we stuck at it and Paul Peschisolido, our tiny Canadian striker, scored a late winner at the Kop end to send us through. Pesch scored a few late, dramatic goals that season and Warnock didn't fancy taking the risk with Wilko again, because I was back in the team!

Brownie was an incredible player, but that season was something special, even for him. He finished with 22 goals from midfield and that lad did not score tap-ins. Forget the Sheffield United goal of the season – Brownie had his own individual awards. "Which one of these was his best goal?" He scored volleys and free-kicks and a few penalties. There were screamers with his left foot, away at places like Walsall and Grimsby Town. And he scored *that* goal against Sheffield Wednesday, a superb volley in a 3-1 win for us at the Lane. It was my first taste of a home derby against them after we had lost 2-0 at Hillsborough earlier that season. Shefki Kuqi got the opener for them and we battered them before Lloyd Owusu came off the bench and scored. He had been so nervous when he came on that he was sick on the pitch. I could understand why.

Every game was huge for me, considering where I had come from, but Sheffield derbies were something else. The Bramall Lane derby that season was on a Friday night in January and a young female Wednesday fan was hurt when a flare was fired from the south stand into the away end. I remember seeing it go across into the Wednesday fans and thinking: "Fuck me. That's not good!" Howard Webb, a part-time copper from Rotherham who later refereed the World Cup final in 2010, had been drafted in to help to police the game, but missed the moment the flare was fired because he was watching the match. I was the opposite – I took my eyes off the game to watch the flare! I didn't need a reminder of how much bad feeling there was between United and Wednesday fans but, if I did, there it was – right in front of my eyes.

There were fireworks on the field as well. Wednesday hadn't won at Bramall Lane since the 1960s and hadn't done the double over United since 1914, so it didn't look too promising for us when they went 1-0 up. Their Irish midfielder Alan Quinn, who would later become a good friend of mine, got the goal, breaking through at the Kop end and scoring. I didn't know him at the time, but he rubbed it in my face later on, giving me all the "I gave you the eyes and sent you the wrong way" bullshit. I had actually read where he was going to shoot: he just put it too far away from me and I couldn't get there quick enough.

At the other end we couldn't get the ball past Wednesday's goalkeeper, Kevin Pressman, who always seemed to save his best for when he played against United. Pressman was a great goalkeeper, but he wasn't a small bloke. Even I looked like an athlete next to him and I used to look forward to playing against Wednesday because I wouldn't be the fattest goalkeeper on the pitch!

Again Pressman was unbelievable that night. Dean Windass and Steve Kabba, who we signed shortly after he tore us apart playing for Grimsby, were both denied by Pressman, who then made stunning saves from Brownie and Peter Ndlovu. Kabbs eventually got the better of Pressman with a great finish before Brownie produced one of his moments of magic by smashing a volley that even Pressman couldn't get anywhere near. The Chief, big Wayne Allison, scored a tap-in late on to make it 3-1 and it was another memorable evening under the lights at the Lane.

That was typical Brownie. Throughout that season, whenever we were in a bit of trouble, he always seemed to come up with something out of absolutely nowhere. He had the biggest pair of bollocks on him. Literally. If he was sitting in front of you now, they would be scraping on the floor. But he showed balls on the pitch, too, whenever we needed a moment of magic. Even away from matchday he was still the main man. He organised all the nights out and helped the younger lads, like Jags, Nick Montgomery, Michael Tonge and Grant Smith, to gel with the more senior pros in the changing-room.

United had a good crop of youngsters coming through at one time and those four all lived together – Monty was the sensible one who owned the house and looked after the other lads. They gave him a set amount every month to cover the rent, bills and food and Monty took care of them. He used to buy two lots of bread when he did the big shop for the house – cheap, supermarket own-brand stuff for toast and Warburtons to make sandwiches. Monty took it really seriously as well. If he caught any of the lads using the Warburtons for toast, he wouldn't speak to them for weeks! They were all really close off the pitch, but could play as well. Warnock later described Jags, Monty and Tonge as United's equivalent of Manchester United's "Class of 92" with Giggs, Scholes and the Neville brothers. It's all relative, I guess, and Jags, Monty and Tongey all had great careers. Grant didn't quite make it to the same level, but those three all played in the Premier League and Jags stayed there for well over 10 years and won a shitload of England caps. He even captained his country once, which isn't bad for a lad who had no interest whatsoever in playing at centre-half!

Jags could play anywhere, and often did. He even had a long stint as my back-up goalkeeper, but was more often used at right-back and in midfield before Warnock switched him to centre-half. Jags wasn't keen at all and used to moan all the time about it, but you can definitely see Warnock's thinking. Jags was good in the air and good on the ball, but it was his pace that stood out the most. There weren't many centre-halves on the scene with Jags' pace, which is why Warnock switched him there. He looked like an Olympic sprinter compared with the likes of Chris Morgan and Rob Page, who looked as if they were pulling caravans when they were running back!

Jags was still playing right-back when he enjoyed his finest hour that season, an unbelievable strike in the League Cup against Leeds United. We had beaten York and Wycombe at home in the previous rounds – weirdly we were drawn at Bramall Lane for every cup game we played that season – and were paired with our rivals from just up the M1 in the third round. Leeds were in the Premier League at the time and had some unbelievable players.

Their starting line-up that night was Robinson, Mills, Lucic, Woodgate, Harte, Wilcox, Bowyer, Bakke, Barmby, Kewell and Viduka. They had a £5m striker in Michael Bridges on the bench, but I was only beaten when our defender Mark Yeates scored an own goal. Then we came alive in injury time. Jags scored from about 30 yards and Ndlovu netted the winner from about six. Both felt so, so sweet. Bramall Lane was absolutely rocking, but Jags was only in a position to score that goal because of his pace! We were throwing everyone forward and kept him back in the hope he would get us out of trouble with his speed if Leeds broke with numbers. The ball was cleared into his path and it sat up beautifully after he chested it down. "Hang on," I remember thinking to myself. "He's going to hit this!" A split second later I was sprinting upfield to celebrate with him and the rest of the lads. Then Ndlovu tapped home from a few yards out and we were in the next round.

We never really looked back. We'd actually had a pretty average start to our league season, but the momentum of our cup run took over and we just rolled from game to game. People in football talk about league form suffering from cup runs, but it was the complete opposite for us. Soon after beating Leeds in the League Cup, we went to Bradford and battered them 5-0. We beat Sunderland, also a decent Premier League team at the time, in the League Cup.

We turned over Leeds again, this time in the FA Cup. We certainly didn't have an easy run to the semi-finals of both competitions – we were just an unbelievable team. In hindsight the sheer amount of games we were playing probably took its toll in the end, but at the time we just kept ticking over. When everything on the pitch is going well, everything else tends to look after itself. It's often when things start to turn on the pitch that real problems arise.

Our League Cup adventure that season ended at the hands of Liverpool, who eventually won the trophy. We beat Crystal Palace in the quarter-finals to book our semi slot and again were first out of the draw to have our home leg first. Neil Mellor put Liverpool ahead and, even though many watching on maybe expected the floodgates to open from there, we knew what we were made of. There were more than 30,000 packed into Bramall Lane for the game – over twice the crowd that had seen my home debut a few months earlier – and it felt as if the roof was coming off when Tongey equalised.

That season the crowd helped us out so much when we got a head of steam up. It's one of the biggest clichés in football, but from where I was standing, being so close to the fans, I really felt it for the first time. No-one on the outside gave us a chance of getting anything against Liverpool. But Warnock had us bang up for it. "If we go out there and do what we can do," he said to us before, "at Bramall Lane in front of our crowd, we'll turn these over." He was right. Tongey smashed home the winner on the night and gave us a lead to take to Anfield. It was ridiculous how we played that day and I was 90 minutes away from a League Cup final in my first season at the club. Frightening.

Tongey's second goal summed up how good a player he was at the time. The ball broke to him from a corner and he shaped to shoot, but had the presence of mind to know that Didi Hamaan was sliding in from his right to block the shot. Tongey took a touch, let Hamaan slide right past him and smashed it into the bottom corner. At the time there was a lot of talk about Tongey going right to the top of the game and there's no doubt he was good enough. He came through in the same group as Jags and Monty and in my opinion was the best out of the three. Tongey eventually got a move back to the Premier League with Stoke in 2009, but only started five games in five years and was sent out on loan five times.

I don't know if it was because of the type of player he was and the way Stoke played at the time. I guess that's a question for Tony Pulis. But I am surprised that Tongey didn't do more in the game. On the ball he was ridiculous. A great passer. Maybe he lacked a little bit of pace, but he definitely had the skills. The difference is maybe that Jags went to a club that suited him and Tongey didn't. That can be all it boils down to sometimes. As a footballer, if you go to a club and don't play for a year to 18 months, you can soon be forgotten about. But he was certainly appreciated at Bramall Lane, especially after scoring two goals to give us a lead to take to Anfield.

What a place that is, by the way. I grew up supporting Manchester United, but you can't deny the history that Liverpool have. I remember people saying to me that the Kop at Anfield would be brilliant with me, especially as an Irishman. It was probably one of the best greetings I ever got from home fans as an away player although that's probably not saying much! I remember going to Leeds as an away player and seeing fans behind my goal applauding me. But I had already been tipped off that, as soon as I clapped back, I would get shitloads of abuse thrown my way. So Leeds never got a clap out of me as an away player because I knew what was coming! Anfield could not have been more different.

We prepared for the second leg of the semi-final on the Mersey. Not in a hotel on the Mersey or on the docks – on a ferry going across the Mersey. I think Warnock had sensed a bit of tension among the lads on the morning of the game, so he took us up on the top deck of a ferry to practise some set-pieces. Poor Chief was seasick and ended up throwing up over the side of the boat. As huge underdogs it was obvious that we needed to hold out for as long as possible so it wasn't exactly in the script for us when El Hadji Diouf put Liverpool ahead. All of a sudden it was 2-2 on aggregate and I *really* started to take in the standard of players we were up against. Diouf, Michael Owen, Steven Gerrard, Jamie Carragher... *wow*.

But at the same time it never really felt as if we were being pummelled and I certainly wasn't making save after save, as many probably thought I would have to do. The game's big moment came in the last minute of normal time when Chris Kirkland, Liverpool's goalkeeper, deliberately handled the ball outside the area under pressure from the Chief, who'd recovered from his seasickness. Everyone watching – including, I bet, Kirkland – expected a red card to follow. But the ref, Alan Wiley, completely bottled it and just showed a yellow.

No player likes to see a fellow player get sent off, especially a 'keeper. But the rules were clear and Kirkland should have walked. Maybe we would still have lost the game: who knows? But it might have given us a bit more of a chance. Put it this way, if that had been me who handled outside my area at the Kop end in the last minute, do you think I would have walked? Absolutely 100 per cent I would have. Tommy Mooney, another Warnock striker signing, took the free-kick and it was deflected just wide. Six inches the other way and we were in the final. Instead we went to extra time and, as we started to tire, Gerrard played in Owen and he finished past me to seal Liverpool's place at Cardiff.

I was devastated that we'd lost, but at least I could finally get rid of my gloves. I had somehow got it in my head that I couldn't change my gloves during our winning streak, which had begun when we beat Leeds thanks to Jags and Ndlovu. By the time we lost at Anfield, I had worn them in 15 games straight! They had holes in them and rips all over. I never washed them. I chucked them into the away end at Anfield and whoever caught them must have thought: "How the fuck has he played football in these?" I had let the superstitious thoughts get into my head, but the gloves were in such a bad state that I wouldn't let my gardener wear them.

Saying that, though, I would have given anything to be able to wear them in one more game.

It wasn't to be and I was also saved the hassle of having to sort out tickets for the final. The amount of people who came out of the woodwork for the big games that season was unbelievable. I never realised I knew that many people! When we played against Leeds, I got orders for tickets from what seemed like half of Halifax, which I paid for before collecting the money later. I got the tickets in an envelope and chucked it in the boot of my car with all my other kit. At the same time I had an old TV that I needed to get rid of. This was still in the era of fat-back TVs that were pretty chunky and I was driving home when I saw a skip up a side street. *That'll do*, I thought. I had no idea whose skip it was, but I got the TV out of the boot and chucked it in.

Job done.

After training the next day I started getting messages from people telling me they were dropping the money off for the tickets. I couldn't find them for love nor money. I found out later that someone had found the envelope of tickets on the floor by the skip and had been flogging them around Halifax for a tenner a pop! I had to tell the club that I had lost them. They cancelled them and reprinted them for me, but people who had bought the originals still turned up to the game and couldn't get in. I hope they managed to see the game somehow. I guess the whole thing was karma for me trying to chuck the TV in a random skip in the first place!

Our second game against Leeds that season was the FA Cup quarter-final at Bramall Lane when Kabba scored the winner to seal our place in another semi-final. I had never known a season like it before. Back then semi-finals weren't played at Wembley and ours, against Arsenal, was at Old Trafford. I had watched my first football game there, on the Stretford End with my brother. Now I was getting ready to play there in a fucking FA Cup semi-final. I don't think I ever got past the first or second round with Bury. It's another cliché, but it really was the stuff of dreams.

At the time Man United and Arsenal had a lot of rivalry and Sir Alex Ferguson couldn't do enough for us to make sure we had any advantage we could over Arsène Wenger's side. Ferguson let us use their training ground in the build-up to the game and originally suggested we train on the actual Old Trafford pitch before the FA intervened and said we couldn't. Warnock told us later that Ferguson had even phoned him to ask how we would like the grass cut and watered!

I met one of my early heroes, Peter Schmeichel, before the game and had a photo taken with him, but we weren't there just to enjoy a day out at Old Trafford. We genuinely believed that we could beat the mighty

Arsenal and reach the FA Cup final. Warnock believed, too. "Listen," he told us before the game. "According to everyone, you'll get beat by four or five today. But we know different, don't we? How have we been this season? We beat Liverpool: we took them to extra time in a semi-final of the League Cup. Why can't we do it today?" It turned out to be another game that I felt we deserved more from. We probably should have won it actually. Again I didn't make a shitload of saves. I was probably tested more often in the previous league game when we lost 1-0 at Wimbledon. But in the slightly more glamorous surroundings of Old Trafford we lost by that scoreline again.

Freddie Ljungberg scored the winner, but the build-up to it was an absolute shambles. The Chief was wiped out by Sol Campbell at Arsenal's end of the pitch. The ref, Graham Poll, waved play on and then ran straight into Tongey, who was about to pick the ball up. Arsenal took possession after Poll's tackle and Sylvain Wiltord had a half-shot, which hit the post and bounced out. Wiltord had another shot, which hit Pagey's backside and could have fallen anywhere. The ball dropped straight at Ljungberg's feet and he smashed home what ended up being the winning goal. Warnock was absolutely spitting with rage, especially when he saw Poll walking off the pitch at half-time with a huge, daft grin on his face, but we had our chances in the second half. The best of them all came with just six minutes left on the clock.

We forced a corner on the right, which Pagey headed back into the Arsenal box after the ball had been cleared. Carl Asaba helped it on towards Pesch, who was only a few yards out and perfectly placed to bring us level. But Pesch didn't make the best contact with the ball and somehow David Seaman managed to arch back and get his hand behind it before dragging it to safety. Pesch couldn't put the rebound in and Jags, who was rushing in, blasted the follow-up out of Manchester from about four yards out.

At the time I didn't appreciate how good the save was – I probably had the worst view in the ground from the other end of the pitch. But I must have seen it a million times since and I don't think there are enough words to do it justice. It was ridiculous. Seaman was nearly 40 at the time and the game was the 1,000th of his career. What a time to pull off the best save I have ever seen in my life! He did well enough to even get to the ball, never mind having the strength to claw it back from the line with his fingertips. It's tinged with a bit of regret when I see the save because, if Pesch gets a better contact on the ball, he does not give Seaman a chance. But, with Seaman hanging in mid-air and his ponytail flapping all over the place, it was still a freak of a save.

Seaman was good enough to give me his shirt after the game and I wonder now if he had got caught up in the emotions of the day because a couple of days later, I got a call on my mobile just as I arrived at Bramall Lane before our game against Nottingham Forest. "Hey up, Paddy, it's Dave Seaman," said the voice on the other end. "Yeah, good one!" I laughed down the line and put the phone down. Then someone from the club called me. "Paddy, we've had Arsenal in touch," they said. "They've passed your number over to David Seaman." *Oh shit,* I thought. I rang the number back and apologised. "Sorry, Dave, I thought someone was taking the piss!" He just burst out laughing. Maybe it happened to him all the time.

"Listen," he said. "I am going to be cheeky here, but with everything that happened with the save and my 1,000th career game... I couldn't have my shirt back, could I?" I could hardly say no! But to be fair to him, he promised to send me his other shirt and a pair of gloves. He signed them both: "To Paddy, Safe Hands." I've got them framed on the wall as a nice memory. He kept in touch with me as well. Before the play-off final later that season, a game we had to win to reach the Premier League, he sent me a nice message to wish me good luck. "See you next season," he said.

If only.

8

AGONY AND ECSTASY

As our team coach pulled away from Old Trafford, we knew that the only way to make up for our second cup semi-final defeat of the season was to go one better in the league and win promotion. We were third in the Division One table when we took on Arsenal and, although we had a game in hand on Leicester, who were second, they were also 16 points ahead of us. We had six games left so they were basically promoted and our best hopes of joining them were through the play-offs. But the FA Cup semi was our 52nd match of the season and physically and mentally, we were knackered.

It didn't help that after the Arsenal game on Sunday we played again on the Tuesday. We faced Nottingham Forest, who were also sniffing for promotion via the play-offs, but didn't even train on the Monday. Warnock knew we were running out of gas and gave us the day off. We beat Forest 1-0. A win over promoted Leicester basically sealed our play-off spot and by the time we played Watford on the last day of the season, we were guaranteed to finish either third or fourth in the league.

Either would guarantee us a home tie in the second leg of the semi-final, so I enjoyed a rare and very welcome day off as we lost 2-0 on the final day. Gary Kelly made his only United start in that game, against Watford, and the result didn't matter anyway because Reading lost as well. So we finished third, 12 points behind Leicester, and set up a semi-final against Forest.

Their fans absolutely hated me. I was used to the usual stick from fans, all the "You fat bastard" stuff, but against Forest – and at the City Ground in particular – it stepped up to another level. It all stemmed from the league game at their place earlier that season. Forest scored first and a ball boy behind my goal started to waste as much time as he could. We were chasing the game and trying to get the ball back as quickly as possible… and you can probably see where this is going. The multi-ball system Forest had mysteriously disappeared and in the end I was having to walk up to this kid to get the ball back and take a goal-kick. Otherwise we might still have been playing now.

This lad was only young but knew all the tricks, pulling his hand away and dropping the ball when I reached out to get it. The crowd loved it. It was classic shithouse behaviour and, to be fair to the lad, certainly no worse than anything I did when I was about his age and taking the piss out of older blokes with my dad's Sunday League team. But when you're on the other end of it, being mugged off, it isn't as much fun!

It happened a few times – I would go for the ball, he would drop the ball, the crowd would cheer and laugh – until one time I gave him a little nudge as I turned away and he fell backwards over his little stool. It looked far worse than it actually was and I felt terrible, but their fans understandably jumped on it and I got absolute pelters from them after that. I wrote to the lad to apologise, but I can't remember hearing anything back from him.

Maybe he has forgiven me since, I don't know. But those fans behind my goal certainly didn't! I knew what to expect from their supporters in the first leg at their place and we were delighted with a 1-1 draw. We knew that we could beat absolutely anyone at Bramall Lane.

I was rooming with Dean Windass before the first leg and we both woke up at about half-four in the morning because of the excitement of the game. We were like a couple of kids on Christmas Day. David Johnson, who later played for us as another Warnock striker, put Forest ahead, but Brownie equalised from the spot after he'd been fouled.

We fancied ourselves completely at a packed Bramall Lane for the second leg, but going 2-0 down after an hour was definitely not part of our script. Johnson scored again with a shot that swerved in the air and beat me before Andy Reid put Forest 3-1 up on aggregate. "Holy shit," I thought to myself as the Forest fans cheered behind me. "We've fucked it up. We've come this far and we're going to lose. What have we done?"

That man Brownie got us back into it again, about a minute after Reid's goal, with a deflected free-kick. It was probably his scruffiest goal of the season, but also one of the most important. You could feel the momentum shift. We knew all about our reputation for coming back from the dead in games and so did Forest. You could almost feel the tension grow and sure enough, we were soon level.

And the move began with my cultured right foot! Forest were camped so deep, defending a free-kick I was standing over, so for some reason I tried to play it short to our right-back John Curtis. He gave it straight back to me, so I took a touch and lumped the ball forward. Carl Asaba flicked it on and Steve Kabba controlled it beautifully before smashing it home, blowing kisses to the crowd who were going mental. I celebrated by rubbing my belly in front of the Forest fans, who had been all over me. It was 2-2 on the night, 3-3 on aggregate and game on.

In extra time we went ahead for the first time in either game. Another long punt downfield from me set our little sub striker Paul Peschisolido free. He teased the Forest defence, turned them inside and out and then mis-hit a shot that wrongfooted Darren Ward and dribbled into the net in front of the Kop. Pesch, bless him, had no idea how to celebrate so ended up throwing his shirt in the air and running around like a madman, screaming: "Oh my Gaaad" in his Canadian accent. It has become an iconic goal in United's recent history and it makes me laugh every time I see it. Little Pesch had only been on the pitch for seven minutes.

We went two goals clear when Des Walker – the ex-Wednesday defender – headed into his own top corner and Bramall Lane was absolutely rocking. No-one could quite believe that we had pulled it around and to this day I still do not know how we managed to do it. We just had an unbelievable belief in ourselves and knew that we could get something if we kept going right until the last whistle. It was a truly special evening. I remember celebrating with Phil Jagielka after Walker's own goal and ending up on the floor. Our skipper, Rob Page, marched over and picked us up by the scruff of our necks. "Get the fuck up," he growled at us. "We've not won this yet." Me and Jags looked at each other and laughed like a couple of schoolkids. There were three minutes left.

We weren't laughing a minute or two later when Pagey scored an own goal of his own to make it 4-3 on the night. I asked Pagey afterwards if he had done it on purpose to show me and Jags that the game *really* wasn't over! But it made the game a lot tenser than it needed to be and about 30 seconds later Forest should have equalised. Matthieu Louis-Jean got his head to Reid's cross at the back post and you could almost feel the whole ground holding its breath. But the header was straight at me and I made the save, holding the ball tighter than I ever had before!

We saw out the three minutes or so of injury time without too much late drama – which was lucky really because I don't think I would have been able to handle much more – and we were in the fucking play-off final. Some fans invaded the pitch to celebrate with us while others sat in their seats, crying their eyes out. Most could not believe what they had just witnessed and, while the players did a lap around the pitch to soak up the celebrations, Warnock was interviewed on Sky Sports. "Never write us off," he said, wagging his finger at the camera. "That's all I'll say."

Typically with Warnock, it wasn't all he said! He gave a little speech in the dressing-room after we had eventually dragged ourselves away from the pitch and the fans and told us how proud he was of us, as players and as people. We all ended up in the giant bath in the changing-room, surrounded by soap suds and our teammates and bottles of beer and even some champagne that someone had found from somewhere. For what seemed like ages, we just sat there in disbelief. Did that *really* just happen? No-one was quite sure. Then someone broke the silence. "Are we going to get pissed tonight, lads?" Now that was a question we definitely knew the answer to!

From the Marriott Hotel, where a few of us were staying that night, we went to Bed nightclub on London Road and then to a casino before reconvening at the hotel bar in the early hours when everywhere else had closed. People were coming down for breakfast the day after and we were still boozing. It was carnage. I didn't go to bed until about eight in the morning. We felt we had earned it and were determined to make the most of it. After about a thousand games and months of hard graft we were one game away from reaching the Premier League.

The play-off final against Wolves was 11 days after the Forest game, but the wait felt 10 times longer. I know there is so much to sort out for the final, but ideally from a player's point of view it would have been a lot sooner. We'd have played the final a couple of days after the Forest game if we could – once the fuzzy heads had gone! Instead after the massive high of that semi-final it was back to training ahead of the biggest game most of us had ever played.

Back then United trained at Abbeydale, an old and decrepit place with buckets everywhere to catch the rain which came through the leaky roof every time the heavens opened over Sheffield. It was horrendous, but it did also have a few benefits, including the fact that it was on two levels. The main pitch was up on the top, where the outfield players trained, but the goalkeepers went down the slope and did their work on the lower level. I remember being down there with Andy Leaning and Gary, doing a few drills. It was only a couple of days after the Forest game and the adrenaline crash had hit me hard. My body was struggling as well and I could not get going, no matter how hard I tried.

Andy volleyed 10 balls at me to warm up. I spilled every single one and he sussed me straightaway. "You can't be arsed, can you?" he asked. "Not today, no," I admitted. That may sound a shit thing for a professional footballer to say, but I was absolutely done in. I was aching everywhere and felt as if I had nothing left in the tank. I was still a young man, at 25 years old, but playing so many games at that intensity was completely new to me, and towards the back end of the season had started to take its toll. Andy understood. We all knew that Kevin Blackwell, Warnock's assistant, was a busy little fucker and would soon be peering down the hill to make sure we were working. We marked all the cones out to make it look like a proper session for when Blackwell checked up on us, and did absolutely nothing. It was exactly what I needed.

Blackwell used to play under Warnock as a goalkeeper before he moved into coaching and, because me and Gary were the club's only 'keepers, Blackie was registered towards the end of that season as an absolute last resort. One day Blackie decided to come out and train with us and was giving it the big 'un in his Luton accent. "I'm gonna facking show you how it's done, aren't I?" and all that. He joined in with the fast feet and handling and tried to step it up. "Are you lot gonna facking hit it harder or what?" So Andy wound it up a bit and let loose with a volley, which went straight through Blackie's hands and smashed him flush in the face. The ball bounced miles away and there was blood everywhere, squirting from his nose. Blackie wiped his face with his gloves. "Facking love that," he said, through mouthfuls of blood.

As the days ticked by, the final just didn't seem to get any closer and I started to worry that the momentum we had built up around the Forest game was completely gone. Instead all the stuff that goes with a big game like that took over. We got measured for new suits at the training ground and worried about ticket allocations for our family, and which hotel they were going to be stopping in. The club had to sort out selling tickets for fans and there was a toss-up for which dressing-room to use and which kits to wear. Us and Wolves ended up playing in our home kits anyway and I wore a black and light-blue shirt. Black is apparently supposed to be slimming, but I'm not sure if it worked for me. I was the only bloke who could put on a "slimming" black shirt and somehow look fatter!

Before the final we went away for a few days – if nothing else, just for a change of scenery and to think about something else than the game. We visited The Belfry, which had hosted the Ryder Cup the year before and has a signature 10th hole that's known all around the golfing world. Seve Ballesteros was the first person ever to drive the green on that hole and it will have witnessed so many magic moments since. The sight of Dean Windass wiping his arse next to the tee box is probably not one of them! The story goes that Warnock dropped Deano for the final after he found out about that, which isn't true.

Warnock had shit himself about the idea of me getting injured or sent off in a play-off final, so broke his own tradition of not having a sub 'keeper in the squad. Deano was the unlucky man who had to make way for Gary Kelly to sit on the bench. Understandably Deano wasn't exactly thrilled to hear the news and was in floods of tears by the time he got in the car for me to drive us back to Sheffield. It was shit to see how devastated Deano was and I think he was actually pretty close to chinning Warnock when he told him the news. Deano had done well for us all season, on loan from Middlesbrough – he was just the unfortunate fall guy when Warnock felt he couldn't take the risk. Mind you, if Warnock was nervous about me getting injured *during* the game, he'd have shit himself if he knew about our game in the hotel the night before it. The lads were cooped up in their rooms – bored, nervous, restless – and obviously couldn't sneak out, so someone came up with the idea of a race, to pass a bit of time.

Before Andy could stop it, I was lining up on the imaginary starting blocks against Gary. I could see the thoughts running around Andy's mind. *What if they both get injured? What would I tell Warnock? Would me or Blackie have to play in goal?!* He was shitting it and tried to stop us. We told him to shut up and me and Gary limbered up. Someone shouted "Go!" and Gary set off like a train. I calmly walked to the first door and waited there while Gary sprinted all the way around the hotel floor.

"When did you pass me?" he spluttered after making it back. "I never set off, mate," I laughed. I'm surprised Andy's sigh of relief didn't wake Warnock up in his hotel room!

We lost the final 3-0. I've heard a few theories since about what went wrong, but simply we just did not turn up on the day. Our preparation for the final was spot-on and we were full of confidence before the game. We felt that there was only one winner, especially after we had gone so close in the two semi-finals that season. But Wolves started brilliantly and were 3-0 up at half-time, from three chances. It's difficult to explain *why* we played like we did without sounding as if I am just making excuses. But we were absolutely burned out. Our squad wasn't the biggest and a lot of lads played most games that season. The Forest game took a lot out of us as well, both physically and mentally. And Wolves were a damn good team as well, which shouldn't be overlooked.

Kenny Miller got their third goal just before half-time after Mark Kennedy and Nathan Blake had scored earlier in the game. Kennedy's goal is one I look back at, wondering if I could have done any better. It was in the sixth minute and I should have taken another step to my right. He caught it brilliantly, though, and, even if I had stepped across, I don't know if I would have saved it. Everything's a lot easier in hindsight, isn't it? Who knows what would have happened if Brownie had scored his penalty in the second half?

There was no blame put on him by us, because he was brilliant that season. I would have put my life on him scoring that to make it 3-1 and I would have backed us to get at least another goal and see how Wolves coped with the pressure. That was the message at half-time: *What have we been like this season? We know how good we have been and so do they. We haven't even got going yet. Get one back and see how they handle it.* Then the penalty was awarded for handball. "Here we go!" I thought from the other end of the pitch. But their goalkeeper Matt Murray guessed right and our dreams of reaching the Premier League were over.

The feeling of losing a play-off final is difficult to describe, even for someone like me who has been unfortunate enough to experience it more than once. The whole day is just really strange because of how much is riding on the match. No player wants to lose any game, but normally there is another chance around the corner to put it right in the league. Miss the chance in a play-off final and it's gone for good. That is difficult to put out of your mind – if you imagine for a second something you have dreamed about since you were a kid and worked your whole life for. Imagine you're now 90 minutes away from getting it – and then try not to think about it! The pressure is unbelievable. You could be the hero or just as easily be the villain. You might achieve your boyhood dream or cost the club millions. *Don't worry about the pressure?* Yeah, good luck with that.

The best way I can sum it up is that the whole day just did not seem real. It was almost like an out-of-body experience, as if I was seeing everything through someone else's eyes. I would have absolutely loved to have won a play-off final in my career, just to experience that feeling on the right side of it. Everyone who has done it says it's the best way of getting promoted and I can *imagine* it is. Unfortunately that's all I will ever be able to do.

Our changing-room afterwards was a tough place to be. I can't remember much being said: what could be said, really? Collectively we weren't good enough that day and we just wanted to get out of there as quickly as possible. A big party had been planned for us at the team hotel in case we won and we still had a few drinks afterwards – even if things were a little more low-key than we hoped they would be. The owner Kevin Mc-Cabe got up to say a few words, about how we would build from this and come back stronger. People told us how proud they were of us and what an amazing season it had been. It was one full of memorable moments, but without the ending we all wanted. And no amount of plaudits could take away the feeling that we had failed.

9

GOING AGAIN

For so long afterwards I could never bring myself to watch a re-play of the 2003 play-off final when it was shown on Sky. It still felt incredibly raw when I thought about it, so I knew deep down that I was nowhere near ready to see it actually unfold again in front of my eyes. But I have seen it since and I am able to sit through it now if I have to. It's a little bit like the feeling of watching a horror mov-ie. You know that the victim will end up dying a horrible death at some point, but you can't tear your eyes away from the screen. We had our fair share of thrillers that season, but they, too, all ended rather predictably for us. In fact, pretty much every time Sheffield United were involved in a big occasion during my time there, it somehow seemed to go against us. We always seemed to drop short somehow, which was baffling and frustrating in equal measure.

My first wife, Karen, was pregnant with our son at the time of the play-off final, so she went to bed early the night of the game and I ended up at the hotel bar with Andy Leaning, Gary Kelly and Stuart McCall. Our plan was pretty simple: get as pissed as we could and forget about the pain. I even chucked a full pint down the chairman Chris Steer's back by accident while me and Andy's lad Jack were giggling about an almighty fart I couldn't hold in during Kevin McCabe's speech. For a few hours we managed to forget about the defeat – until the morning at least. For a brief few moments, as I groggily opened my eyes, I wondered if the game had all been a dream. Then I remembered that in our case, it had been a truly horrible nightmare.

When we got back to Sheffield from Cardiff, we were ferried around the city centre on an open-top bus parade. I found it really strange be-cause we hadn't actually achieved anything, but the club wanted to do something for the fans. I'm not sure many of the players wanted to do it and I know I certainly didn't. I had allowed myself to dream of a fairy-tale first season at United, ending in promotion to the Premier League – and here we were, waving to cheering fans from an open-top bus after reaching two semi-finals and a play-off final and losing them all. Defeat in Cardiff took a while to leave my system, although I was chuffed to bits to be later voted player of the year in a season when Michael Brown scored a million goals from 30 yards and seemed the obvious winner. Now all we had to do was go again.

But could we? A season like 2002/03 could only really be topped if we won promotion or maybe reached one of the cup finals. And on a personal level, *could I?* The triple-assault season was absolutely brutal on me and I could have done with an extended break through the summer to recover. Instead the time I did get off through the off-season was actually cut in half because of the play-offs. I know how it sounds. Poor footballers, right? The truth is that I was absolutely cooked, both in body and mind. It had been the craziest year of my life – up to that point anyway – and I remember returning to pre-season training feeling really lethargic. I hadn't had enough rest throughout the summer and I have wondered ever since whether that contributed to the injury that ended up keeping me out for four months of the 2003/04 campaign.

It happened away at Crystal Palace. I had saved a penalty earlier in the game and then made the decision to come off my line to cut out a ball over the top, colliding with Palace's Shaun Derry in the process. I came sliding out, he came sliding in and the result was damage to my knee ligaments and cartilage. As usual we had no goalkeeper on the bench, so Phil Jagielka took my gloves and was beaten only from the penalty spot as we won 2-1.

That injury wasn't fun. They have changed the way they deal with problems like that now, but at the time I was in a leg brace for eight weeks and the next challenge was for me to be actually able to bend my knee again. The physios, Dennis Pettitt and Nigel Cox, used to have me in all sorts of positions while one of them tried to force my leg back a certain number of degrees. I would lay on the bed, either crying or laughing at the pain, and sometimes a mixture of both. They were struggling to get the bend in the knee when me and a lad called Ben Doane went on a bike ride from our training ground down towards Hillsborough, where

Sheffield Wednesday played. I was still something like 15 degrees off full bend in my knee, so I was still a way away from any kind of match fitness and walking with a bit of a limp. Me and Ben were pissing about on the bikes and I hit a branch, flying arse over tit. I landed on my knees, prayed that no-one had seen and recognised me so close to enemy territory, and gingerly pushed the bike back up the hill towards our training ground.

My injured knee was killing me and, as I iced it, I prayed. *Please tell me I haven't fucked it up.* I iced it again overnight and went back in for treatment in the morning, hoping for the best. It felt okay, but who knew what damage I had done underneath when my knee was still recovering? Coxy got me on the bed. "Right, let's see if we can get a few more degrees, eh?" He grabbed my leg and it bent fully, straightaway. He couldn't believe it. "How has that happened?" he asked out loud. I lied and told him I had no idea. Luckily Coxy is thick and fell for it! So I ended up fixing myself and returning to the first-team quicker than anyone imagined. Who needs a fancy medical degree anyway!

Ben is a player United fans might not remember, but is a great example of how fickle fate can be, especially in football. He was another member of the highly-thought of group of young players that also included Jags, Michael Tonge and Nick Montgomery, and Warnock had sent Ben out on loan to Mansfield to give him a taste of men's football. By all accounts Ben was doing well and ended up being recalled. We had played Crystal Palace on the Saturday and had Wimbledon on the Monday, and the two clubs shared Selhurst Park at the time. We stayed down in London between the games and went out to Walthamstow dog track on Saturday night, but Warnock told us we couldn't drink. Kelly and Rob Ullathorne got caught sneaking out, so Warnock sent them both home. Ben took Rob's place in the team against Wimbledon and fucked his ankle in a tackle. He never played a professional game again. He shouldn't have even been back with us, never mind in the side. And who knows where his career may have taken him?

Being injured was a horrible experience, but seeing a lad like Ben being forced into retirement made me realise that I had been fortunate my knee problem was not worse. And at least my spell on the sidelines gave me the chance to wind up Coxy a bit more. All the injured lads at United had to report to Ponds Forge, a leisure centre in Sheffield city centre, on a Thursday afternoon. To a man everyone hated it. Lads used to get verrucas because the pool was so scruffy and, to make it worse, it was the middle of the school holidays. I knew I had to do something, so I called Sue on reception at Bramall Lane and made up a name.

"Hi, it's so-and-so from Ponds Forge," I said in some ridiculous accent. "We've had a booking for Nigel Cox, but we've been double-booked because it's the school holidays, so we'll have to cancel." Sue said she would let Coxy know and I waited with my fingers crossed. Eventually he came to tell us that we had the afternoon off. What a result. I didn't tell him until a few years later when we were both at QPR and he was on my case about something. I told him how I had tricked him that day and he hadn't forgotten. "You twat!" he said. "We got charged for the lane as well because we didn't show up!"

I had to do something to keep my spirits up because being injured is shit and slowly starts to eat away at you. I remember losing my head with Dennis, a lovely old bloke, when I was still about three or four weeks away from returning to training. I was in the gym with a few other lads, just having a bit of a mess about, and Dennis came for me. I took it and took it until he went just that bit too far. I stormed into the physio room with steam coming out of my ears and called him a silly old twat. There were other players pissing around, I said, and he came for me because he thought I was an easy target. I told him I would rip his head off and walked back out to calm down.

A bit later one of the lads came in and told me that Dennis wanted to see me. "I hope he's apologising," I said and it turned out Dennis had gone one better than that. Dennis knew I was frustrated and went to Warnock to suggest sending me on holiday for a week. "That's one of your best ideas ever, Gaffer!" I told Warnock when he suggested it. I rang Karen and told her we were going to Tenerife. After 10 weeks of treatment, the same shite day after day, it was exactly what I needed. I came back refreshed, blasted my treatment for a few weeks and was back playing sooner than anyone thought.

Although I did not miss that gym when I got back out on the training pitch, there were some sights in there. Warnock used to come in sometimes after training when he was on a health kick, with his sweatbands on and the headband like the blokes off that old 118, 118 advert. Warnock was on the walking machine once when Rob Kozluk made a 118 sticker and slapped it on his back. Another time Warnock was in the gym, lunging with these tiny weights, and went outside to take a phone call. Kozzy swapped the weights for much heavier ones and Warnock didn't realise until he was mid-lunge and it was too late. He wobbled side to side under the weight before toppling over.

Warnock gave as good as he got with those kinds of things, though. The story about him taking us bowling has been retold by a few people and, every time I hear it, the figures seem to change! He took us away to Scarborough and arranged a 10-pin bowling night for a bit of team bonding, convincing us all to chuck a few quid into a pot to make it interesting. When everyone in the squad had chipped in, Warnock left and returned with his own ball, his own bowling shoes and a weight under his arm. He even had his own cloth and everything. He bowled a few strikes, won the game and took the pot, thanking us all for coming as he walked out.

Me and a few other lads took the train up to Scarborough and Warnock's only rule was that we were not allowed to drink on the way. I'm not saying we ignored that, but we all turned up at Sheffield train station with four cans apiece and someone came up with a rule that they all had to be drunk by the time we arrived in York. We had a 45-minute wait in York for the next train, so the next rule was that we had to have three more pints in that time. Kozzy was pouring shots of vodka in Simon Francis's pints every time he went to the toilet and the poor lad was struggling. We got four more cans for the train from York, which took about an hour. By the time we got to Scarborough we were absolutely steaming.

We bowled through the hotel door, absolutely pissed out of our minds, and bumped straight into Warnock. "You bastards," he hissed at us. "I told you, no fucking drinking on the train… You all take the piss… but I can't fine you all, can I?" Somehow we ended up getting away with it. Mind you, Warnock took us to a Chinese restaurant owned by someone he knew that night… and got as pissed as anyone else did on the entire trip!

While we were in Scarborough, I was rooming with Phil Barnes, our other 'keeper and a Sheffield lad. Back then you could still bet on football games you weren't playing in, so we stuck £500 each on Spurs to win at home at even money. Pubs back then didn't have football on every TV as they do now, so we had no idea what the score was. I told Phil to ring

Betfair and ask them if Spurs were winning yet. "I don't know how drunk you are, Phil," said the voice on the other end of the phone, "but they don't kick off for another hour and a half." For the record, Spurs won 1-0 once the game eventually did start!

Those bits didn't make the Warnock documentary when it was aired on TV, but the cameras did catch me having to run into the freezing Scarborough sea after losing a game of rock-throwing on the beach. Tongey had to go in the sea with me after being beaten in a skimming contest and Danny Cadamarteri joined us after losing a vote amongst the rest of the lads. Poor Tongey looked like death when he made it out of the water. A film crew followed us around for a lot of that season, giving an insight into the dressing-room and life behind the scenes, but they also missed a lot of stuff. That was probably just as well for us – although 10 pissed-up players crashing through the door of the hotel, giggling like schoolkids while Warnock told them off, would have made brilliant TV!

Barney was a big Blades fan and almost ended up playing for his club at a packed Bramall Lane against the mighty Arsenal in the FA Cup. He was out on loan at Torquay when we drew 1-1 at Highbury in the fifth round and earned a replay. But before Arsenal came to town, we played away at Plymouth and I injured my hip. Jags again went in goal and we lost 3-0, so Barney was quickly recalled and told to get ready for Vieira, Ljungberg and Co. But there was a problem. I got a call at 6pm, the day before the Arsenal replay. "Barney can't play tomorrow," Warnock said down the phone. "He weren't registered for the first game. He can't play in the replay 'cos he were out on loan."

I asked him if he was joking, but I could tell he wasn't. He told me to get up to the hospital for a scan, to see how bad the injury actually was. The specialist told me that it was pain-bearing and wasn't going to get any worse, so he thought I could play. "What the fuck?" I thought. I was in absolute agony. He gave me an injection there and then with another one to follow from the club doctor just before kick-off. Arsenal at the time were the reigning Premier League champions, who had won the title the season before without losing a single game. And here I was, at 10pm the night before facing them, getting jabbed just to get me through the game!

The alternative was to put either a 16-year-old kid from the youth team in, or Jags, so I really had no choice. Somehow I managed to keep a clean sheet as we drew 0-0 and the game went to penalties. Jags might as well have been in goal to face them – I could only dive to my left side because of the pain in the right side of my hip. Sooner or later, I thought, they would *surely* go the other way. But they put every spot-kick to the side that I couldn't dive and we lost 4-2 on penalties. Players like Thierry Henry and Dennis Bergkamp were missing for Arsenal, but we still took Patrick Vieira, Ashley Cole and a young Cesc Fabregas all the way to penalties. A few years later we played Arsenal's kids at the Emirates in the cup and got done 6-0. Carlos Vela was about 14 and scored a hat-trick before later scoring about a thousand goals in the MLS. You have to laugh sometimes!

Every goalkeeper has days like that. We signed a lad called Lee Baxter in December 2003 when I was close to recovering from my knee injury and Paul Gerrard went back to Everton. Warnock had originally lined up Ian Bennett on loan from Birmingham, but that fell through and he eventually signed Alan Fettis and Baxter, who had been playing in Sweden for Malmö. We had Burnley away at the weekend and Warnock couldn't decide whether to pick Fettis or Baxter. It came down to whoever trained better on the day before the game and Warnock went for Baxter. It didn't go well. He let a long-range shot from Robbie Blake through his hands and into the net before a routine header squirmed past him for 2-0. Burnley's third, a penalty, was hardly Baxter's fault, but the damage was already done. He was taken off at half-time and never played for United again.

I think what happened in that first half at Turf Moor broke him, which is why Warnock tried to spare his blushes a little bit and bring on Fettis for the second half. Any goalkeeper knows that it can easily happen. Baxter was just unfortunate enough to have one of those days on his debut. Who knows what might have happened if he had a decent game? He might have gone on to have a good career at United and I might have struggled to get back into the team. I look back to my debut against Coventry when I dropped a cross, but managed to keep the ball out of the net. I could easily have been in the same boat as Baxter, who was gone by the time I was fit again.

I never even had a training session with the lad and did feel for him a little. He had been thrown in at the deep end and judged solely on 45 minutes. He had only been in England for two days when he played against Burnley. He had trained for one day and didn't know anyone. But that's the life of a goalkeeper!

That 2003/04 season was our first without Kevin Blackwell, who had walked out on us soon after the play-off final defeat to join Leeds as Peter Reid's assistant. Warnock and Blackwell had worked together for 16 years when he left and what hurt Warnock the most was finding out about his "defection" to Leeds – in Warnock's own words – from a journalist rather than Blackie himself. Blackwell was the kind of bloke who would take a mile whenever Warnock gave him an inch. I used to smile to myself when Warnock brought Blackwell down a peg or two, blowing his whistle in the middle of one of Blackwell's training sessions and telling him to shut up when he complained. But I know the Gaffer felt incredibly hurt and let down that he didn't hear the news from Blackwell himself.

I can only imagine how sweet it felt for Warnock when Blackwell became Leeds manager, and we went to Elland Road and stuffed them 4-0 in their own backyard. We absolutely tore into them from the first whistle and Danny Webber scored after 93 seconds – after Blackwell had helped to fire us up before the game. In the build-up he had done a big write-up on all our players, slagging us off in some detail. Because football is how it is, a copy of it ended up being sent our way. It felt really sweet to go there and ram his words back down his throat with a 4-0 win.

Even Monty scored! Monty was a great lad and a great player, but I think it's fair to say that he was not exactly renowned for his qualities on the ball. He knew his strengths and knew his limitations as well and he would probably be the first to admit that he was no goalscoring midfielder. But he got our second that night with a well-timed run into the box and a poacher's finish which, as a Leeds lad, must also have felt pretty sweet. It took everyone by surprise, except one man: my dad, who always used to back Monty to score first, for reasons only he would be able to explain.

The odds must have been about six million to one, but my dad had a fiver on him every game. One weekend my parents were stuck in terrible traffic coming over to a game from Halifax, so my dad didn't have time to get to the bookies. We were 1-0 up when they got into the ground and you can imagine who had scored our opening goal. My dad was absolutely raging!

Monty may not have been the most talented teammate I played alongside in my career, but he is exactly the kind of guy I would pick to go into battle with if I had to. Chris Morgan is another from that squad: genuine men who would put everything on the line for their team and their teammates. In football there are less people like that than you might think. When I had a bit of a scrap with Kevin Muscat in the tunnel away at Millwall, Morgs was straight out of the changing-room and right in the middle of it as soon as he heard something going off. That was caught on camera and included in Warnock's documentary and it summed Morgs up as a captain and as a bloke.

The Den isn't the nicest place for opposition teams and players at the best of times and Millwall have, let's say, a certain *reputation* that I don't think their fans – and players – mind trying to play up to. The biggest shithouse of them all at the time was Muscat, who liked to try and prove himself as Millwall's "hard man" and had smashed a couple of our younger players in the first half. As we walked off at half-time, he was just in front of me. "Fucking hell, Muscat," I chirped at him. "Bullying young lads and trying to smash them. Why not smash someone your own age?" He turned around to look at me and, out of nowhere, headbutted me. As you can imagine, it took me a little by surprise. Then I regained my bearings and went for him.

By now we were in the tunnel and all hell had broken loose. I was trying to get at Muscat, he was trying to get at me and Danny Dichio, who was in a suit because he wasn't even on the bench, was hitting me over the head from behind with a fucking Lucozade bottle. That was brave of him. Andy Leaning, our goalkeeping coach, tried to control me by pinning my arms behind my back, so I couldn't even defend myself against Muscat, Dichio's plastic bottle or whoever else was involved. All I had done was defend the young lads in our team!

In hindsight I should have been the bigger man and walked away. But I was in the moment and anyway, if someone headbutts you out of the blue, I think it is a natural human reaction to stand your ground and give some back. The tunnel at Millwall isn't the biggest and I think the cameras caught only the aftermath of everything that went on. In the middle of it, it was madness.

Eventually all the bollocks fizzled out and we were dragged into the changing-room to calm down. Warnock had missed it all, so Morgs told him what had gone off. "Gaffer, Muscat's headbutted Paddy. Paddy's had a bit of a go back. We've backed him up… We stuck together." Warnock was all over that. "Brilliant, lads. We're a team, we stick together. Well done, Paddy. Muscat's a shithouse. Don't fucking take no shit off him. Fair play to you… Well done, boys… Brilliant."

Then the referee knocked on our dressing-room door. "Er, Neil, can I have a word with you and Paddy in my room please?" Muscat was in there with Dennis Wise, their manager who wasn't shy of a scrap himself when he was a player. The ref told us that Millwall's security guys in the tunnel had reported to him what had gone on. God knows what they actually told the ref because they worked for Millwall and were hardly going to be the most objective witnesses. They probably saw Muscat headbutt me and realised he was going to be sent off, so why not try and take me down with him? We were both sent off at half-time. I sat back down in the changing-room with a giant bump above my left eye growing by the second and Warnock looked over at me. "What are you fucking doing?" he asked.

"What do you mean, Gaffer?" I replied.

"Get out of my fucking sight. You've fucking let me down, you've let your fucking mates down…"

"Gaffer," I said. "You've just said I did right for sticking up for myself, Muscat's a shithouse, we're a team and all this."

He wasn't having it. "Get out of my sight… Go and get in the shower."

I stayed out of the way until the lads went out for the second half. We were 1-0 down at the break and as usual we didn't have a sub goalkeeper on the bench. Barney had travelled down with us, but him and Rob Kozluk weren't in the squad, so I went to find them and watch the rest of the game in a room. Jags went in goal again and made a really good save from Paul Ifill, which kept us in the game. We had equalised by that point and then late on, little Del Geary scored from outside the box to win us the game.

"Who needs Paddy?" joked Warnock in the changing-room afterwards. My ego was almost as bruised as my eye! Muscat had given me a lovely early Christmas present, which I sported on our Christmas do in Dublin. We flew straight out after the game and a few Millwall fans tried to get on the minibus that was taking us to the airport, to get at me. I had been headbutted and sent off and now I had fans trying to fight me because I had tried to defend myself. And I mean *tried.* Thanks again, Andy!

I was banned for three games for being on the other end of Muscat's forehead and a few days later a story came out in a newspaper claiming I had smashed up the room that me, Barney and Kozzy had watched the game in. What a crock of shit! We were giddy because of everything that had gone on and, when Del scored, Barney and Kozzy – who'd had a few beers already – were jumping up and down, banging on the ceiling. Four or five of these cheap panels came out of the roof and we legged it. Then the story came out claiming I had smashed up the room! I hadn't done a thing. Any win at Millwall was always nice, but after Muscat's antics we were absolutely delighted to ram it down their throats.

I got well-oiled in Dublin on our Christmas do and, when we got back, Warnock pulled me into his office and told me that the club wanted to fine me two weeks' wages. "Fuck off, Gaffer," I replied. "I'm not having this. I didn't do anything wrong. We won the game anyway... who gives a toss?"

"Paddy, listen. The club want to fine you but if you want to put some money towards charity instead, I'll go back to the board and smooth it all over." He wanted to make out that he was looking after me, doing me a massive favour! So I paid a grand "fine" that ended up going to charity. I went back and told the lads. "The club don't want to fine you!" was the general gist. "The Gaffer just wants to look like a good guy and make it look like he's doing you a favour." Maybe he did, but at least some cash went to charity – and some good came of my meeting with Muscat!

We finished the 2004/05 season eighth, the same position as 2003/04. Warnock told the board that we were missing something that only a few more quid would fix, but it didn't help that we had lost Michael Brown in January 2004. Brownie's contract was running down and it was an open secret that he would go sooner rather than later. It was a case of when, not if. In the end he got a brilliant move to Spurs and not one lad in the dressing-room could fault him for taking it. He had almost left the season before and moving to the Premier League was reward for everything he had done for us.

We were constantly sniffing for the play-offs in both 2003/04 and 2004/05, but fell just short and another season in Division One beckoned. Considering where United were when Warnock took over a few years before, finishing eighth two years in a row in Division One was not actually that bad. But we had overachieved in 2002/03 and anything we did after that – apart from get promoted – was always going to look crap, compared with two semi-final runs and a play-off final appearance. We had not got any closer to promotion than that miserable day in Cardiff, but there was a sense that we were very close and we just needed something to click. Eventually it did.

10

GOING UP

It might not be your fault lads, eh? I'll just have to make sure it just doesn't fucking happen again. I tell you now, I'm more determined than ever. I'll have a chat with all of you next week before you start flying off to fucking Majorca and all these other places. We'll have a chat about the game and about your game. I stick up for you lot every fucking week in the Press... but you blame everything. Blame me, blame the fucking pitch, ref, system, tactics... You want to have a look at your fucking selves, some of you, in the fucking mirror because there's some of you that could have done fucking better and we should have been up there. You're also-rans and you're happy. You'll be off flying away next fucking week. It doesn't hurt you: you're picking a wage up. I'd fucking die for you lot. I've got to bring the players in now and I'm going to fucking do. No reputations... We won't be a fucking soft touch next year.
- Neil Warnock, Sheffield United dressing-room, April 2005

Warnock was right. We weren't a soft touch in our promotion season in 2005/06 even if things didn't exactly fall into place from the very start. Instead of our usual trip to Cornwall in pre-season we flew to China. United had signed a deal with a club over there and saw it as a good chance to make a name for themselves in the Far East – and probably a bit of cash, too. Football was just starting to become huge in China back then, but the tour was absolutely horrendous for us players. It was the worst I experienced throughout my entire career. The heat and humidity were ridiculous. Some lads were losing half a stone in training because they were so dehydrated.

We weren't allowed off the training pitch until we had downed two litres of water and we had so many flights between matches that I lost count in the end. It was too much for Andy Gray, who was so jetlagged that he had to fly home after about three days. The Press were told that he had some kind of injury, but really his head had gone. Big time. He just couldn't deal with it at all.

I can't blame him in the slightest for leaving early. The tour was a shambles right from the very beginning. Our flight from Manchester down to London was delayed, so we were late checking in for the leg to China and the players ended up being dotted all around the plane rather than being together. It was a 10-hour flight and we were sitting with random Chinese families and businessmen. When we eventually got there, we were looked after brilliantly and visited the Great Wall of China and things like that. But it was the longest 10 days of our lives.

I saw the appeal from a business point of view. Look at someone like David Beckham, who was mobbed at an airport over there when he touched down in the early 2000s and had over £1billion worth of shirts with his name on sold during his career. Admittedly we were not on the same level – I can't imagine many kids running around in China with Kenny, 1 on their backs! – but our equivalent of Beckham was a lad called Hao Haidong, who we had signed the previous season. I called him a "lad," but he must have been about 59 by the time he rocked up in Sheffield. He was only a small bloke, but over in China he was a giant. He had played a shedload of games for the Chinese national team and everywhere we went in that pre-season there were thousands of people who had queued just to get a glimpse of him. It was mad. The rest of us could pretty much stroll about wherever we wanted and no-one had a clue who we were!

As a lad, Haidong was quiet and kept himself to himself a lot. To be fair to him, he could still finish despite actually being 34 when he signed for us. The only problem was getting him in front of goal. His legs had gone completely. He was like a Subbuteo man. If you could have flicked him into place, he would have been flying. He ended up playing only one proper game for us, coming off the bench in an FA Cup match at home to Colchester United. We lost as well and I can't imagine it was a game that had millions of people in China staying up to watch!

Haidong scored the winner in our last match on that tour, but his biggest contribution was sorting out a bottle of Jack Daniel's one night when

Warnock had banned us all from drinking in the hotel. No-one could say no to the country's most famous footballer. The hotel we were in was unbelievable, but it was in the middle of absolutely nowhere and the lads were bored out of their minds. Me and Phil Barnes, my roommate and fellow 'keeper, loved a beer anyway and got stuck into this bottle of JD until it went missing. Our skipper, Chris Morgan, had taken it from us, like a parent taking a toy off his naughty kids. Rob Kozluk brought it back to us. "Kozzy, what are you doing, you dickhead?" Morgs asked. "Leave them, Morgs," Kozzy replied. "This will be funny, this."

He knew what we were like. Me and Barney were steaming and Andy Leaning had to come and get us and help us to our rooms. Whoever called him obviously thought we were Andy's responsibility off the pitch as well as on it! He took us up to our rooms and we watched through the hole in the door for him to go, shouting: "Night Phil..." and "Night, Paddy" at the top of our voices. Eventually he went, so we snuck back out and spent three hours searching for a casino. We had no idea where we were and, looking back, anything could have happened to us. For some reason I decided to act the dickhead and jump on top of this car. "Phil, watch this!" I said as I jumped and fell straight through the roof. I was stuck in this fucking car at three in the morning, somewhere in the middle of China. Barney had to pull me out – and we later found out that gambling is illegal in most of the country anyway.

I needed a release because the whole trip was starting to get to me. We had barely touched a ball before Warnock asked Andy to put a shooting session on. The strikers were smashing the ball at me and Barney from 12 yards and the more shots that flew past us, the angrier we both got. It was absolutely roasting and eventually I started volleying every ball that came near me into the stands of this ground we were training at, which had a running track around the edge. Eventually we ran out of balls and the session had to be called to a halt. Andy lost his head at us a little bit for getting him in trouble, but the lads just wanted to get the tour over with. Before we flew home, we had some food and a few drinks and chatted about how horrendous it had been. We were genuinely worried that we might get relegated that season if we didn't pull our fingers out and liven up. Then, when the season began for real, we won 10 of our first 11 league games and had 30 points on the board by the end of September!

The worst trip any of us had experienced had somehow inspired us to make a start no-one expected. We started like a train. Warnock kept his word about bringing in players in the summer, spending about £700,000 on Paul Ifill from Millwall and later in the season splashing big money on Ade Akinbiyi and Geoff Horsfield to feed his striker addiction. I got on really well with Geoff, who had made his name at my hometown club Halifax Town, and we met up for yearly trips to Dublin even after he left. Ade was another good lad with a body a bit like myself at the time. I think Warnock wanted someone to be able to compete with me in the gym! But seriously, he was an absolute animal. When he was in the gym, he used to pull these weights on a wire with one arm and I couldn't pull them with two. He scored some important goals that season and won us some important games, including one just down the road at Hillsborough.

We beat Wednesday 2-1 to do (another) double over them with a stunning free-kick from Michael Tonge and then a volley from Akinbiyi. They scored a late penalty to make it interesting, but we held on for a famous and memorable win. We'd had a bit of a crisis in defence – probably because Warnock only signed strikers! – and had to get a lad called Neill Collins in from Sunderland. The day before the game he was on a drip in hospital after an infection in his leg. Warnock called him and asked him if he'd like to play in the Sheffield derby. Neill agreed, against his doctor's advice, and signed just in time for the game. We met him for the first time as he got on the bus on the morning of the game, and he looked a bit ropey – exactly as you'd expect someone to look after three days in the hospital.

Ade shook his hand and asked him if he was ready for the game. Neill casually replied: "Yes," so Ade gripped his hand tight, gave Neill a terrifying death stare and looked into his soul. "ARE YOU READY?" he boomed. Neill shit himself. If he didn't know what he was letting himself in for before, he certainly did now. Ade, I think, just didn't want a new lad coming in on loan, tossing it off and costing us. There was no chance of that. Ade missed a sitter to put the game to bed and they pulled a goal back, enough to put us on edge a bit. But we held out and Collo certainly played his part in the win before heading back up north.

He had been given a few quid by the board to spend in the summer, but some of Warnock's best signings that season didn't cost a penny. Neil Shipperley was an unbelievable bloke. I was delighted when we signed him because he took a bit of the pressure off me in terms of weight and body fat. I looked a million dollars next to him! When we had the team photo that summer, I asked if I could stand next to him. Everyone thought I had lost weight. Shipps obviously wasn't the fittest player in the world, but he knew what his game was about. He was a target man who could finish and was unbelievable that season. He scored a few goals and created so many more because he used to cause carnage up there. I can't remember him running many channels, mind!

Keith Gillespie also came in. He was nicknamed Bestie because of comparisons with George Best and struggled to find a club after being falsely accused of rape while he was a Leicester player. He had a trial at Leeds under Kevin Blackwell – who Bestie absolutely despises – before Warnock offered him a deal at United on the back of a good second half in a pre-season game against Scarborough. Bestie was a brilliant lad who loved to gamble. He'd bet on raindrops if he could and in his book, he worked out he'd frittered away more than £7m during the course of his career at the bookies.

Warnock wasn't shy of making a surprising signing and probably the most left-field of all came when he signed two lads directly from that lot across the city the season before. Alan Quinn and Leigh Bromby left Wednesday on free transfers and came to us. A third, little Del Geary, went to Stockport County first for a few months before we signed him for about 25 grand. Quinny was a fiery lad – two of his brothers, Stephen and Keith, also ended up in our academy – and, like Del, had that Irish mentality about him. Pretty-boy Brombs was useful, too, mainly for his long throw! He is the stiffest man in the world. You couldn't help but like all three of them, though – especially for having the bollocks to move across the city to their old club's bigger and better rivals.

I remember there being a few boos for Brombs on his debut – mostly from me behind him! – but on the whole the fans were brilliant with them. They came in and got on with things. And because of the kind of players they were, always putting a shift in and being able to play as well, the fans soon took to them. That's all supporters ask for, isn't it? It doesn't matter who you've played for before.

Or at least it shouldn't, and I don't think it did for the majority. Although having said that, I could not have ever imagined me making the move the other way! Not just because of my feelings for United, but because of the trouble I had with Wednesday over the years. I couldn't see that going down too well!

All of a sudden, our squad was as strong as it had ever been with the new lads adding to what we already had with Morgs, Phil Jagielka and the rest. We battered Leicester on the first day of the season – Bestie set up one of the goals, which he was delighted about after all that had happened – and didn't look back. Steve Kabba started the campaign like a train with seven goals in his first 11 games and over breakfast one day, someone pointed out that we could afford to win, lose and draw our remaining games that season and still get promoted because of the start we'd had. That was the last thing on our minds, though. We had experienced the taste of winning game after game, and found that we quite liked it.

There was also talk of a new contract for me, my first since I had joined United. I was on £1,200 a week at the time, which was a huge jump from the £400 I had been on at Bury, and my agent helped me to get a new deal which, to me, was ridiculous. I found with a lot of agents that, when there's a sniff of a contract in the air, or maybe a deal, they will be all over you. Then, when there is no money to be made, they are nowhere to be seen. I'm not saying they are all like that, but ones I had early in my career were. The best one I had was a lad called Lee Payne, who represented Nick Montgomery at the time. By this point I was an international with Ireland and Lee had done a deal with Ben Foster around the same time. He never told me exactly how much Ben was on, but made the point that I was more established than Ben at that time, and was a full international. He told me he was going to push for seven grand a week for me.

"What, from £1,200?" I said. I thought he had got it wrong. United, I later found out, had told Lee what they valued me at. I never found out what that figure was, but Lee told United that, if they sold me and bought another goalkeeper for that same amount, he would want £7,000 a week. "So they've got to pay you what your level of player would be earning," he told me. The first contract offer we received was £2,200 a week. A thousand pounds a week more. I thought that was unbelievable! But my agent turned it down. "Not even close," he said.

United then upped their offer to £3,000 a week, more than double what I was on before. Lee gave the same answer: "Nowhere near." At this point Warnock and Terry Robinson, the chief executive, started to kick off at me a bit. "We took you in at Bury on £400 a week… We've offered you ridiculous money… It's a fucking joke that you've turned it down… We can't believe it, we've stuck by you and brought you here." I didn't know what to say. They were right. They had both done a lot for me. They came back and offered £3,500. Lee turned it down. Warnock properly lost his rag and kicked off at me. Apparently I was a greedy twat and he was done with me. Terry was the same. "Fuck you," I remember him saying to me.

Agents get a bad rap in the game, but this, I think, is where they earn their money. If it wasn't for Lee, I would have signed a lot earlier, and for a lot less, because I was shitting myself. I don't blame Warnock or Terry because that was their job. There was obviously a budget and they could afford seven grand a week for me. But if they could get me for £3,500, that meant there was £3,500 left in the pot for another player. I knew how it worked and knew they weren't trying to screw me over. Warnock probably thought he could get another striker or two with the leftover cash! At this point I had a year left on my original deal and thankfully I was away with Ireland when Warnock found out we'd turned down £3,500. He ended up going mental at me down the phone. "Thank fuck I wasn't there," I thought. I would have been in his office, and I would have ended up signing whatever they wanted me to.

I had a lot of respect for Warnock and Terry and the club as well. And a three-times wage increase is absolutely ridiculous, isn't it? Here I was turning it down! But it was never a case of being greedy. Lee was right. If the club valued me highly, then it was only right that they paid me a salary to reflect that. The club had been good for me, but I had also been good for them. Apart from my knee injury, I had played pretty much every game since I arrived. I wasn't a player who was in and out of the team all season, playing 20 times and downing tools when I wasn't picked. I had played week in, week out for three seasons and we had started like a house on fire, going for the Premier League. I played injured, like the cup game against Arsenal when I had the injection to play and couldn't dive to one side. It wasn't a case of Warnock asking if I could play through it. It was: "Paddy, you're playing through it."

Eventually there was a breakthrough. Apparently after three offers had been turned down, the deal had to go up to Kevin McCabe at the top of the club. "This is the situation," McCabe was briefed. "We've offered him X, Paddy wants Y and we've got up to £3,500." Apparently McCabe turned around and said: "Give him what he wants!" As easy as that. We had been fucking about for weeks and it got sorted with a click of the fingers. I came back from Ireland duty and was told they'd agreed a deal, so I was told to be at the club on our day off on Wednesday to announce it.

I was waiting in Warnock's office before we faced the media and he walked in. The last time we spoke, he had absolutely battered me and called me every name under the sun. This time he came up to me and put his arm around me. "Paddy," he said. "If anyone deserves this, it's you, son." And he walked off laughing! I thought: "You fucker. You've battered me for about four weeks for being a greedy twat and now you're saying this!" It was brilliant, and typical Warnock.

With a new deal sorted, it was time to get back to the business of getting United promoted. Our form didn't show much sign of slowing down even after I messed up away at Crewe and the lads had to get me out of trouble. We won 3-1 and two sides of the ground were packed with Blades fans. The stand down one touchline had only about 10 rows, but it was an unbelievable sight. Crewe had a free-kick and floated it into the box. I was under no pressure at all and heard Jags shout: "Cherries," which he always did whenever I went up for an easy catch. But this time the ball went straight through my hands and their lad scored in the empty net. I said to Jags afterwards: "Don't you ever fucking shout: 'Cherries' again in your life!"

Around the time I signed my new deal, there was real talk about Warnock leaving us to take over at Portsmouth. There was a lot of speculation and as players we thought it was very close to happening. Warnock met Portsmouth and they offered him twice what he was on at United on a three-year deal. He was Cornwall-based, so it would have been closer to home for him, but he ended up staying with us. With how the season was going at that point, it would have been horrible if he had just left. He wanted an answer from Portsmouth before we played Wednesday in December, but didn't get one. So he stayed and we were delighted.

Victory over Wednesday was the perfect way to celebrate and it just had to be Quinny who scored the winner. He smashed home a volley on his left foot – although it hit Shipps close to the line and there were a few nervous looks towards the linesman – and made history as the only man to score for both sides in a Sheffield derby. His goal for

Wednesday came in our memorable 3-1 win back in 2002 and, with the stick he was getting from the away end, I wouldn't have been surprised if he had celebrated in front of them. If it was me, I would probably still be celebrating now. But instead he sprinted the whole length of the field to jump into my arms.

If anyone wondered why, it went back to a few weeks earlier when we had lost 2-1 to Reading, our rivals at the top of the table. It was a fiery game and Jags had lost his man for both Reading's goals. Warnock would rant and rave for fun in the dressing-room in those days, but for some reason he was just battering Quinny. He had given away the free-kick for Reading's second goal by trying to stop the cross. We used to joke that Jags was the manager's blue-eyed boy and Warnock's son – just ahead of me! – and he was off the hook despite being at fault for both goals. Quinny was a fiery little fucker, but for some reason was quite restrained and only had a little go back. If I was in his shoes, I would have lost my head. After a few more minutes, I did.

"Look, I'm not having this," I said, rising to my feet and pointing at Jags. "The blue-eyed boy's man scored two goals and you've not said a fucking word to him. Quinny has tried blocking a cross and given a free-kick away by accident and you're caning him." It calmed down then and, when Quinny scored the winner against Wednesday, he headed straight to me. "That's for you for backing me up at Reading," he shouted in my ear as he jumped into my arms. There is a brilliant picture of the moment and I had Quinny sign it for me later on.

We were looking great value for promotion until we approached the final straight and had a little wobble in late February and early March. We lost three games in four and only drew the other against Crewe. In mid-March someone had sorted us a box at the Cheltenham Festival with a free bar and the works. Like most footballers we didn't mind a flutter, and the card school on the bus could get very interesting when the cash began to pile up. We played three-card brag for £10 and £20 and, when there were eight lads around a table, there might easily be £500 in the middle at any point.

It probably won't come as a big surprise to hear that Bestie was really into the card school. His betting habit began when he was a kid at Newcastle and on one day, which he called *Black Friday,* he lost £62,000. He told us that it was actually nearer £65,000 because his first bet that day had won £3,000. By the end of his career he worked out that he had blown exactly £7,215,875 in bets and ended up bankrupt. I liked a bet as much as the next man – unless I was next to Bestie – but thankfully things never ended up as bad as that.

On that Cheltenham trip, Phil Barnes pulled me to one side before we set off. "Paddy, I've got a grand in cash on me," he said. "Do you reckon that's enough? £400 for the horses, £300 for cards, £300 for drinking."

"Jesus, Phil, that'll be ample," I told him. We were late setting off from Bramall Lane but the cards came straight out. Barney had lost the whole grand before we even reached the bottom of the Parkway. We weren't an hour into the day and he was already borrowing from the other lads. Barney probably doesn't remember the day at Cheltenham very fondly, but it certainly did the trick in terms of our promotion push. We came back to Sheffield and didn't lose another game for the rest of the season.

We battered Southampton 3-0, drew away at a freezing Stoke and then came out on the right side of a mental game at home to Hull City. We went 2-0 up and thought we were well on the way, but then we went to pieces. Stuart Elliott pulled one back when the ball was deflected into his path and I was lucky to escape giving away a penalty when I pulled back Stuart Green's leg in the box. I also managed to injure myself in the process, but as ever Warnock didn't have a sub 'keeper on the bench, so Dennis Pettitt patched me up and I carried on. Then Hull equalised. Darryl Duffy got it from close range and my head smashed against his knee as the ball came across the box.

We looked as if we were cruising, but had now conceded twice and narrowly avoided giving away a penalty in the space of five minutes. I was seeing stars: if that happened nowadays with concussion protocols and all that, I wouldn't have played again all season. But with Dennis working on me and Jags looking over nervously, I played on. It was like my league debut when I got knocked out and finished the game. My mentality was to play through injuries, even though I had no real idea where I was that day.

Not long after I was on the deck again when Morgs smashed into me and sent me flying. He picked me up and gave me a hug before Jags came over. I have no idea what he said, but I can imagine it was along the lines of: "Don't you dare go off!" I didn't, and watched in a daze from the other end as David Unsworth smashed the ball home in the 93rd minute to send Bramall Lane crazy. There were bodies everywhere, but I was the calmest man in the dressing-room when the final whistle went. Not for any great reason – I just didn't know that Hull had made it 2-2. I thought we had pissed it 3-0 and Unsy's goal was just the icing on the cake!

The fun and games really started then and I was reported to the police by some Hull fans after the game. Apparently – again I have no recollection – I was rubbing my belly in front of them and giving them some stick back because they'd been abusing me all game. A few of them took a dislike to it and reported me. The police actually came to see me about it, but by then I didn't know what they were on about. One man who did remember was Howard Webb, the referee who was working as a copper on the Hull end that day. In his book he wrote about me taking dog's abuse all game, from grown men with children standing next to them. He says he was back at the station when 20 irate Hull fans turned up to report me. One said something like: "My kids shouldn't have to witness that." Talk about irony!

A number of Hull fans also supported me over the incident, if you can really call it that, and no action was taken. When I eventually came round from my daze, I wasn't thinking about any Hull fans or anything they had been chanting at me. We were on the brink of the Premier League.

11

THE BIG TIME

T he race to reach the Premier League that year ended up being a three-way shootout between us, Reading and our old friends, Leeds United. Reading eventually pulled away and pissed the league title, but the battle for second place became very interesting – and not just because it was Neil Warnock against Kevin Blackwell, his former No. 2 and old friend. That may have given a bit of extra spice to the season run-in, but we didn't really need it. The prospect of playing in the top flight was enough of a carrot for us.

The chance to achieve it at Blackwell's expense was just a bonus.

Our mini-wobble actually meant that Leeds got to within a few points of us in the table, but they lost the game that could have sent them level. It's a funny thing, pressure. When you're chasing, it is off a little bit and it is much easier. When you're ahead and being hunted, everything is magnified and any little mistake seems so much worse. To make it even more interesting, we were due to play Leeds at home three games before the end of the season. It would have been a fascinating showdown in the race for promotion. But it didn't end up going that far.

We all but sealed our Premier League status on Good Friday at Cardiff. Danny Webber scored a brilliant winner with 14 minutes left and we had one foot in the top flight. The coach journey back was brilliant – we were all as giddy as anything, thinking about what might happen the following day. I didn't sleep a wink, knowing that we were up if Leeds didn't beat the champions Reading. All the lads met up at the training ground to watch *Soccer Saturday* on Sky, but Leeds went 1-0 up with Rob Hulse scoring. Bastards, we thought. The clock ticked down and we thought it might not be our day.

We knew we were still in the driving seat, though, and more than fancied our chances of turning over Leeds in midweek. Then Jeff Stelling, who knew we were all watching him from the training ground, piped up.

"There's a goal at Elland Road," he said. "Who is it? Are Sheffield looking at promotion or are they going to have to hang on?" He was dragging it out. But before he revealed all, the score flashed up in the bottom of the screen. Stephen Hunt – who, like Hulsey, was to play a part in the story of our next season – had equalised for Reading with just five minutes left. We went absolutely mental and, when the full-time whistle blew, the champagne came out. We were in the Premier League.

What a night that was. I don't think I've ever been as pissed in my entire life. Still feeling the after-effects a little, we drew 1-1 against Leeds on the Tuesday and then went to Luton the following weekend. There was a mad scramble for tickets for Luton as thousands of Blades turned up in fancy dress. Our last game in the Championship wasn't until the following Sunday, so we flew out to Marbella after the Luton game and didn't come back until Wednesday. We would meet up at 12 o'clock every day to get on it. There would be 25 to 30 of us in every bar, together.

Reading were out there at the same time, celebrating winning the title. We would go in one bar and see three or four of their players there. In the next place there would be four or five more. They were all in their little groups, but we went everywhere together. It just showed the kind of group we had and how we had managed to win promotion. The trip was brilliant. The only time lads dropped out from the group was when they were absolutely fucked and had to call it a night. Above Linekers bar there was a bookies that Vinny Samways' dad owned and, as a team who didn't mind a flutter, we took full advantage – getting the beers in from Linekers and watching the horse-racing upstairs. Don't get me wrong – Reading were unbelievable that season. We managed 92 points and still didn't win the league. We actually finished 14 points behind them! Which shows how good they were. But in terms of team spirit – and drinking – we were streets ahead.

Why did it work? How did that rag-tag bunch of journeymen and youngsters win promotion? I think it was a gradual thing after the ups and downs of that "triple-assault" season a few years before. We had a lot of experienced players and a lot of good lads. There were no dickheads in that team, which is more important than you may think. Every so often you get them, trying to cause trouble, but we didn't have a single one.

You see players sometimes spoiling training and all that because they're all in it for themselves or getting into arguments with players because they aren't playing and they can't handle it. In this squad everyone knew his place. We had older ones like Geoff Horsfield and Neil Shipperley who knew they were at the back end of their careers and wanted to play a part when they were needed.

There was still one game to go before the celebrations could really begin as we signed off from the Championship against Crystal Palace at a packed Bramall Lane. We landed back from Marbella on Wednesday and Warnock gave us Thursday off before we went into training on Friday and Saturday. We did absolutely nothing but still won 1-0 on the Sunday, our skipper Chris Morgan heading the winner before lifting a silver platter we were given for finishing second.

One of the most memorable parts of that game was seeing Craig Short in white boots. He'd played under Warnock when they were both at Notts County back in the dinosaur age and was supposed to be retiring after the game. He had never worn anything but black boots in his career, so as a squad we all decided to wear white ones. He had no choice, but he was raging! A proper old-school pro who knew the game inside out, Shorty signed on again for our Premier League season before eventually calling it a day.

Shorty was one of the few players in our squad who had actually played in the Premier League, so it was a case of stepping into the unknown for me and some of the other younger lads. It certainly felt a long way from the youth club at Pellon, the rejection from Bury and my dad booting a chair over before telling me to fetch my gloves. I'd had the shit kicked out of me on park pitches and prepared for life as an engineer and now I was going away for the summer as a Premier League footballer, thinking: "I'm coming back to a Premier League club." A real "What the fuck?" moment. There was also another wage rise on top of the bump from my new contract. In six months I went from earning £1,200 a week to nearly £12,000.

It sounds like a fortune and it was. Footballers' salaries at the top level had not quite exploded to the levels we see now, but the boom had definitely begun. Top players like Steven Gerrard and John Terry were earning £150,000 a week even then and Wayne Rooney was on even more. In no way am I comparing myself in terms of ability – or anything, for that matter! But that was the level we were going into – I had watched players like Gerrard and Terry on TV in the past, but they were now equals. In a way at least.

People sometimes ask me where all the money went. I wasn't daft like a few footballers I know, but, as a young man with a few quid in your bank account, you live to your means. You buy a better car, go on better holidays. It can actually be difficult sometimes to spend the money, though; in football it seemed at times as if the more you had, the more you got for free. From little things like free copies of the FIFA video game when it came out. There would be piles of them on a table at the training ground and players could take home as many as they wanted. One year I ended up taking eight, four apiece for Jonjo and my first wife's son, so they had a copy at every house. They should have cost about £50 each.

A better example is probably cars. When United got into the Premier League, the training ground became a free-for-all for hangers-on. One of the things on offer was a deal for Alfa Romeo cars. I never had one, but lads were leasing them for 50 quid a month. They hated them and hardly ever drove them, like – they felt the steering wheel was off-centre and a few sent them back early, just paying whatever was owed because it was so cheap. £50 a month? For Premier League footballers, earning thousands? It was mad.

Later in my career, when I was back in the top flight with QPR, Mercedes got involved and I leased a brand-new, top-spec C63 – which was probably worth around £70,000 to £80,000 – for two years. The cost? £178 a month. I paid more for my insurance than the car itself. I had a white one for a year and then they offered me an upgrade to a new one in black. I paid just a £1,000 deposit and kept the same payments.

The first time I really splashed out and treated myself was after promotion. I wanted something to show for the achievement, so I spent nine grand on a watch. Morgs met a bloke who used to come to the training ground with watches for the lads and I picked this Franck Muller, which was supposed to be worth £15,000. I went to Dubai and had about a grand's worth of diamonds put in it, which I thought would make it worth even more. Not as daft as you may think, see!

I showed someone the watch and they asked if I had it insured under my house insurance in case I lost it or had it nicked. I had no idea that was even a thing, and my insurers told me that anything worth more than

£10,000 had to be valued independently. I sent it off, and it came back with a note. I had paid £9,000 for it and had a grand's worth of diamonds added to it. The value? £3,300. That was just what the diamonds were worth. The watch was fake.

I had worn it for two years and was raging. I phoned Morgs. "Tell your watch guy I'll smash his fucking shop up," I said. "He's ripped me off." My head had gone big time. Morgs told me he'd sort it and to be fair to the guy he told me he didn't know it was fake. He gave me the same watch again – which I had valued straightaway – and three-and-a-half grand cash back. Maybe me threatening to smash his face in and nick every watch out of his place did the trick, but the feeling of being ripped off isn't a pleasant one.

A few other lads bought them off him as well and I don't know if any of theirs went back. I had also bought another watch from him, a £4,000 Chanel that was supposed to be worth five or six grand. It was for my second ex-wife, so I didn't bother getting it valued – I thought it was best to leave it for everyone's sake!

As we relaxed on a beach and prepared for our big Premier League adventure, Blackwell's Leeds were being stuffed 3-0 in the play-off final. I'm sure it was a popular result in the Warnock household – not least because it allowed us to raid Elland Road for players. Rob Hulse joined us and Ian Bennett arrived as competition and cover for me before Warnock went back in January and signed Matt Kilgallon. Hulsey got off to the best possible start when he headed home on the opening day against Liverpool, who had won the Champions League a couple of years before. For 25 minutes or so we were top of the Premier League. Then – not for the first time that season – a decision cost us.

Hands up anyone who has ever seen a penalty given for "intent," either before or since August 19, 2006? Me neither. I dread to think how many games I've watched or played in my life and it was completely new to me, too. But that's how Liverpool got back in the game. Gerrard played a one-two and, under pressure from Morgs, shot softly, straight at me. I held it comfortably and looked to launch an attack, but then heard the whistle go. "What the fuck's that for?" I thought. Rob Styles gave the penalty and Robbie Fowler did me completely from the spot.

He used to jink in his run-up and I fell for it three times against him that season. I think I was getting up from my dive before he'd even taken the penalty and we had to settle for a point when it could, and possibly should, have been three.

After the game Styles said he felt Morgs had intended to foul Gerrard and couldn't even remember Morgs' name, calling him something like "the Sheffield player." The same referee didn't give us a nailed-on penalty later in the season when Luton Shelton was wiped out against Manchester United at Old Trafford. There was certainly "intent" there as well as contact; make of that what you will! Luton had pace to burn and was unbelievable in that game. Seeing a video of him recently, struggling to speak as he battles ALS, or motor-neurone disease, was heartbreaking and just another reminder that football isn't everything.

After the disappointment of the Liverpool game we took one more point from our next five. The draw was a crazy 0-0 at home to Blackburn in which I saved a penalty from Lucas Neill. Unfortunately Brad Friedel saved two at the other end, from David Unsworth and Hulsey. I had a good laugh with Brad after the game, saying he had to take the limelight off me, and I got his shirt. But when you're given two penalties, you really have to win the game and it was another moment that cost us in the long run. Unsy, devastatingly for us, recovered his shooting boots from 12 yards later in the season. We got off the mark with a good win over Middlesbrough, Jags smashing a shot home from long range late in the game, but finished October with back-to-back defeats on the road at Everton and Chelsea.

We were already 1-0 down at Everton when Claude Davis, who'd joined us in the summer, gave away a penalty and was sent off. James Beattie beat me from the spot and we lost 2-0, but the fall-out didn't end there. Claude and Ade Akinbiyi had mutual friends and Ade, who hadn't been in the squad, had said something about Claude costing us the game when he got sent off. Claude came back with something insulting towards Ade, which was a brave thing to do, and Ade didn't take too kindly to it. "We'll fucking sort it out on Monday," he said.

When we got back in for training on Monday, I was upstairs – eating breakfast, would you believe? – when all hell broke loose downstairs. I was told later that Claude knew that Ade was probably going to have a go at him, so put a razor blade in his sock. Claude walked into the gym and Ade went for him, so Claude whipped out this fucking cut-throat razor, like something off a prison film. I don't think Claude went for Ade with it – it was more of a protection thing – and a few lads managed to get in the middle of them to break it up. Claude and Ade sorted it out afterwards, but a razor blade? That's serious shit. Warnock denied anything had happened in the media, but I suppose he had to really. At the time we would have all closed ranks and said that nothing had happened. All fun and games in the dressing-room – it would have taken a brave man to get in the middle of those two, by the way!

Our first away win came in early November when we beat Newcastle, followed by a point against Bolton and taking the lead against Manchester United. The games just seemed to get bigger and bigger as we went on. Our mentality had to change because we were used to winning week in, week out. We were now dealing with bigger grounds and more attention. Everything is a lot more public and tense and, put simply, you have to accept that you will probably lose more games than you're going to win.

We even had to get used to new balls. In the Championship we'd used good old reliable Mitres, but Nike had the deal in the Premier League and there was one game, against Chelsea at home, when Frank Lampard did me with a free-kick from miles out. I saw it well and went to my right, but it swerved in mid-air and made me look a bit stupid. It was a bad goal and I should have saved it, there's no doubt about it. But those balls were a nightmare. We had to change how we trained because of how they moved in the air. We had to start learning to parry balls that we would normally try and catch, that kind of thing. It may sound easy, but, when you have done something a certain way for years, it becomes ingrained. All because of a new ball!

I was sponsored by Nike at the time for boots and gloves and they said that they were always a couple of years ahead with the new balls. Every season they were told to make a new ball that scores goals and basically screws goalkeepers over, so suddenly no shot was straightforward any more.

Especially not from the boot of Wayne Rooney. Man U were my team as a boy and Rooney was hot property at the time. A few days before playing us, he'd scored for England away in Holland, but we went ahead when Bestie headed home against his old club. Rooney then smashed home two goals to win a game probably best remembered for a horrific miss by Cristiano Ronaldo at the back post. The ball came over from the right and Ronaldo somehow put it over an open goal as our defence tried to play offside for some reason. He was about four yards out. People say to me how bad a miss it was all the time and I tell them I put him off – he had one eye on the fat cat flying back across goal at him!

I remember the day Ronaldo signed for Man U, with his dodgy jumper and blonde hair. We were playing Macclesfield in the League Cup and we went to Mottram Hall. We pulled up and there were cameras everywhere, which obviously weren't there for us! We were hoping to have some food and sleep in the afternoon, but it was carnage. We were asking: "What's going off here?" and someone said: "Oh, Man United have signed someone called Cristiano Ronaldo." We saw him and were all "Who is he?" He was some spotty little kid wearing a dodgy jumper, who went on to become probably one of the best to have ever played the game!

I think it's difficult to pick one save that's the best you've ever made, but one I made against Ronaldo at Old Trafford is right up there for me. He shot low and hard, down by my feet, and I tipped it round the post. Just after he looked at me and said: "What a fucking save!" I've got a video on my phone just in case anyone ever asks me about it and if they don't, I show them anyway. The commentators are on Fox Sports and they pull themselves off over Ronaldo's movement in the clip. And then one of them eventually says: "Good save in the end." *Are you for real?* I think, every time I hear it. Is that all I get? It's still a good memory – I had two games against one of the world's best that season, and he didn't score. He should have, though!

After that home game against Man United, we went to West Ham and lost 1-0. We scored a perfectly-good equaliser late on which was ruled out – Mike Riley, this time, saying Rob Kozluk had fouled Rob Green – and it started to feel as if things were not going our way. Back-to-back winners in the 88th minute, away at Watford and at home to Charlton, lifted us, especially Gillespie's winner against Charlton. It was a superb strike from Bestie, whose technique was flawless as he waited for the ball to drop and volleyed it home. Not everyone was impressed, though – in the celebration, for whatever reason, Colin Kazim-Richards told Bestie that the goal was a fluke.

Bestie was not Kazim-Richards' biggest fan and I agreed with him. Warnock took a gamble on Kazim-Richards from Brighton and I wasn't too keen. His attitude riled me. He used to come into training with T-shirts that had a big picture of himself on the front. We had our squad numbers on our training kit, but he asked the kitman to put "Kaz Man" on his. I wasn't having it one bit. I hated all that shit. One day he came in with another T-shirt with his face on – I have no idea how many he actually had – and I was injured, so while the lads were out training I found a black marker and drew all over it. There were face tattoos, dodgy earrings and all sorts. He was raging when he found out. He probably doesn't know it was me to this day. After one year with us he went to Fenerbahçe and I don't think there were many tears shed.

Another goal from Hulsey, who looked right at home in the Premier League, gave us a precious win away at Wigan before successive defeats over Christmas brought us right back down to earth again. We wanted to sign off on 2006 on a high and had one last chance to do so.

12

BACK DOWN TO EARTH

Christian Nade wasn't someone many people had heard of when he arrived at Sheffield United. I will admit that I didn't have a clue who he was when he arrived in the summer after promotion. Of course he was a striker, apparently from Troyes. He had played for France under-21s, so obviously had something about him, and he was another who looked slightly on the larger side for a Premier League footballer. I lapped him in pre-season, which shows how fit he was! A few hours before the game against Arsenal he didn't think he was playing so he went to McDonald's. Christian polished off his Big Mac, or whatever his weapon of choice was there, and headed to Bramall Lane, where Warnock told him that he was starting!

It was like something out of *Roy of the Rovers* that he went out and scored the winner. Kolo Toure was a serious defender, but Christian bullied him that day and his goal was a classic. Out of nowhere he dropped short for a pass, let it run through his legs and rolled Toure. The defender was treading water and, when Jens Lehmann came racing miles out of his goal, Christian finished superbly past him. Bramall Lane went berserk. Then my groin went. I took a routine goal-kick and felt it straightaway. Dennis Pettitt, our physio, tried to strap me up, but there was no way I could carry on. Our centre-half Phil Jagielka took over the gloves again. It was a role he had played a few times before in the past, but it was a little bit different in the Premier League!

I think Jags, like many outfield players, looked at us 'keepers and thought: "That looks fun." It might do until they have to do it and it hurts! To be fair to Jags, he wasn't bad – he is like that annoying kid at school who is just naturally good at every sport he tries. He used to join in with the 'keepers when we trained a few times, just do 20 minutes here and there of basic handling. He had a little bit about him, to be fair – he could catch it all right, which sure helped. So, with a little less than half-an-hour of normal time remaining, he took my gloves and shirt and I limped to the changing-room to watch the rest of the game on TV.

Early on he came and confidently punched a corner away to safety and then made a great reaction save to push Robin van Persie's shot over the bar. We saw out a famous win and Warnock was at it again in the dressing-room. "We don't need Paddy any more... Jags is staying in!" My groin was in bits, but I was buzzing for the team. Christian swapped shirts with Toure after the game and it was probably the nearest the defender had got to him all evening.

We hoped the Arsenal win would inspire a bit of a run, but we took one point from the next three games thanks to a great free-kick from Stephen Quinn against Portsmouth. Then we went to Reading and made history – or rather, Keith Gillespie did. He'd been on the pitch for 12 seconds when he was sent off for elbowing Reading's Stephen Hunt in the face. The ball had gone out for a throw, Bestie had come on, the ball had barely even come back into play and he was off again. It was bizarre. I've never actually got to the bottom of Bestie's problem with Hunt. Maybe he has forgotten himself. I used to get changed next to Bestie and we had conceded on the stroke of half-time to go in 1-0 down. In the dressing-room Warnock said to him: "Bestie, keep warm because if it's 1-0 in the next 10 to 15 minutes, you're coming on. I want you to get at Hunty." For whatever reason that was music to Bestie's ears and he turned to me.

"Paddy, the first chance you get, hang the ball over Hunty's head," he said to me. "I want to smash him." I just laughed. "Paddy, I'm being serious," he said. "First chance you get, hang it up for me to run on to. I'm going to fucking do him." Fair enough, I thought, and in the end I didn't even get the chance. Bestie came on with us 2-0 down and decided he couldn't wait to smash Hunt. Hunt went down as if he'd been shot, Bestie was off and then all hell broke loose on the benches when Wally Downes came for Warnock. Those two famously didn't get on.

I remember laughing when Chris Kamara showed the touchline "handbags" on his show and paused it at a certain point. Players and staff from both sides were piling in, apart from little Del Geary. He had been subbed for Bestie and sat on the bench, sulking. "You wouldn't want that kid in the trenches with you, would you?" Kamara laughed.

Ahmed Fathi was another signing United fans probably didn't know too much about when he arrived in January. He was an Egyptian lad who played in midfield and Warnock's master plan for our game away at Liverpool was to give the ball to Fathi whenever we could. Everything in training the week before the game revolved around Fathi. "Give it to Ahmed and he'll win us the game," we were told over and over again. "Whatever happens, get the ball to Fathi." We went to Anfield, Fathi started in midfield and we were battered 4-0.

Robbie Fowler did me again with a stuttering run-up for his second penalty of the game after 25 minutes and it didn't get much better from there. Fathi kept his place for the next game against Everton, but didn't play for us again and was sold back to Egypt a few months later. In fairness I didn't have my finest hour against Everton either. We were 1-0 up, through Hulsey again, when I lost my bearings and fouled Andy Johnson. He never needed a second invitation to go down, but it was a shocker from me. I was worrying about carrying the ball out of my area and took my eye off it for a split second. Mikel Arteta scored from the spot and we dropped two more points at home, but soon had bigger problems.

Hulsey was our talisman that season and, according to Warnock, was on the verge of an England call-up on the back of his form. Then, away at Chelsea in mid-March, he broke his leg and as a team we never recovered. He had scored eight goals for us by that point, a decent return for a newly-promoted team, and we won just two of our 11 games without him, scoring seven goals. Three of those came in one game. I didn't think we were down as soon as Hulsey broke his leg – the human side of you takes over and you just hope the lad is all right. But it made a bad day even worse. We got stuffed 3-0 and one of their goals came from a corner that was swung in. Me, Morgs and Didier Drogba went for it and I ended up in a heap with Morgs on the floor. I opened my eyes and heard cheering. "Where's the ball, Morgs?" I asked. "In the net," he said. "For fuck's sake!" I said. "Well, we can't do anything about it now," Morgs said before giving me a kiss on the lips and dragging me to my feet!

Looking back, there is no doubt that Hulsey's injury cost us our place in the league. Because of how well he was playing, I have no doubt that he would have scored three or four more goals before the end of the season and we would have stayed up. He might have got into the England squad and who knows what could have happened? He was superb that season; he was a threat in the air, he could hold the ball up and crucially he could score goals as well.

Another factor in our relegation was without doubt West Ham and the Carlos Tevez affair. About the time of the Chelsea game West Ham, one of our relegation rivals, were charged over the signing of Tevez and Javier Mascherano. It had come out that both players were owned by a third party, which goes against Premier League rules. Mascherano had moved to Liverpool, who bought him outright, but Tevez stayed at West Ham and crucially was allowed to continue playing for them even though his signing broke the league rules. He didn't have a kick when we played West Ham at Bramall Lane and beat them 3-0. There was a brilliant moment when Tevez had a bit of a tangle with Morgs. Morgs span him around in mid-air and dumped Tevez on his arse. But the striker had the last laugh in the end.

We could not believe that West Ham escaped a points deduction regarding Tevez and Mascherano. Tevez was found to have been owned by a third party, which was bad enough, but people at West Ham were also proven to have lied to the Premier League to cover it all up. They were fined £5.5m but weren't docked any points and Tevez was somehow allowed to play for the rest of the season. There was some bullshit from the panel that a points deduction would have hurt West Ham's supporters. What about the fans of the other teams all scrapping to stay up and playing by the rules?

I wonder if the panel thought that West Ham were already down anyway. They were rock-bottom when they were charged – 10 points off safety. But the whole thing stunk. Tevez scored seven goals in his last 10 games of that season and West Ham won seven of their last nine to stay up.

Even then our fate was still in our own hands going into the last two games of the season. We were 15th, three points above West Ham and three goals better off, too. Our second to last game was at Aston Villa and Fulham, another relegation rival, played Liverpool, who were in the Champions League final. Liverpool rested all their big guns, like Gerrard and Carragher and Fulham won 1-0. I found it strange that those two both played in Liverpool's next Premier League game, but we walked out at Villa Park for the evening game knowing we were still in control of our own destiny. A win would have seen us safe. A point would have virtually kept us up. Jesus, even a 1-0 defeat wouldn't have been the end of the world because of our superior goal difference. Instead we fell apart and lost 3-0.

I remember having an argument with Matt Kilgallon after a ball went between us and I called for it. He headed it out for a corner and I told him to listen to me. He said he didn't hear me, so I got angry and threw the ball in his face, with a few words for good measure. It was the pressure of the situation getting to me. Even a 2-0 defeat might have made everything play out so differently. Instead we went into the final game of the season just three points and one goal above Wigan in the table. And they were our visitors to Bramall Lane.

It had become a lot tighter than we wanted, but there was still hope. We were also above West Ham in the table and they were away at the champions Manchester United. We were something like 7/1 at the bookies to go down that day because everyone expected our game against Wigan to be irrelevant. Surely Man United would beat relegation-threatened West Ham at home, on the day they got their hands on that Premier League trophy again?

At Bramall Lane, it absolutely battered it down. Wigan went ahead before Jon Stead made it 1-1 with one of the bravest goals you'll see. He went up for a cross and was punched square in the head by Mike Pollitt, but didn't pull out and was rewarded with the equaliser. As it stood, we were safe. Then on the stroke of half-time Jags jumped for a cross and handled it. Penalty. *Shit.* My old pal David Unsworth – by now a Wigan player after leaving in January – took it. Funny how football works sometimes, isn't it?

You couldn't script it really. Unsy had missed that penalty for us earlier in the season against Blackburn and was back at Bramall Lane, facing me from 12 yards with my team and his team both fighting for our Premier League lives. I knew he liked to strike the ball the way he did. When someone hits the ball at pace as he used to, you tend to kick across yourself. I had seen him take so many penalties before and thought: "He's going right." It seemed as if the eyes of the world were on us at that moment, just me and him. He was under more pressure than me because a penalty-taker is expected to score. I felt strangely calm, considering the circumstances. "Right, what am I doing? Which way do I go?"

I went the right way, but Unsy could strike a ball. Pure power beat me that day and we were 2-1 down at half-time. Still there wasn't too much panic. Surely Man United would beat West Ham? Then news filtered through. West Ham were winning. Tevez had scored. The longer the game went on, the tenser the atmosphere became. Surely we would score soon? Surely Man United would get back into it? The closest we got was when Danny Webber went clean through and lifted his shot over Pollitt. It took an absolute age to hit the post before bouncing away from Webbs and skidding across the wet grass to safety.

It wasn't our day. We were relegated.

I remember sitting on the pitch for what seemed like an eternity, watching Wigan's players celebrating with their fans and taking in what had just happened. It seemed forever until anyone spoke. You could see what everyone was thinking: "How the fuck has that happened?" It's easy to look at the league table and say that our away form cost us, but I have turned it over so many times in my mind and I just think it was destiny that we were relegated. We needed just a point at home on the final day to stay up, and failed. But even from the first day so many things had gone against us. The penalty for "intent." Missing two spot-kicks against Blackburn. A perfectly legitimate equaliser at West Ham disallowed. Hulsey breaking his leg when we needed him most.

By March West Ham still hadn't won away from home. They eventually did so by beating Blackburn 2-1. Their first goal was never a penalty. Their second was a shot by Bobby Zamora that hit Tevez on the goalline and didn't cross it. The goal was given anyway. Then they went to Man United on the final day and Sir Alex Ferguson left Giggs, Vidic, Scholes and Ronaldo on the bench because they had already won the league. As I mentioned before, I was a Man United fan as a kid and until that day. After that, I couldn't give a shit about them. I was thinking solely about us – and facing up to the fact that, after just one season, our Premier League dream was over.

13

ONE NIGHT IN HALIFAX

He's let himself down and I think he's more embarrassed about it than anything else. This should have been avoided. I've told Paddy in the past he shouldn't be going out in Halifax. All of a sudden he's back out and it isn't a coincidence. He's let himself down. He won't be going out in Halifax again. He knows he's let me down, but things happen with young lads like that. The lads have got to learn that wherever you are when you're a Premiership footballer, you're news.
- Neil Warnock, BBC, November 2006

Warnock always hated me going out in Halifax. I suppose I was a fairly recognisable bloke anyway because of my frame, but I could have been five foot and weighed 10 stone and I still wouldn't have been able to blend into the background. I had a real problem with walking away from trouble whenever it flared up. And back in my hometown it had an unfortunate habit of flaring up too often whenever I was out.

I introduced my teammates to the delights of Halifax a few years earlier after my kid's christening. A few of the lads, including the skipper Rob Page, had come up from Sheffield and we went out afterwards. We walked into the first pub, a Yates, and it was full of Leeds fans. The lot went off, both inside the boozer and outside on the pavement, and the police ended up being called. We had only gone for a few drinks on our night off and we had dickheads wanting to take a pop at us.

In hindsight I know I should have walked away. But I'd had a few beers and felt someone was having a go at me for no reason. I was fiery and I couldn't back down from things like that, so I ended up getting into trouble. Looking back, it was my own fault – I just wasn't strong enough to laugh at them and walk away. I was a dick.

It was difficult, but it shouldn't have been. I was the professional foot-baller and should have been able to rise above it. But when someone was having a pop to your face, it was different from the feeling of thousands abusing you from the stands. But I know I did myself no favours. I just reckon it was jealousy, plain and simple. I had come from the same working-class background as a lot of these people – the difference was that I had become a footballer, which seemed to make some people quite resentful. Perhaps it was also as simple as a lot of Leeds fans also went out in Halifax and they were United's big rivals. Either way, as we stood outside the Yates with blue police sirens everywhere, I smiled at Pagey. "Welcome to Halifax."

Later in my career I did get a bit better at learning when to walk away. One Sunday I was on West Street in Sheffield with a few of my mates when a group of Sheffield Wednesday fans came into the boozer we were in. There was a bit of banter flying about before the smallest lad of the lot came over and started giving it the big 'un and generally being a prick. For a few seconds I weighed up knocking the short-arse out before real-ising that it wasn't worth it and leaving. We got outside and into the taxi when the lads came out and threw pint pots and bottles at the cab.

The taxi driver wouldn't move with fear until I reminded him that his car would get smashed up if he didn't get a move on. Halfway down West Street he spotted a police van and pulled over. The copper came out of the Black Maria and, when the driver explained what had happened, he looked at us lot in the back of the taxi. He recognised me straightaway and reached for his pocket to get out his black book.

"Ey up, Paddy," he said. "How you doing? Listen, you couldn't sign this for my little lad, could you?" I signed his book and the copper turned back to the taxi driver. "These are good lads," he said. "Take them wherever they want to go." The night could have ended up very differently if I had made a different decision with that gobby short-arse, but instead we went for a curry – and, on that occasion, I didn't end up with brawling with an old mate who then bit off my eyebrow.

That happened in 2006, a few months into my new-found status as a Premier League player, and Warnock was right. We were big news now. Once we had got into the Premier League, Warnock remembers getting wind of a plan for two girls to infiltrate our Christmas do and sell the story to a newspaper. Luckily we were tipped off beforehand so we didn't get caught out but stories of "the curry-house brawl," as *The Times* described my eventful night out in Halifax, did end up all over the telly and the newspapers. Some of the reports were true, some were half-true and some were complete and utter bollocks. At the time I laid low, hoping that the whole thing would blow over quicker that way. Now I can tell the story of that night and what *actually* went off. But to understand it fully, I think it's important to start right at the beginning.

It was back in Halifax that I met my first wife, Karen. We had some mutual friends and ended up stumbling into each other on a night out in our hometown. I was 21, she was 19 and things went from there. They moved quickly. I was still playing for Bury at the time and that summer, when I was in Tenerife with seven of my mates, I nipped out of our apartment to call home and check in on Karen. I didn't have a mobile at the time, so had to chuck a load of change into a phone box, which wasn't far from our rooms. The lads weren't happy that I was calling my missus and absolutely caned me. But after a few minutes of the call I stopped taking any of it in. I wandered back to my room in a daze, trying to get my head around what Karen had just told me.

I'm pregnant.

Shit, I thought. A child? I was still a kid myself. Karen was only a teenager. We had known each other for a couple of months and it's fair to say that having a baby at that point wasn't exactly top of our list of priorities. But we went with it and I do not regret a second. Karen gave birth to a beautiful baby daughter, Beth, and, before we had our second child, a lad called Jonjo, our lives had changed forever. By that point I was earning a relative fortune, on £1,200 a week at United, and we'd swapped our first house in Halifax for a four-bedroomed detached place in Sheffield.

The move to South Yorkshire happened quickly: I had got into the odd bit of trouble on nights out in Halifax and Warnock threatened to sell me unless I bought a house in Sheffield. For the first time in our lives we had a few quid in the bank, so we were able to. Once Karen learned to drive, we had two big cars on the driveway and we had gone from having absolutely nothing in Halifax to being able to afford everything we wanted in Sheffield.

Can that change a person? People will have their own opinions on that, but I think it can. We had become parents for the first time at such a young age and a lot had changed in what seemed like a short space of time. I made my first start for Ireland a few days before me and Karen got married and, although it was a bit of a whirlwind at times, life felt good. On the surface at least. Looking back, the cracks were obvious.

Me and Karen clashed massively and argued like cat and dog as a result. We were both fiery – we were probably as bad as each other in that respect – and stubborn as well. We were similar characters: probably too similar. But I was a young man with a young family and didn't really know any different, so we just got on with things. We had colossal arguments about tiny things and it was like World War Three at times in our house. Then the following day we would forget about it and carry on until the next little thing blew up massively. Then the cycle would repeat and repeat, on and on and on.

It was a very volatile marriage, but I can understand that it wasn't particularly easy for Karen. Before she learned to drive, she was stuck in the house while I went to training and did the nursery and school runs. She was very close to her mum, dad and grandma Winnie, who was lovely, but they all lived back in Halifax and she couldn't get back over to see them. Me and the kids were all she really knew and I think that eventually started to take its toll.

We went up to Leeds for our Christmas do one year and Karen told me she wanted me back for midnight. There was no chance. I had one eye on my watch for a bit, but the beers were flowing and we didn't end up leaving Leeds until 12am to get back to Sheffield. "I'm already in the doghouse now," I thought, "so I might as well make the most of it." I staggered home at 4am.

Karen had put some pans behind the door, so she knew when I was home and came rushing down the stairs. Then a can of Coke came flying through the air and missed my head by inches. If it had hit me, I reckon it would have knocked me clean out. Instead it smashed against the walls in the hallway and stained them. That summed up our marriage pretty well. When it did eventually end, I was devastated to lose Beth and Jonjo, but wasn't too bothered about losing anything or anyone else.

Things eventually came to a head towards the end of 2006. I had been picked to go away on international duty with the Republic of Ireland to play Cyprus and the Czech Republic and a mate of mine had asked me if I could bring back a few shirts from the Manchester United players in the squad. Like me, Paul Binns was a big Man U fan and someone I had known for years. We had grown up together in Halifax and he was at the wedding when me and Karen got married. He was texting me about the shirts on the Saturday night after our game against Cyprus. We had been stuffed 5-2. It was a result that proved to be a big turning-point in my Ireland career, but at the time I was more concerned about some tightness around my groin and thigh that I had felt towards the end of the game.

I couldn't train after that and the decision was taken not to risk me for the Czech Republic match. I felt pretty low after the Cyprus result, but didn't speak to Karen until Sunday morning. We had just bought two brand-new houses, one in Sheffield and one in Halifax, but Karen told me she hadn't been at either of them for the weekend and had stayed at my cousin's instead. Back then she had one of those old mobiles that wiped everything when you took the SIM card out and she kept making a point of saying her phone wasn't working when she took out the SIM card and blew on it. I didn't think anything of it at the time, but slowly I started to piece things together.

I eventually confronted her on the Monday when I got back and she went to Meadowhall shopping centre while I looked after Beth and Jonjo. She was gone for about three or four hours and told me her phone battery had died. It was on 80 per cent. I decided to bite the bullet. "Have you had another SIM card in this phone?" I asked her. To be fair, she was shit at lying. She burst into tears and sprinted upstairs. I knew then that she had been up to no good, but she wouldn't come clean and admit it. *Fuck this,* I thought. I got in the car and drove to the house in Halifax.

On my way I phoned my cousin, David. "There's something dodgy going on," I said. "I've not spoken to her all weekend, she stayed at yours and..." David interrupted me. "What? She hasn't been here." Some more of the pieces suddenly fell into place before I played my trump card. I had a bit of dirt on one of Karen's mates, who had been playing away from home, so I phoned her and threatened to tell her fella everything I knew if she didn't come clean with whatever the fuck was going on. It did the trick and I finally had the truth.

Karen *had* been up to no good. With Paul.

It turned out her and my so-called mate had been together in a hotel on the Saturday night while I was away in Cyprus. The same night he was texting me about his fucking shirts. I phoned Karen and she admitted what had gone on, but said that it *only* happened once. Only. As if that mattered. As far as I was concerned, we were done. I went in for treatment on my injury at United on the Tuesday and called her on the way in from Halifax. "Right, I want you out by tomorrow night," I said. "Get your car packed and whatever vans you need for your stuff. I need to live in Sheffield for work... You can have the house in Halifax and I'll move back to Sheffield."

On the way back to Halifax I phoned Warnock. We had a big game that weekend, away at Manchester City, and I thought he had a right to know what was going on. My head was up my arse by this point, completely – my marriage had broken down and I was worried about losing my kids. Warnock had a bit of a laugh about it and asked me if I'd be fit for the weekend. Dennis Pettitt, our physio, had told me I should be fine, but Warnock asked me if I wanted a weekend off. No chance, I told him. "The last thing I want to do is miss a game, Gaffer." He agreed and told me to have a few days off after the City game. In the meantime, I called a bloke who used to sort me out with cars and ordered a new Porsche. It was my way of trying to cheer myself up after my life had been turned upside down.

The first night alone was the worst. I had got a text to say all Karen's stuff had been moved out and suddenly I was all on my own in this big house. The place had only half my stuff in it anyway because we had only just moved in and I hadn't even spent a single night there with my wife. I was used to the chaos of the kids running everywhere, bathing them every night and putting them to bed. Now the house was completely silent. I somehow got through the week in training – a few lads knew what had gone on, but kept it to themselves – but on the day of the game I woke up at the Lowry Hotel and it was all over that day's newspapers. *Bastard*, I thought. It couldn't have happened at a worse time. A year earlier, when I was in the Championship, no-one would have cared at all. Now I was in the Premier League, it was apparently big news and all of a sudden everyone knew my business. It was right up there with the toughest times of my life.

I made a joke of it with the lads who didn't already know. "I don't care... Plenty more birds out there... The only thing I'll miss is my kids." But I did care about Karen. The relationship just wasn't good for either of us. I had actually been telling my cousin for months that I couldn't keep going as I was, but it was difficult with the kids and the houses and the marriage we had committed to. I thought we had to try and make it work somehow, but there was no going back from what she did. Perhaps if it had happened with a complete stranger, it might have been something we could have worked on. I don't know. But with one of my best friends? No chance.

I consoled myself at the time by thinking it may be a blessing in disguise. I have seen plenty of couples stay together for the benefit of their kids and it doesn't always work. All parties just end up resenting each other and are even more miserable. I knew this was it. This wasn't just another argument, when I could get the hallway repainted and carry on as if nothing had happened. I couldn't even grieve in private. For whatever reason the tabloids felt that my personal life was worth splashing all over their pages and I was counting the hours until I could pull on my gloves again and forget about everything else – for 90 minutes, at least.

We went to the City of Manchester Stadium and picked up our first away point of the season. City weren't the force they are now, but still had some good players. They gave a 19-year-old lad called Joe Hart his debut against us, but we drew 0-0 and Warnock kept his word by giving me a few days off before I went back to training on the Thursday. Me and my cousin went to Puerto Banús in Mallorca, just to try and get my head right. My head was up my arse by this point and I just needed a blow-out. I got it and, after we had boarded the plane back on the Wednesday, I put my head back and looked forward to putting the whole horrible chapter behind me.

At the time I thought I was coping well with it all, but deep down I wasn't in a good place at all. I ended up seeing the kids every other weekend and, when I dropped them back off on a Sunday, Jonjo would scream the house down as I left. It absolutely killed me, as anyone who has been in a similar situation will understand. I would cry all the way home from Halifax and was in no mood to sit in an empty house, wallowing in how much I missed my children, so my solution was to ring round the lads and see who fancied a few beers. Before I knew it, I would be pissed up and wouldn't be in bed until the early hours before getting up for training the morning after.

I like to think I am a mentally tough person – with all the shit that has been thrown at me over the years, I have had to be – but at times in that period, I was a wreck. My kids are everything to me and hearing Jonjo screaming when I said goodbye to him was unbearable. Karen and Paul stayed together for a while after and he used to come and watch Jonjo play football. When it first happened, I told him that I would rip his fucking head off the next time I saw him. Just a few weeks later we were in the same bar in Halifax. He shit his pants when he saw me, but I put an arm around him. "I just want to thank you for what you did," I said. "I've got a right life now." I walked off and he ran out of the bar, shaking his head as he went.

By that point I had calmed down and could look at the bigger picture. The situation with the kids had improved with time and I began to realise that he had done me a favour. He had helped me to get me out of that shitty life, when I wasn't even allowed out past midnight on my Christmas do. Karen later did an interview with *The Sun* and they both had their photo taken under the headline: "I was a baddy to my Paddy." They're not together any more. And he never got John O'Shea's shirt off me either.

Paul and I started our relationship in October after exchanging text messages. Paddy knew nothing about it and was very upset when he found out. He is a brilliant dad and footballer and has been a good husband. He has done nothing wrong. The ones who have done wrong are Paul and me.
- Karen Kenny, The Sun, November 2006

A newspaper later offered me decent money to sell my side of the story – about £25,000, just for an interview. But I wasn't interested. The whole thing had calmed down by that point and I wasn't daft – I knew they didn't give a shit about me as a person. They were interested in the Premier League footballer. I lost my head a bit when Warnock let a journalist from *The Times* come to the United training ground and do an interview with me, supposedly about football. All he wanted to talk about was my divorce and my personal life. Warnock said later that he advised the journalist to take cover in his car while I calmed down. As far as I was concerned, I'd had enough of it all. And then I made the mistake of going out in Halifax.

I met up with a group of mates I had gone to school with and had known forever. One of them had his own business and was worth a few quid, but for whatever reason was acting like a bit of a dickhead that night. He was off his tits and getting a bit lairy, so the rest of us left him to it and went for a curry. The lad we left behind eventually caught up with us, at Ziggy's Spice House, and was pissed off that we had left him behind. "Fucking hell," he said suddenly in my direction. "I bet he's giving it the big 'un, buying all the beers and the curry and that."

"What are you on about, dickhead?" I asked him. "They're paying for their own… If you want to be the big man, why don't you treat all the boys?"

By this point I had a few beers in me and after a few words someone suggested we should take the conversation outside. So we both got up and, according to the version of the story that was in the newspapers, this was the point that my mate told me that he had been shagging my wife as well. Utter nonsense. It was a stupid, drunken scrap about who was giving it the Billy big bollocks and escalated into an early-hours street brawl. My pal took the first swing before we'd even left Ziggy's, hitting me from behind. I turned and went for him; we were both rolling all over this table with food flying everywhere.

The lads broke it up and we went outside. There was another bit of a fight, which got broken up again. Then a bit more of a fight, neither of us backing down. Then suddenly I felt blood gushing down my face. He had bitten me in the eye.

I obviously couldn't see *quite* how bad it was, but I had an idea. It was bad. My best mate, Gordon Farrar, suggested it might be a good idea to go to the hospital and, with blood squirting everywhere, I couldn't really argue with him. I ended up with 12 stitches at Calderdale Royal Hospital and a pretty nasty scar, which is still there to this day. My eyebrow was gone and my left eye became slightly lazy. You can see it literally drop a bit lower, especially when I'm tired. But it could have been a hell of a lot worse. A few millimetres lower and he could have hit my eye with his teeth. I could have lost my eye and, with it, my career.

The police came to see me at the hospital and wanted the name of my mate who had bitten me, to charge him, but I refused and haven't named him here, for obvious reasons. He didn't have a clue what he was doing, and didn't go out that night to bite my eyebrow off – he was pissed out of his head. Warnock was not as understanding, though. When he got wind of what had happened, he was understandably raging. As I said earlier, he already hated me going out in Halifax. "Tell him to stay out of my fucking sight until Thursday" was the message, relayed to me by my agent.

That gave me even more time to stew over everything that had happened. I'd had a bit of a do with my Ireland manager Steve Staunton after the Cyprus game and had flown home injured to find out that my wife had been shagging one of my oldest mates. Then I had gone out to try and take my mind off everything and another of my old pals had bitten my eyebrow off. Surely it couldn't get any worse. And then it did! When Thursday eventually came around, Warnock had me in his office at the training ground and absolutely battered me. He was completely right. I didn't have a leg to stand on. And amongst all that had happened, possibly the worst part was the feeling that I had let him down.

So for a change I sat and took what he was throwing at me. Took it, took it, took it. Then Warnock delivered his knockout blow: "And you won't be playing against Man United this weekend." I had officially hit rock-bottom. It wasn't even that Man United were my boyhood club; football was the only thing keeping me going throughout such a shit period. Now that was being taken away as well. I pleaded with him helplessly: "Gaffer, I'm out of order. I know that. I accept full responsibility. But I've just broken up with my wife… I'm not going to be involved with Ireland any more… This has happened with my mate… And you're not going to let me play against Man U? You're killing me off slowly here, you know."

Warnock looked at me for a minute and then put his arm around my shoulders. "D'you know what, Paddy? I feel sorry for you. Tell you what, you can play Saturday. But you'd better play well!" He got up and walked out of the room, chuckling his head off. My eye was patched up and I played the game. One of the physios said to me: "We'll put something over your eye to disguise it." They did a great job of that. I faced Rooney, Ronaldo and Co., the biggest team on the planet, with a big, white plaster over the top of my left eye. It couldn't have been more obvious if they had tried! I stood out like a sore thumb on a day that I just wanted to blend in and get through the game. Fat chance of that.

I woke up on the morning of the match to hear Steve Greaves, a lad I used to run marathons with to raise money for a local children's hospice called Bluebell Wood, talking to my mum and dad, who had come over to help me with the kids and help me to focus on the game. "Fucking hell," I could hear Steve saying from downstairs. "It's all in the 'papers about what happened last weekend." I closed my eyes again, hoping I was dreaming. *Not again*, I thought.

I went downstairs and looked at the story – a "close source" talking absolute bullshit about what went on, saying the fight happened when my mate told me he'd been shagging my wife as well. The truth obviously wasn't exciting enough and apparently did not matter. It certainly didn't to the Man United fans behind the goal when the game kicked off. It didn't take long for the first chant to go up. "If you've shagged Paddy's wife, clap your hands." I looked round and they were all clapping away. *Ruthless bastards!*

It was all still very raw. But what can you do? I had to get on with the game. I couldn't acknowledge it – I had to try and blank it out and continue the game. If I had let it get to me, they had won. That was the whole point of it. I also did not have a leg to stand on. Everything that had happened was out there in the public domain – with a few half-truths and inaccuracies thrown in for good measure to make a better story. There's no other job quite like it, is there? You live your life in public and then have thousands of people taking the piss out of you about it.

Then when players react, as some inevitably will, they get hammered for that as well. Eric Cantona took it a bit far when he kung-fu-kicked that Palace fan, but players are only human beings at the end of the day. I'm probably a bit fortunate in that I never really minded the abuse. But in what other environment would you sing: "You fat bastard" for 90 minutes at a bloke you have never met? If someone said that to you on the street, you'd probably want to go for them. It really is a funny old game.

I tried to not let it get me down too much and as my scar began to fade, I had other things on my mind. I was newly-single, in my footballing prime and playing in the Premier League, in a city like Sheffield. Looking back now, I maybe went out too much, but I enjoyed myself and did what I had to do. I wasn't stupid with it, but I did meet a lot of good-looking women who were way out of my league.

I knew full well that I wouldn't have had any chance with them under normal circumstances. But I thought: "Fuck it" and used it to my advantage. These women wouldn't look at me twice if I had been Joe Bloggs in the street, or an ordinary engineer back in Halifax. But I was in the Premier League with United – and milked that for all it was worth.

That may sound crass or whatever else, but I didn't give a shit. Not one bit. I knew these girls were only half-interested because of who I was and what I did for a living, but I could not have cared less. If they are going to be that shallow, I thought, then so am I. I had become a dad at 21 and had to grow up quickly because of that. And all of a sudden I had a second chance to go out and enjoy myself again – and you can bet your life I took it!

A few years later I bumped into the lad who had bitten my eyebrow off. It was my elder brother's funeral: he knew our Tony as well because we all went back years. It was more than a decade since that night in Halifax and we had a beer together at the wake. That day, of all days, showed me that life is too short to hold grudges. Sometimes it is just better to let go and move on.

14

CAPTAIN MARVEL

It may have proven to be short-lived in the end, but I absolutely loved my first taste of playing in the Premier League and it gave me a desperate sense of wanting to get back to that level as soon as possible. But there's no denying that it was really tough as well. I thought I did all right up there – there were certain games when I let goals in that were my fault, but I certainly didn't embarrass myself and neither did any of the other lads. For a lot of us it was our first time in the Premier League and, although we'd had a bit of a taste of it in my first season when playing sides like Leeds and Liverpool and Arsenal in the cup, they were one-offs. In 2006/07 it was week in, week out. All of a sudden the speed of games was a lot quicker; the games themselves more intense. We were playing against players like Didier Drogba, Frank Lampard and Steven Gerrard – every squad had ridiculous quality really and we had to get used to it quickly.

The majority of promoted teams struggle with that step up and, although we'd got used to it as the season went on, we were relegated by one fucking goal and had to face up to life back in the Championship again. The morning after the Wigan game I jumped straight on a flight to Marbella with Alan and Stephen Quinn, just to get away from it for a few days and lick our wounds. We were over there when news filtered through that Warnock had left, which was really disappointing to hear.

It wasn't the best way for his time at the club to come to an end and I think he deserved better. It was a lot to take in. We'd had the gut punch of relegation on the final day of the season with all the injustice of Tevez as well and then the manager – the man who brought me to the club and took us on this remarkable journey – was suddenly gone. All of us had been in football for long enough to know how it worked, though, and deep down we knew it was inevitable that the team would be broken up.

The highest-profile departure was Phil Jagielka, who stayed in the Premier League with Everton. No-one could fault him for doing that. Jags had shown that he was capable of playing at that level and, when you look at what he went on to do in the game – playing so many Premier League games and even captaining England – there is no doubt that he made the right choice. For other lads, though, it was the end of the road for them as far as the Premier League went and the knock-on effects of relegation were huge. Players' wages went back down, but more importantly some people who worked at the club behind the scenes lost their jobs to save money. The club planned to make improvements to the ground, which didn't happen. Being relegated is never a nice feeling, but the way it happened made the whole experience even more bitter.

United tried to go through the courts and get reinstated to the Premier League, but never for one minute did I ever think that would be successful. There was a small moral victory eventually when United went through the courts to sue West Ham and won. The settlement might have apparently been higher, but Kevin McCabe settled for £20m to avoid the risk of West Ham going bust. It didn't do us players any good, though, and the only thing on our minds was regaining the place in the Premier League that we felt was unfairly taken from us.

Looking back now, I find it unbelievable that we didn't. We had a right squad; the team was probably stronger in the Championship than it had been in the Premier League. We had kept a core group of players from the top flight and added players like a young Gary Cahill, Billy Sharp and James Beattie, who smashed the club record at the time when he arrived for £4m. Beatts rocked up at Bramall Lane in a Lamborghini with a personalised number plate resembling his nickname and I can understand why people thought he might come across as a bit flash! But he was a great lad and I really got on with him. He scored some unbelievable goals for us – there was one free-kick from miles out to earn us a point late on in a derby against Wednesday – and, if I made a save to keep us in the game, he was always the first one to make a big deal about it. A player like that, on big money dropping into the Championship, might have just been in it for himself, but that was never the case with Beatts.

Gary Naysmith, Beatts' old Everton teammate, was another player we signed with bags of Premier League experience and it seemed that the board's decision of new manager was starting to pay off. Bryan Robson was a legend of a player with Manchester United and England and I think the directors thought having such a big name to replace Warnock would help to attract players to get us back in the Premier League. He certainly didn't let us down on the "name" front – Ugo Ehiogu, who played for England, and Gary Speed joined us in January – and, having grown up as a Man United fan, it was a little bit surreal to say the least to think that "Captain Marvel" was now my new manager.

Our relationship, though, could have very easily got off on the wrong foot. I had bought a new house that summer, but the builder had ballsed up the drains. My house was the bottom one on the estate and, because all the shit water had nowhere to go, it all ran down the slope and settled in my garden. I was having a conservatory built at the time and the fresh-ly-dug foundations just filled with shit straightaway. I had to have the environmental health people round and all sorts, so I wasn't particularly pleased. The builder said he would get a machine to come and suck up all the crap and it would be sorted. Instead he used buckets to scoop it all up and poured it over the fence , all over next door's garden. I caught the whole thing on my cameras.

I rang him to ask what he was playing at and the day before I was due back for pre-season, we ended up fighting. We were rolling around on the floor outside my house, and under my car. I ended up with a huge graze on my face and afterwards I remembered that I was due to meet a new manager – and a childhood hero of mine – the day after. *Shit.* What do I say? For hours and hours that night I ran through some different plans in my mind. Do I say I've been out on the bike and fallen off? Or I've been out running and tripped over? I made a decision on the first morning of pre-season. No, I thought. I'll just be honest. "I've had a bar-ney with someone who's being dodgy with my house, he's denied doing anything wrong and we had a scrap. Maybe no-one will even notice?"

I walked into the changing-room and Robson came straight around the corner. "What happened to your face?" he asked straightaway in his Geordie accent. I braced myself and came clean, telling him all about the house and the builder and the fight. Robson punched me in the stomach with a huge grin on his face. "Love all that, Paddy," he said. "We're gonna get on, me and you." I was completely lost for words. We hadn't even said hello to each other!

Under Robbo there was another Man United legend in the form of Brian Kidd, who had come in the previous season and stayed when Warnock left. Kiddo had won the European Cup with Man U and later worked under Pep Guardiola at City, so he clearly knew his stuff. But for me his training was really basic and he always seemed a bit insecure. We would do a session and then he'd ask us afterwards: "Was training all right for you? How did the lads enjoy it today?" It was a bit bizarre because you would imagine a man of his experience and standing would already know.

Robson joined in with training occasionally, in the circle with the lads, and his touch and some of his passes were frightening. But other times, he looked like a bag of shite. Almost every day in training we would be waiting for him to come out because he was always last, and you could always tell when he'd had a skinful the night before. Budweiser was his poison, and he absolutely loved the stuff. On our pre-season tour, not long after he took over, I was offered a new contract and went to Robson's hotel room to sign it. While I was in there, I must have had about eight bottles of Bud and I was half-cut by the time I put pen to paper. I staggered out of that room and, when I sobered up, I thought: "Shit, I hope I signed the right contract!"

I don't know if it was something that was done at Manchester United when he was a player, but Robson had a horrible habit of naming the team on the day of the game, about an hour-and-a-half before kick-off. The lads hated it. The teams are released to the world an hour before the game and we as players only knew it half an hour earlier. A couple of times lads came into the team after not playing for two or three weeks, so had no family there. They were scratching around for tickets and ringing their families, trying to get them to the game. Under Warnock we knew the team on a Thursday, so lads could prepare properly and we could go through things like set-pieces in training. All of a sudden it was chaos.

One game, away at Bristol City, sticks in my memory from that season and not just because we lost 2-0 to leave us with just two wins from our first 10 games. It was an hour before kick-off at Ashton Gate and Robson came into the dressing-room, asking why no-one was getting changed. "Gaffer," one of the lads said. "You haven't named the team." We had no idea who was playing. He'd handed the teamsheet in to the referee and all that, but forgot to actually tell his players. I bet that never happened at Man United!

We went 1-0 down in that game at Bristol just before half-time and me and Lee Hendrie disagreed over who was at fault when the whistle went. It became an argument as we walked off and then a full-on scrap once we reached the dressing-room. The both of us threw a good few punches at the other before it was broken up by the rest of the lads. After the game we had a cuddle and apologised to each other, and ironically we became really good mates after that. I still speak to Lee now. We just both wanted to win so badly, but defeat in Bristol left us just outside the Championship's relegation zone and the pressure looked like it was starting to show with Robson.

"A number of our players are not as good as I thought they were when I took the job," he told the media after the game. "I didn't expect to be in such a lowly position after 10 games, but we are where we deserve to be. It is disappointing for the fans because they expect us to be higher in the league, but our performances mean we are not." It was a tough time. When a team is relegated from the Premier League, there is always an expectation that they will go straight back up without taking all the other issues into account. For whatever reason we couldn't get it together and had a horrendous run around Christmas when we lost four and drew twice in seven games.

We recovered a bit in January with back-to-back wins, away at Bolton and at home to QPR, before we lost 2-0 to Wednesday at Hillsborough. I don't think the fans appreciated Robson describing the Sheffield derby as "just another game" and I'll never forget hearing the Wednesday fans singing: "There's only one Bryan Robson" when they were 2-0 up. He had another not-so-subtle dig at us in his Press conference after the game. "I gave all the players new contracts in the summer to keep everybody from last season and I'm not so sure that was the right decision," he said. "Maybe we're not good enough to be up there, maybe the expectations at the start of the season were more than the players could take on board. The league table doesn't lie."

We bounced back to beat Premier League Manchester City in the FA Cup with the help of a deflection off some balloons for one of the goals, but after four draws in a row United's patience ran out. Robson was sacked on Valentine's Day, and the board turned to a familiar face to replace him at Bramall Lane.

15

WEMBLEY WOE

I went back a long way with Kevin Blackwell. We had been together briefly at Bury under Warnock right at the start of my professional career and then had been reunited at Sheffield United when Warnock signed me in 2002 and we enjoyed that unbelievable season. He had jumped ship for Leeds a year later, but, after leaving there and having a spell at Luton, Blackwell was back at the Lane as Bryan Robson's successor.

I think Blackwell still thought of me as the Paddy he knew from Bury – a shy kid who didn't really know his place in the game and could be bossed around. But he was wrong. By the time he returned to United, I had played a lot of career games and was a lot more experienced, both as a player and as a person. So it was no surprise really that we clashed a lot. Me and Blackwell either got on fine or hated each other's guts, and there wasn't really any in-between. He would try things with me that he would have got away with when I was younger, but I wasn't having it any longer.

He used to hammer me for goals that were never my fault in a million years, and I would take it. Not now. I was no longer the quietest lad in the dressing-room, the kid that Rob Page thought was called Kenny Paddy. I was now one of the biggest characters at the club. And without being cocky, I had also played at a much higher level than Blackwell had ever done.

To be fair to him, though, I thought Blackwell's training was brilliant. It was full on and sharp every day – 100 miles an hour and full speed. There were no easy days. Some players couldn't handle it, but I enjoyed it. His detail in preparing for games was always on the money. I can't fault him for any of that on the coaching side, but I hated the way he spoke to people sometimes when he was in charge. Even worse was the way he did it. His trick was always to pick on young players and people he knew wouldn't say anything back rather than the senior boys.

Keith Gillespie devoted an entire chapter in his autobiography to Blackwell, and his thoughts on him as a man and as a manager. Bestie remembers one game, away at Norwich, when Blackwell sent Kyle Naughton – a young right-back – off the bench to play on the right-wing instead of him. We lost 1-0, in the 90th minute, and Bestie and Blackwell went at it in the dressing-room after the game. Gary Speed intervened and told Bestie to shut up. Blackwell kept chirping, so Speedo told Blackwell to shut up as well. The manager went silent instantly.

Me and Blackie nearly came to blows ourselves, in a bar in Spain before the play-off final in 2009. It was my birthday and we had gone out for a drink before Blackwell turned up for whatever reason. Our fitness coach was a guy called Carl Serrant, who wasn't drinking that night for whatever reason. I overheard Blackwell snap at him with this horrible, arrogant tone in his voice: "You go and get my car *now*, I want bringing back."

I knew Carl well from our early days at Bury, and got on really well with him. I also had a few beers inside me, and I wasn't going to stand for it. Blackwell was the manager, so maybe I shouldn't have said a word, but again I couldn't let it go. "Don't speak to him like that," I told Blackwell. "Show him some fucking respect." That was like a red rag to a bull and the whole place nearly went up. Chris Morgan ended up pulling us apart.

Another time Blackwell tried to use me to make a statement to the rest of the players and make out as if he was in charge. We had gone on a bad run – not playing badly, but not well either – and he pulled me into his office. "Paddy, listen," he said. "I'm going to have a meeting today and I'm going to come for you. You're one of the main characters in the dressing-room and I want people to know that I'm not afraid to go for one of the top dogs. So I'll come for you, but it's nowt personal. I'm not digging you at all. It's purely for the other lads."

Are you for real? I thought. I agreed to it but, when it actually happened, I stood my ground and argued with him. I wasn't going to let him use me like that – especially after he'd tried to set the whole thing up beforehand as well. I always thought the way he went about things was strange, and his bizarre idea for kick-offs sticks in my mind. When it was our kick, we had someone charging down the touchline and looked to clip it into him. But whoever was making the pass was told to deliberately over-hit it and send the ball out for a throw-in, deep in the other team's half. Then we would squeeze them and try and force an early mistake from their own throw-in. It was madness.

But whatever anyone thinks of Blackwell as a bloke, there's no denying that his methods did help to turn our season around after Robson had left. We were 16th when Blackwell came in, with 11 league games left, and won nine of them. When we went to Southampton on the final day of the season, we actually had a shot of getting in the play-offs if a few results went our way. It proved a step too far, though, and we couldn't take the momentum from those last 11 games into Blackwell's first full season in charge.

We were fifth when we went to Hillsborough to play Wednesday in the Sheffield derby, and the team we put out that day was ridiculous for Championship level: Kenny, Naughton, Ehiogu, Kilgallon, Naysmith, Cotterill, Speed, Howard, Quinn, Beattie, Sharp. Naughton had just come through the academy at that point, with Kyle Walker to follow him later in the season. But the turning point came before half an hour had even been played, when Matt Kilgallon was sent off by Mike Dean for a very soft foul – a moment that proved to be huge in the context of our season as well as that one game.

We lost 1-0 that day and Wednesday's winner came when me and Morgs collided going for the same ball. Morgs admitted afterwards that he *had* heard me call for it, but thought it must have been someone trying to trick him because I never came off my line. The ball instead fell nicely for Steve Watson, who lobbed home the winner. Wednesday had a man sent off themselves later on – although Jermaine Johnson had already been substituted when he kicked a water bottle into the crowd and was shown a red card – and I actually saved a penalty from Deon Burton to keep us in the game, but their goal is all that's remembered! I was so down after the game and called my mum and dad who were heading back to Halifax. They had taken my kids to the game and put the phone on loudspeaker so I could say hello to Beth and Jonjo.

"Dad," Jonjo suddenly shouted.

"What, son?" I asked.

"Just stay on your line!"

I burst out laughing. He was four years old, and shouting at his dad for making a mistake! To be fair I needed it because it managed to cheer me up a little. I had cost us the game, simple as that, and felt so low. It was a ridiculous finish from Watson under that pressure, but deep down I knew Jonjo was right. *Dad, just stay on your line...*

My up-and-down relationship with Blackwell hit rock-bottom a few months later when he put me on the transfer list, after it properly kicked off between us on Christmas Day. Beth and Jonjo lived in Halifax with their mum, so I had spent the day with them before travelling back to Bramall Lane for training at 6.30pm. The weather was horrendous on the journey down from Halifax and I got to the ground at 6.03pm – three minutes late for the six o'clock meeting time, but 27 minutes ahead of actual training. I walked through the door and Blackwell was standing there, looking at his watch.

I could tell he was ready for something and we looked at each other for a few moments before I broke the silence. "Everything all right?"

"No," he said. "Are you taking the piss? You're late on Christmas Day for training."

"Bloody hell, it's three minutes past six. We're not training for another 27 minutes."

"Don't be patronising with me," he said. I told him I wasn't.

"I'm telling you how it is... I've just come from Halifax, seeing my kids on Christmas Day, and I'm not late for training."

He accused me again of taking the piss. "Get out of my sight," he said.

I couldn't understand why he was making a big deal of it. I walked into the changing-rooms, calling Blackwell all the names under the sun, and a few lads were still getting changed when he walked in with Sam Ellis, his assistant. "I've had enough of you," Blackwell said to me. "You've always got something to say. You've taken the piss today. Get back changed, get in your car and fuck off home."

It was the final straw. "All right," I said. Blackwell stormed out and Sam tried to keep the peace. "Paddy, stop being stupid," he said. "Put your training kit back on."

"No," I said. "He's the manager. If he wants me to go, and tells me to, then I will. Unless he tells me to stay, I'm going home."

On the way out I bumped into Blackwell again. He pulled me into a room and asked me to hit him. "Come on then," he said. "Let's have it."

This was on Christmas Day! And the manager was offering me a fight in the physio room. I told him: "If you want to go, then you hit me first, because you're the manager. And then we can go." He didn't, so I went home. I missed the game at Wolves on Boxing Day and a couple of days later we had a meeting in his office. "It's not working, this," he said before slapping my name on the transfer list.

Andy Leaning, our goalkeeping coach, rang me later in an attempt to persuade me to come down to the hotel overnight. Apparently all the lads were asking after me, but I dug my heels in. I wasn't going to go anywhere the manager didn't want me to. Andy had to tell Ian Bennett, our other goalkeeper, that he would be playing against Wolves. "That's just my luck, Andy," Benno said. "I've had an extra Christmas Day brandy and an extra bowl of trifle and suddenly I'm playing!"

I think Blackwell blamed my Boxing Day absence on injury and that was actually half-true. Instead of playing at Molineux, I was out running on my own and twinged my back ever so slightly. I came in for treatment before our home game a couple of days later against Charlton and after the physios had checked me out, they told me to get myself home. It would do me no good to sit out in the cold with a muscle injury, they said. So just as most of the fans were turning up to Bramall Lane, I was seen driving away. It was another situation where people put two and two together and ended up with 10.

All of a sudden fans were ringing up the local radio station and saying that I had stormed out of the ground and refused to play. I was being caned and my mum heard it. So she rang up. "Listen, he's hurt his back running on Boxing Day," he said. "Get your story right, get the facts right!" She's a crackpot, but she couldn't bear to sit there and hear me getting hammered for something that was blatantly untrue. I missed two games in total and was back in the team on January 10th, keeping three clean sheets in my next four games.

Blackwell pulled me back in his office, but the mood was very different. "See, I knew I'd get a reaction out of you," he said. I wasn't having it for a second. He had tried to bully me, failed and was now trying to take the credit. I still don't know why he had the face on that day and tried to take it out on me. Maybe he'd been given the wrong socks for Christmas or something.

Again, whether by accident or design, Blackwell's methods seemed to work and I do believe that we would have won automatic promotion that season if Beatts hadn't been sold in January. Instead we finished third, just three points behind Birmingham in second and with a better goal difference.

After Beatts was sold, we drew eight games and I have no doubt that he would have made the difference in at least one of those. His move was worth a few million quid, but how much did it cost the club to miss out on promotion back to the Premier League? Instead of keeping him, we took the money and replaced James Beattie with Craig Beattie. I know who got the better end of the bargain: James scored six goals in half a season for Stoke in the Premier League and we got one goal out of Craig.

Craig was a good lad, but he couldn't hit a barn door for us. Selling his namesake was similar to the feeling of losing Rob Hulse to injury a few years earlier in the Premier League season. Beatts wasn't only a big character in the dressing-room; all of a sudden you look around and think: "Where are the goals coming from?" But to be fair to us we didn't let it derail us too much and we again went into the last game of the season with everything to play for. This time we went to Crystal Palace with an outside chance of automatic promotion. We needed to beat Palace and hope Birmingham lost, but it wasn't to be.

About 7,000 Blades followed us down to London, but we couldn't find a way past Palace – managed, ironically, by Warnock. We had to settle for the play-offs. We edged past Preston in the two-legged semi-final, Greg Halford scoring the winner to send Bramall Lane absolutely crazy in the second game and set up a Wembley final date with Burnley. Me and Blackie had our set-to in Spain before the game and a couple of other things he did before the final pissed me off.

First, he came out and slagged off the referee who would take charge of the final, Mike Dean. Dean had sent off Killa at Hillsborough earlier in the season and Blackie called his appointment "stupid" and "absolutely inexplicable" for whatever reason. The tit. It was stupid of him. The FA weren't likely to change their minds on the back of a manager slagging off the referee, were they? I'm not saying it made a difference to Dean's decision-making on the day but I don't think it did us any favours, either.

Then in the build-up to the game he made the decision for us to stay at Luton Hoo Hotel. It was almost 30 miles away from Wembley by road and on the day it took us an hour-and-a-half to get to the stadium. We were sweating our bollocks off on the coach. What kind of preparation is that? It was a shit way to get ready for the biggest game in English football. We all knew what it meant – the game is life-changing. I had been involved in our last play-off final against Wolves in 2003, so had an idea of what to expect. It's absolutely impossible to put out of your mind what the game means, for so many other people as well as yourself.

My abiding memory of Wembley that day was the heat. It was piping. It was energy-sapping just warming up. At least we made a better start than we had in Cardiff against Wolves when we were a goal down after six minutes. This time Burnley had to wait 13 minutes before they went ahead. Wade Elliott ran from halfway and shrugged off both Nick Montgomery and Stephen Quinn. He played in Chris McCann, but Killa had got a toe on the ball to stab it away. It rolled perfectly to Elliott, who curled the ball at pace into the top corner. *Bastard.*

I am my own biggest critic, but there was no saving that in a million years. After the early goal against Wolves, we went to pieces, but this time we settled down a bit and started to get on the ball. We had a long time to get back in the game and threw everything at it, but couldn't break through. Again, if we'd had Beatts, maybe he would have come up with a moment of magic. If we had kept him, we would likely never have been at Wembley that day anyway.

It's all ifs, buts and maybes, I guess.

We had a good go and had about four penalty appeals turned down by Dean. Burnley had a few chances as we pushed forward and the two Kyles, Walker and Naughton, really came of age that day. They both went on to do amazing things and, although no-one predicted the success Walker would have, it wasn't a surprise to anyone that they moved to a higher level. I just wish it had been with Sheffield United.

After the best penalty appeal of the lot, when Walker was brought down after getting in behind, there was a sense that it might not be our day. When Jamie Ward came off the bench and was sent off for two handballs, it confirmed it. Lee Hendrie, another substitute, also saw red after the game for telling Dean what he thought of his performance and, as the final whistle sounded and Burnley players celebrated all around us, a familiar feeling was forming in the pit of my stomach. Another horrible day.

Back where it all began – with my brother, Sean

An early family holiday – check out those outfits!

Chilling out with Mum beside the seaside – I had no idea I would later wear the Irish jersey for real!

Picking up the Boothtown player of the year trophy early in my career

Lining up with Dad before one of his games when I was only a kid

Playing 'Thunder Blade' at the arcade in my 'United' T-shirt - pretty ironic, really, considering I played for the Blades later in my life

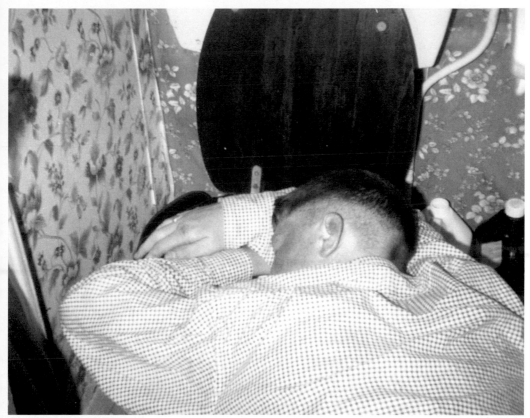

This is how my first night out in Halifax ended! I was 16 – and it didn't put me off

I've always been a sucker for a bird... this one didn't cost me a fortune, though!

☐ A GOAL by Gerard Horner five minutes from time against Wibsey Middle School won the Diamik West Yorkshire Schools U13s FA Cup for Halifax Catholic High School when the two sides met at the Shay. The winners now join three other Yorkshire schools in their bid to win the Yorkshire Cup.

The Catholic High School team are, from the left, back row: Jason Kendall, John McGahey, Neil Grant, Craig Armstrong, Danny Megson, Ronald Briggs, Gerard Horner and Dean Finelli. Front: Daniel Montgomery, Daniel Farrar, Craig Whelan, Andrew Laheney, Andrew Pearson, Noel Horner, Patrick Kenny and David Manley.

A write-up in the Halifax Courier of our school team's West Yorkshire FA Cup win. We won the Yorkshire Cup, too

The early days at Bury - and some proper facials as I came off my line for a change against Wigan!

The Gaffer – a brilliant man, and an incredible manager

Moving to Sheffield United was a huge step up, both on and off the pitch

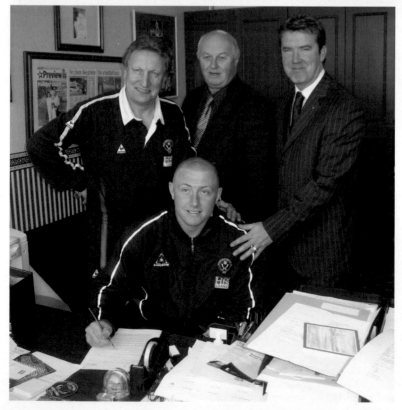

Above left: On United debut, in front of thousands of fans in a friendly at Baslow

Martyn Harrison

Above right: Clowning around with the legend, Stuart McCall

Sheffield United

Left: All smiles with The Gaffer, Terry Robinson and my agent after signing a new contract – even after Warnock called me all the names under the sun because of our negotiations!

Sheffield United

PLEASE R
BOOTS BE
ENTERING
THANK

Trying my hand at modelling in a few photos for
the front of the programme throughout the year.
They had us players doing all sorts!

On international duty with Ireland - here, Klaas-Jan Huntelaar beats me in a 4-0 defeat to Holland in 2006

Meeting a hero in Peter Schmeichel before the
FA Cup semi-final against Arsenal at Old Trafford

Despair after the 2003 play-off final defeat to Wolves

Michael Brown was unbelievable in 2002/03 as we
reached two semi-finals and a play-off final - but I
somehow beat him to the player of the year award

A frustrated, injured goalkeeper in 2004 - until
one day, I managed to fix myself by accident!

Alan Quinn scored the winner against Wednesday – and sprinted the length of the pitch into my arms!

Phil Jagielka – a top man and part-time 'keeper! Here he took my shirt and gloves in a quiet game at Millwall

Above: Celebrating promotion to the Premier League in 2006 with Jonjo and Beth. Inset: On the piss in Marbella with Jags – we were out there for five days, came back and beat Crystal Palace in our last game of the season!

The pain of the Premier League. Putting my body on the line to save from Wayne Rooney at Old Trafford...

...and feeling my groin against Arsenal. I couldn't carry on but Jags kept a clean sheet in an unbelievable win

Sharing a joke with Jags – but I wasn't laughing inside. I played against my boyhood club, Manchester United, with a huge bandage over my eye after having my eyebrow bitten off by a pal after my wife cheated on me...

Martyn Harrison

Martyn Harrison

Above: Working hard in training... honest! Andy Leaning, right, was my first full-time goalkeeping coach and we had so many good times together. I believe his loyalty to me ultimately cost him his job at United, and we later worked together at Leeds. Below: The elation of victory in the 2009 Championship play-off semi-final against Preston North End at Bramall Lane, to take us to Wembley. My celebrations were cut short by a random drugs test, and my life was soon turned upside-down

Martyn Harrison

Clockwise from left: Game face before the 2009 play-off final, and another defeat; An emotional reception in my first game back after my drugs ban; Getting up close and personal with John Terry while at QPR; Sharing a joke with Warnock after he met the buy-out clause United had inserted into my contract

A dream first season at QPR ended with us winning the Championship title, and me breaking the club record for clean sheets. I got my hands on the trophy for this picture with Beth, Jonjo and the unbelievable Adel Taarabt

My view of Sergio Aguero's goal that won Manchester City the title. To this day, I get people telling me I should have saved it. I was about four yards away from him and he absolutely smashed it into the back of my net

After a messy divorce from QPR, I signed for Leeds and looked forward to another go at promotion

I came back for pre-season in the best shape ever – but a dodgy still from a video suggested differently

Left to right: Making my own squad number at Leeds after being bombed out; Enjoying a few pre-season beers in Slovenia after sneaking out on Brian McDermott; Getting out on the road after setting up my own business

All smiles after linking up with Warnock for a fifth time. Keeping Rotherham up is one of his best achievements

Above: Posing with my Maltby Main shirt after signing on for what turned out to be a short spell. Right: The top that David Seaman sent me after the 2003 FA Cup semi-final against Arsenal. It was his 1,000th game, and he made THAT save from Paul Peschisolido

I was never shy of having a bit of banter with opposition fans behind my goal – no matter what they were singing about me!

My mum and dad, who have been by my side for every step of the journey - good and bad

My children mean the world to me. From left to right: Jonjo, Ashlin, Beth and Kaelin

Wembley must be a great place to win a game like that, but it's horrendous for the team on the other side of it. Everyone just wanted to get out of there. All you want to do is lick your wounds and go again, which I knew from past experience was easier said than done. I ended up in Egypt that summer and slowly tried to get the Burnley game out of my system. I was looking forward to another crack at it the following season. And then out of the blue, my phone rang.

16

BANNED

The Sheffield United goalkeeper Paddy Kenny has been suspended from all football for nine months after failing a drugs test. Kenny could have been given a two-year ban after testing positive for the stimulant ephedrine, which is found in some cold remedies, but mitigating circumstances were taken into account by the FA's judgment. The Republic of Ireland international was found not to have attempted to "enhance sporting performance" when ingesting an over-the-counter medicine without consulting United's medical team. His manager, Kevin Blackwell, has called the punishment "harsh", however, and said the club may challenge the decision.
- Alan Gardner, The Guardian, September 2009

"You've failed the drugs test."

The unmistakably broad Lancastrian accent on the other end of the line belonged to Terry Robinson, then the chief executive of Sheffield United. My reaction was to laugh down the phone. I said to him: "Are you winding me up? I've never touched drugs in my life." He repeated himself: "You've failed the drugs test, Paddy. We don't know what it is yet. We need to find out. And we'll need to speak to you when you get back." I was in complete shock. There had to be a mistake somewhere. Someone had messed up. *Surely.*

It all traced back to the previous season before the play-off semi-final against Preston. In the week leading up to the game I had suffered quite badly with chest infections and I was struggling to sleep at night, having trouble breathing and coughing all sorts of crap up. Louise, my missus at the time, used to work in a chemist and suggested taking some ChestEze tablets to see if they helped. I took six tablets in total over three nights and to be fair, they did the job. They helped me to sleep before the game. We drew 1-1 at their place and won the return leg at Bramall Lane, so were through to the play-off final at Wembley.

At full time the stadium was absolutely buzzing. Fans were everywhere and the lads were bouncing around like mad men. We were 90 minutes away from getting back into the Premier League, which was life-changing for everyone at the club. I couldn't wait to join in the celebrations. And then I got the tap on my shoulder. "You've got to come with us." The random drug test! Typical. It takes forever to piss in the cup and give a sample because of the dehydration from the game. We had got through to the play-off final, my teammates were celebrating and I was sat in a room filling out a fucking form.

Players were asked to write down anything they had taken recently on the paperwork and in the week before the game I had taken ChestEze and Zopiclone to help me to sleep ahead of one of the biggest games of my career so far. I had also used paracetamol and Voltarol to help with a few niggles I had before the game. My head was a blur because of the euphoria of the win, so I left the box blank and went to give my sample. The drug-tester does not leave your side until you've pissed in the cup. If you go in the shower, he's got to stand and watch you. If you go to the toilet, you've got to drop your trousers and lift up your T-shirt to prove you're not hiding anything. Apparently back in the day players went to all sorts of lengths to avoid being detected – fake cocks and bags filled with someone else's piss and all sorts. It wasn't fun – and certainly not how I would have chosen to celebrate getting to Wembley!

I understand that the drug-testers have a job to do, though, and are a valuable part of making sure that sport is clean. I was only young when Ben Johnson was done for doping after taking steroids to beat his big rival Carl Lewis in at the 1988 Olympics and, although we didn't have anything like the coverage of sport that exists now, I remember the fallout after he was stripped of his gold medal in disgrace. Drug cheats bring shame upon any sport. I don't know how they think they can get away with it and in my view, if they feel they need to cheat, then they shouldn't even be involved in the first place.

I got back from holiday after Terry's phone call and the club suspended me more or less straightaway. I think the reasoning was that, if I was eventually banned, the club hoped it would be backdated to the day I was suspended. Then the process began; meetings with the club, the FA, the PFA, my QC from London. We had conference calls every other day, trying to get to the bottom of what exactly had happened. At this point I still didn't know how I had failed the test. Eventually the FA came to interview me at Bramall Lane and that's when I found out that ChestEze contains a small amount of ephedrine. Ephedrine, it turned out, is a stimulant on the list of banned substances and the people from the FA could not get their heads around why I hadn't disclosed taking the tablets.

It wasn't just ChestEze I hadn't told them about; there was also the paracetamol, sleeping tablets and Voltarol. If I was somehow trying to cheat, I would surely have just left ChestEze off the list? The truth is that I was simply not thinking that logically. I was on a high – not literally, I should say – and was thinking about nothing else apart from what we had achieved less than half an hour earlier. My mates and the fans were out there celebrating and I wanted to be with them; the last thing on my mind was some over-the-counter chest medicine I had taken a week earlier.

Eventually a date was set for my hearing and before then me and my agent went down to see my QC in London. This bloke supposedly knew his stuff – which he should, considering that he ended up costing me nearly £30,000 in the end – and told us that, as far as he was concerned, I would get done for negligence at worst and be banned for three months maximum, backdated to when I was suspended by the club. It all sounded so simple and obvious when he said it. I might miss a month or so of the season and, although I obviously didn't want to be banned at all, I would have snatched his hand off for that just to get the cloud from over my head. As far as the expert was concerned, I had nothing to worry about.

The evidence in my defence was overwhelming. Put simply, my levels weren't high enough to get done for cheating. My QC got a scientist to work out the mixture of everything I'd put into my system before the Preston game. His findings said it all. To gain any enhancement in performance whatsoever, I would have had to have taken 50 to 60 ChestEze tablets 20 minutes before the game. Even then that would contain only enough ephedrine to give me a 20-minute buzz and considering I had taken six tablets across three days, I was hardly sprinting around like Ben Johnson. Armed with that scientific evidence, I went into the hearing in confident mood.

Athletes don't take ChestEze the week before a game to try and enhance their performance and in my mind, I could only hear what my QC had told me at our first meeting. *Done for negligence... three months' ban, maximum... backdated to when you were suspended.* It can't be that bad, I thought. This will all be over by the end of the day and I can get back to focusing on football. I couldn't wait.

The hearing itself was held in one of those Club Wembley boxes with big glass panels overlooking the huge stadium with its bright red seats and lush green turf. I looked out and allowed my mind to wander back to the Burnley game when I had walked out onto that pitch for the first time. It was one of the biggest games of my career and yet here I was a few weeks later back at Wembley and preparing to go into a room where I may have to battle to save it. Sure, I was confident – but the nagging doubt at the back of my head wouldn't quite go away just yet.

I sat, suited and booted, in front of a three-man panel on the other side of a U-shaped table and gave my side of the story. My manager, Kevin Blackwell, was also interviewed, as was Robinson and Louise, to explain her role in me taking the tablets. We were called back in after two hours that seemed more like two days. The panel had come to an agreement; I had not used the ChestEze tablets to enhance my performance and cheat. My heart raced. They were going to do me for negligence. My QC kicked me under the table and wrote down on a piece of paper: "No Ban." And then the panel delivered their punishment. A nine-month ban.

Wow.

I have since tried to sum up my feelings in those few seconds and minutes that followed the verdict, but I simply can't. The best I can do is that I felt like someone had hit me over the head with a huge bat. At first all I had were questions. What? Why? How can this be happening? How can the panel be so far apart from my QC? I thought I would get a three-month ban. They agreed I had only been negligent and that I had no intention to cheat, yet I had been banned for nine months. Quick maths told me I would be out of action until April, but my worries extended far beyond the season in front of us. "This could be me done and dusted," I thought. In that moment, as I stared straight ahead in complete shock, I thought my career was over.

Blackwell eventually broke the silence outside the room after about half an hour of dumbstruck silence from everyone present. "I'm sorry," he said. "I can't believe it. I can't believe what's gone on. It's wrong." So many people offered their condolences and expressed anger or shock or whatever else. After a while I stopped taking it all in. Only one thought consumed me now – I was finished as a footballer.

Getting home from Wembley was a complete blur. I remember being taken out of a side door to avoid the media outside, but have no further recollection of driving home. It took nearly three hours, but I didn't say a word for the entire journey. To this day I honestly couldn't say if we stopped off or if there was any traffic. All I could think about was my career, or what was left of it. When I did eventually make it home, I didn't go outside again for days. I don't mind admitting I felt a mixture of embarrassment and fear. But my QC was adamant there was still hope. United wanted to appeal against the decision, so the process began again. More conference calls, more meetings. No football.

I couldn't go to matches and I couldn't train with the boys. I wasn't even allowed at the training ground, full stop. I was still an employee of the club, but could have nothing to do with them. So it was a case of forcing myself up in the mornings to attempt to stay fit. I hired a personal trainer, Matt Sanderson, and worked with him three times a week. A lad I know called Matt Roney, who has played about a thousand games in non-league for Sheffield FC, used to meet me twice a week to do some goalkeeping drills. Both Matts definitely helped me, both physically and mentally, but still there were times when I just couldn't face getting out of bed.

Weekends were the worst. During the week I could occupy myself at the gym or on the course at Bondhay Golf Club, but there was nothing that could replace that feeling of waking up on a Saturday and looking forward to the game. The buzz used to start as soon as I opened my eyes, but suddenly it was gone. Footballers can get a bad reputation – and at times a deserved one – but throughout my career I have never known one who was happy to pick up a wage and not play on the weekend. We have been conditioned since a young age to work towards a matchday, so spending them at the gym and watching the scores come in on *Soccer Saturday* was not an easy time.

It was a little easier, though, that I had a date to work towards. It wasn't as if I was injured and my recovery could take longer than planned if my body didn't heal properly or I was worried in the back of my mind about breaking down again. I had something concrete to aim for and I knew I would definitely be available again when that day came around. In the meantime, it was a case of making sure I was in the best shape possible.

For the record I completely accept the negligence charge. It was so stupid and clumsy of me not to think to check what was contained in the tablets, but I never tried, and would never try, to cheat. The science backed that up as well. What made me feel hard done by, and still does, is the length of the ban. Chelsea's Adrian Mutu got nine months after testing positive for cocaine, a Class A drug. Rio Ferdinand missed a test entirely and was banned for less time than me, eight months. The one that really rankles, though, is Kolo Toure. He took his wife's slimming tablets, which contained a banned substance, and failed a drugs test. The commission accepted that "Toure did not intend to enhance sporting performance or to mask the use of a performance-enhancing substance."

Sound familiar? They accepted the same at my hearing. Our cases were actually pretty similar; except for when the bans were handed out. Toure got six months, which ran through the summer, and he was back playing by September. I couldn't get my head around the panel saying that taking slimming pills doesn't enhance performance and also why Toure's ban was a third shorter than mine, 18 months earlier. I wasn't the only one. "How the fuck has he only got six months for that?" my dad asked. I didn't have an answer for him at the time and I still don't to this day.

I can also still remember vividly a conversation I had with an old United teammate of mine soon after my ban. He was always someone that I had got on well with and I was in the car-park of Bondhay waiting to start another round when he called. He had left United that summer and told me that at his new club he knew four or five players who went out every Saturday and got off their rocker on recreational drugs. They knew that they had Sunday and Monday off training and that whatever they had taken would be out of their system by the time they came back to training on the Tuesday. They would be clean. "You've been punished for nothing, for being negligent, and they're going out and sniffing whatever, knowing they're going to get away with it," my mate said. "And you'll miss a full season of your career even if you carry on in the game." I think he was trying to make me feel better, but the call made it even tougher to take.

The glimmer of hope in the shape of my appeal was extinguished when a three-man panel turned it down, two-to-one. The funny thing, if that's the right phrase, is that I had never even heard of ephedrine before I was accused of taking it. I didn't have the faintest idea what it even was, although I know full well now. It's connected to me, all over the internet. My name is there in a story in the *Daily Telegraph* from 2011, underneath the headline: "Football's drug problem." Most of the articles contained some kind of reference to DRUGS BAN.

Years ago those 'papers would become fish-and-chip paper; gone, forgotten. Now my name is on the internet, forever associated with drugs. The articles themselves contain the full truth, that I was cleared of cheating and was done for negligence. But the papers screamed: "Drug ban" and all of a sudden, people thought I was taking all sorts. That I was some sort of Lance Armstrong-type doper or was off snorting coke in a toilet every weekend with my mates.

It could not be further from the truth.

The other part of the process that pissed me off was the FA's system of communication when I was initially suspended. I had to send them a text message every day, telling them where I would be and when that day in case they wanted to come and drug-test me randomly. In my messages I was literally sending: "Paddy Kenny of Sheffield United will be at home between 8pm and 9pm."

I never saw another tester or heard another word back from the FA, but I sent the text every day. I was determined not to give them another excuse to do me, but they found one anyway. At the first hearing they were accusing me of failing to inform the FA of my whereabouts on 17 different days – because the text messages did not contain my full address.

I was speechless. Why, I asked them, couldn't someone just contact me after the first text and give me a steer that I needed to put my full address? I thought it was fair to assume that the Football Association would have a player's address on file when they were going through a hearing. They couldn't answer me. "This is the system," they said. Surely someone checked the messages every day? I thought it was diabolical and felt as if I was being stitched up.

I sometimes wonder how much of it had to do with the fact that I was a United player, going back to the Tevez affair a few years earlier. Our noisy, northern club didn't exactly back away quietly from that, did we?

Who knows? Being honest, I think it may have played a part – although no-one will ever admit it, even if it is true. I guess I will never know.

The only positive thing I can really remember from the time is how brilliant United were with me. I spoke to the powers-that-be at the club early on in the process and they reassured me that they were going to stand by me. Of course I understand that they couldn't continue to pay me what I was earning before the ban and my contract was winding down anyway. So they cut my wages in half, from 10 grand to five, and gave me another year. They expected me to keep myself fit and, if I did, they promised to go back to my original contract. It wasn't a charity case – they said themselves a few times that I was an asset to the club they wanted to protect – but at the same time I was just grateful that they had stuck by me at such a tough time.

I was so thankful to be getting a deal – any deal – that I signed it without hesitating, although I did find it strange that they insisted on putting a buy-out clause in the new contract. To this day I still don't know why, but I didn't question it at the time. Maybe they thought I would push for a cheap transfer when I came back, I honestly don't know. As far as I was concerned, they could have put whatever they wanted in there as long as they didn't dump me on the scrapheap. The contract was more than just that: it was a show of faith. I might have been an asset to them before, but no-one, least of all me, knew for sure how I would return after the ban – both physically and mentally.

The day finally arrived when I was allowed to train with my mates again. It was six weeks before the end of my ban and I remember laughing at the FA's generosity, giving me a month and a half to get back up to speed. Thanks for that! Blackwell was still the manager and Andy Leaning was in charge of the goalkeepers. As I touched on before, I had known Andy for years and he was brilliant for me. He knew what I needed and what I didn't need to do. If I looked tired or stiff, he knew when to ease off and he knew when to work me hard as well. If I'd had a few beers and still felt rough the morning after, I could tell him. He wasn't a stupid man and our relationship spoke for himself. But I think my return to training, and how close we were, ended up costing him his job at United.

It started when Blackwell pulled Andy into his office one day. "I want Paddy being sick every day," Blackwell said. "I want to see him crawling off that training pitch." Andy refused.

"Let me train him," he asked Blackwell. "I've got six weeks." I was available for the last two games of the season and the plan was to play me if we didn't have a chance of promotion or weren't in danger of being relegated. "I know how Paddy works and I ain't making him sick every day," Andy said. "I'll work him hard, but I've got six weeks to do it. If you ask me to beast him, he'll go the other way and you'll get nothing out of him. His head will go."

In fairness to Andy he was absolutely spot-on. I could be fiery, but that was because I wanted to win – at everything. When I play my son at Xbox, I want to win. When I play golf, it's the same. It's something that I believe is built into you as a sportsman and you can't turn it off. I think, and Andy thinks, that going up against Blackwell and pushing back over what was best for me ended up costing him his job. He was laid off at the end of that season. But he did what he was asked to do and got me fit in those six weeks. He knew I had come through a tough time, physically and mentally, and the last thing he wanted to do was make me crawl off the pitch. What the fuck would that have achieved?

Blackwell was like that sometimes. I felt it was about control with him; a sort of "I'm in charge, so do it my way" kind of thing. Neither of us backed down easily, which is probably why we clashed as often as we did. But he did put me back in the team for the last two games of the season and the first was against Swansea at Bramall Lane. The reception the Blades fans gave me as I ran towards the Kop was amazing. To be honest I wasn't sure how it would go. I had always got on well with the Blades supporters before and I thought, and hoped, they would stand by me. But you never know for sure, do you? The reception they gave me was frightening and, thinking back to it all these years later, I actually get quite emotional even now.

But at the time there was still a game to be played and, although I had no idea how I was going to go, I was determined to give a good account of myself. I had played a couple of practice matches at the training ground – I didn't even have a reserve game – and it was my first competitive outing for 11 months since the play-off final at Wembley.

Early in the game a through ball came down the middle and, without even thinking, I came for it. If I hadn't, their striker would have beaten me easily. I forgot all about that moment until Andy reminded me of it after the game. Like me, he was nervous about how it would go. But from the minute that my instincts kicked in and I came for that ball, he knew that I would be okay.

We won 2-0 and I played my second and final game of the season on the last day, away at Ipswich. Roy Keane, my old Republic of Ireland teammate, was in charge at Portman Road back then and a few years later, when I was at QPR, Brian Murphy told me about Keane's pre-match team talk that day. He went through each player in the United line-up and obviously began with me. "Paddy will be in goal," Keane said. "He's a good 'keeper at this level… a good shot-stopper. But he loves his drugs."

I'm not sure what Ipswich's players gathered from that bit of insight – probably not a great deal, considering that we stuffed them 3-0 – but it just shows how mud sticks in this game. Brian was in goal for Ipswich that day and, when he told me the story a few years later as teammates at QPR, I was able to laugh about it.

The three points saw us finish eighth in the Championship and from a personal point of view I was back doing what I loved. I would have snatched my own hand off if I had been offered two clean sheets from two games in two wins and, if I could, I would have started the new season the following day. I had no idea that another whirlwind summer was just around the corner.

17

FORCED OUT

It started with yet another phone call and by this time I was starting to wonder if I should just turn my mobile off completely during the summer months. This time it was my agent on the line and he wasn't ringing to ask how the weather was on my holiday. "QPR have activated your buy-out clause," he said. "Sheffield United have had to accept it." The contract I had signed while I was banned contained a buy-out figure, put there at the club's request. Admittedly I didn't query it at the time, but any power I might have usually had in negotiations was gone. I was just delighted to have any contract offer whatsoever and signed it without thinking twice.

My first reaction was shock. "That's strange," I thought. Why would they want me to go? It didn't really add up. When I signed the deal, on half my original wages, I had agreed with the club that, when I came back and proved my fitness, my money would go back up to what it was before and they would give me another couple of years. I returned to the side and kept two clean sheets, and had continued the fitness sessions with my personal trainer throughout the summer. I was determined to put a disastrous year behind me and get back to playing at Bramall Lane.

My agent told me that United were looking to bring in Steve Simonsen on a free transfer from Stoke City, and the club thought that they were getting the better end of the deal by cashing in on me. "But I don't want to go," I told my agent – and that was the honest truth. At that point, I owed United everything. My own stupid mistake had cost me nine months of my career and I could only watch helplessly as my friends and teammates struggled to eighth in the league, a year after losing in the play-off final. If United had just cut me loose when I was banned – which they would have been more than entitled to do – I would have been screwed. I would obviously have had a year without a job, which would have been hard enough. But it would have been so difficult to get back in – especially with the stigma of a drugs ban permanently attached to my name.

I later heard that my ban had actually put QPR off signing me a little, but their manager dug his heels in and insisted that the deal went through. It was that man Neil Warnock and, although I obviously owed a lot to him and loved playing under him at both Bury and Bramall Lane, I also had no ambition whatsoever to go and play in London. I always maintained that, whatever happened in my career, I would never go down there. Warnock apparently once recommended me to Arsène Wenger when we were together at Bury. Arsenal may have tested my resolve if any interest Arsène might have had went any further. But he famously banned the club chef from serving burgers and chips when he took over so, in hindsight, I may not have completely fitted in with his methods!

Some years later, by the summer of 2010, I was completely settled in Yorkshire. My kids were nine and seven at the time, living just up the road in Halifax, so moving four hours away to London had no appeal whatsoever. I could shoot over after training and pick them up from school. At any time they were only a short drive away. I had endured enough stress during the previous year and I owed United big time for their faith in me. I wanted to stay.

That stance was fed back to United and the mood began to change. We were told that the club weren't sure how I would react to coming back after my ban and that they wanted me to get the move. They had Simonsen coming in and thought that he was a better 'keeper than me. The message to our camp was clear: "We want Paddy to go to QPR." Maybe they saw £750,000 as decent value for a goalkeeper who had played twice in a year, especially with Simonsen coming down from the Premier League. I told them again I didn't want to go anywhere, but it didn't make a bit of difference – their minds had already been made up.

The thing I found most strange was that I didn't hear a single thing from the manager during the whole process. I had my ups and downs with Kevin Blackwell through the years, but he never picked up the phone once for the two or three-week period that the discussions were taking place. Not to say he wanted me to stay; not to say he wanted me to go. Nothing. Surely the manager of a football club has the last say on his players being sold? Or should anyway. It was a similar story when Michael Tonge was sold to Stoke. Tongey remembers Blackwell telling him that he had been told not to persuade him to stay. I wondered if the decisions were all being taken above Blackwell's head, but either way the messages were pretty clear. I was forced out of Sheffield United.

I began to look at the alternatives. I clearly wasn't wanted. Did I want to sit on the sidelines for another season or even be bombed out completely? I had missed a year of football and didn't want to be out for another minute. Reluctantly, I agreed to speak to Warnock. He told me to come down and said that QPR were going to have a right go that season. He spoke about all the experienced boys he was bringing in to play alongside a talented lad they had called Adel Taarabt. And the more he said, the more wanted I felt. Then he told me I had a day to make my mind up or he was going to sign Julián Speroni from Palace. "Oh, thanks!" I thought. "You've given me loads of time to think about that one!"

From there everything happened quickly and it was a bit of a blur. Warnock offered me a good contract lasting three years and I sat down with my family to discuss it. We decided we could make it work. I would travel down to training rather than move down permanently and get the kids down to London as much as we could when I was down there. Ipswich also wanted me and offered me the same money as QPR, but I called Warnock. "Gaffer, I've made my mind up," I told him. "I'll come down."

The circumstances were strange but in some ways, the move to QPR was pretty standard by football's standards. All players have a shelf life and as much as people love to talk about loyalty in the game, clubs are only loyal to players for as long as they are useful to them. For whatever reason United decided my time was up and I was no longer wanted, although a different story came out at the time. The feeling was very much that I had pushed to leave and it probably suited the people at United who had made the decision to let people think that.

Even to this day there are a lot of United fans who resent me and think that I jumped ship. I can't deny that I earned more money at QPR but, when I factored in travelling to London and renting a place for a couple of nights a week down there, I wasn't much better off financially – with a lot more stress and hassle on top as well as being further away from my family.

The move to QPR was not motivated by money. I was promised a new deal at United and I was happy that the promise would be honoured. Even if they had offered to meet me halfway on the wages, at £7,500, I would have been happy with that. If they had said: "Let's see how it goes in three or four months," that would have been fine by me, too. But from their point of view there was only one option on the table – and after eight brilliant years, that was me leaving.

I had enjoyed so many special nights at United, the biggest and best club I had been at. It's an amazing place, and I still speak to a lot of the staff there now. Without meaning to sound big-headed in any way, I was quite a fans' favourite at the time. The way the crowd reacted to me when I came back against Swansea still gives me goosebumps now. I did an interview after that game and someone said it had been years since anyone had received a reception like that at the Lane. And, no matter what anyone thinks of me, there is no way I would throw that affection back in the fans' faces.

My time at QPR turned out to be a successful one, but in the beginning I must admit that I wasn't looking forward to it at all. The fact that Warnock was in charge did help and there were a few other familiar faces from United there as well. My old United physio Nigel Cox did my medical at QPR, if you can call it one. When I rang Warnock to tell him I was coming down to QPR, he was buzzing. "Right," he said. "I'm away next week, but I want to be here when you sign. Come down the week after, on the Tuesday, and we'll do your medical then and get you signed."

"There might be a bit of a problem there, Gaffer," I said. "I'm on a stag do that week and I don't get back until the Monday... Do you really want me doing a medical the day after I get back from Magaluf?"

"Oh shit," he laughed. "We'd best get you down tomorrow!"

That was how my time at QPR began. I went down and found Coxy at the training ground. We had a coffee and a chat about how everything had ended at United. Then he asked if I could touch my toes. I couldn't, but I told him I could. "Let's get you weighed," he said. I stepped on the scales and he wrote the number down. "Right," he said. "That's your medical passed. Do you want another coffee? We just need to sit around here for a couple of hours and make it look as if we've done a proper medical." No matter what happened, I was signing anyway.

I wanted to come out and tell the real story about my departure from United at the time, and Warnock did hint at it a few times in interviews.

But he advised me to just try and put it behind me. "You've played there now... Just leave it," he said. "Concentrate on what you're doing here. You don't need to open that can of worms. Let people think what they want to think... You know the truth." Now, I am glad to get the chance to get that truth out there, albeit some years later. It was more like a break-up than a transfer – one party had made a decision and the other had no choice but to deal with it and try and move on.

***

I was still settling into my new surroundings when my phone rang again. It was five past eight in the morning on the day the fixtures were released for the new season and Warnock had got hold of them an hour before they were released at 9am. "You're not going to believe it," he said to me. "Second game of the season... who've we got?"

"Fuck off!" I replied.

"Yeah... At Bramall Lane. Get ready."

No time for the feelings to die down! Obviously I knew I would have to go back to United at some point, but the second game of the season? It was just one of those quirks of football and I knew the reception wouldn't be particularly kind whether it was the first game of the season or the last. So I might as well get it out of the way, I thought.

We had only just left the hotel to go to the ground when Warnock got a phone call, passing on some advice from the police. "There are a lot of fans outside the players' entrance waiting for Paddy. He needs to get his head down. Just put his head down and walk in. Do not acknowledge them or it could get heated." Warnock called me to the front of the bus and told me what was waiting for me. I got off the bus, head down, and could hear the hate. Shouts of "Judas!" and stuff like that.

It obviously wasn't nice – I can't lie to you and say that I enjoyed it. I was no stranger to being abused, but this felt different – they still felt like *my* fans. I had spent so long with them on my side and basically, within the space of two or three games at Bramall Lane, I had gone from being loved by everyone because I was back, to being hammered because I had left. But I had a job to do and, just as it had been my whole career, it was to go out there and win a football match for my team.

We won 3-0 and were three up inside 23 minutes thanks to Hogan Ephraim, Jamie Mackie and a penalty from Taarabt. At Bramall Lane

United normally attack the Kop in the second half, but, after winning the toss at kick-off, my old mate Chris Morgan spun us around and stuck me at the Kop end in the first half. I got battered by the fans behind my goal. Then United won an early corner, which I came and caught, before Morgs twatted me and gave away a free-kick. He picked me up and slapped me on the back. "Sorry, pal," he growled. "We got told to smash you early doors by Blackwell." The fans loved that. A lot of them probably wished they could have done the same, but they had to settle for venting their hate through songs. "You're just a fat, greedy bastard" was one that didn't seem to end.

I'm not looking for any sympathy here, by the way. I had been in football for long enough by that point to know how it worked. If I had been a United fan on the Kop that day and thought that my club had paid a player while he was banned for nine months only for him to fuck off at the first chance, I would have reacted exactly the same. I completely understand the reaction I got and why the fans felt the way they did towards me. I consoled myself with the thought that I knew what had *actually* gone on. I knew what I had been told and why I left. And I knew that not one fan behind me, calling me Judas and every other name under the sun, knew the truth.

Despite the 'welcome' I received at Bramall Lane, I didn't celebrate one of our goals that day. Inwardly, I was buzzing but I didn't want to wind the United fans up. Despite what most of them seemed to think of me, I had too much respect for them. Throughout my career I celebrated every goal my team scored as if it had been me who had got the final touch. And usually, going 3-0 up away from home so early on, I would be doing cartwheels. But back at Bramall Lane so soon, and in front of the Kop, it just didn't feel right.

After the game I met my parents outside the ground and I was sworn at in front of my kids. That angered me because I thought it crossed a line. I had no problem with anyone thinking what they wanted about me, but at that moment I was a parent with his children. When my kids were out of earshot, my dad lost it a bit and had a go back at someone who was giving me dog's abuse, telling them to fuck off. He's not normally like that, my dad. But I think the emotions of the day had just started to get to everyone by that point.

They had certainly got to the United board. Before the QPR bus had even pulled away from Bramall Lane, Blackwell had been sacked. United had drawn away at Cardiff on the opening day of the season and lost to lower-league opposition in the cup in midweek, as we did. And after two league games, Blackwell was gone. Warnock and Blackie still had a bit of beef at this stage, going back to how Blackwell had left for Leeds. Warnock let me shoot straight off from the game, because I still had a house in Sheffield and I was coming off the M1 at junction 31 when he rang me, pissing himself down the phone. "What's up, Gaffer?" I asked. "What are you laughing at?"

"You won't believe it," he said. "He's been fucking sacked! Serves him right for what he did all those years ago."

Karma always comes back to bite you, doesn't it? But as much as me and Blackie didn't get on at times, sacking him after two games did seem a little strange. Not that Warnock seemed to mind. He was buzzing - Blackwell had been sacked and we were flying. It was only two games, but the early signs looked good. We had won both, scoring seven goals and, crucially for me, conceding none. It was a far better start than I had expected. I still remember us scoring late on to draw 1-1 with Plymouth in a friendly before the season started, in front of less than 3,000 people.

Everyone knows that pre-season results don't matter but as we were walking back to our cars after the game – there's no parking at the ground, only at a school down the road – me, Shaun Derry and Clint Hill were absolutely battered by a group of about 10 QPR fans. The three of us were getting on a bit, at the back end of our careers, and the supporters were calling us has-beens and journeymen. "We don't want you here," one of them said. "Fuck off back to Palace... Fuck off back to Sheffield United!"

"This is going to be a long season," I thought. "We've not even kicked off yet!" But Warnock knew exactly what he was doing. Our team was solid, especially straight down the spine of me, Clint, Dezza and Heidar Helguson upfront. Helguson had been on loan at Watford when Warnock brought him back in from the cold and he was brilliant. He had the best leap I had ever seen and made my kicking look unbelievable that season because he was capable of hanging in the air forever! We were relentless. We won eight of our first 10 games and our belief was unbelievable. We were 2-0 down at Derby after 90 minutes and scored twice in injury time to win a point.

Warnock managed us brilliantly. After the Derby game there was an international break and we had already been given the schedule: Sunday and Monday off; back in Tuesday and Wednesday; off Thursday, Friday, Saturday and Sunday; back in Monday at 1pm. We got back in the dressing-room at Pride Park and Warnock was off his tits at our late equaliser. Carl Serrant was our fitness coach at the time and Warnock asked him what the plan was. Carl reeled off the schedule. "Fuck that!" Warnock shouted. "Lads, see you a week on Monday... You've been brilliant so far." I packed a bag and went to Dubai for five days! It was unreal.

When Monday eventually rolled around, the lads were blowing a bit. Warnock strode out and blew his whistle in the middle of a session, completely messing it up. He didn't care. "Lads," he barked. "We've had a while off, so we'll only train for an hour. But when we've finished, I want you to stay and have something to eat and then we're going to have a meeting." We all filed into a room after training. "Right, there's another international break coming up," Warnock told us. "Get me three wins before then and you can have another week off." We walked out of that meeting with six games before the next international break. We played on Saturday, Tuesday and Saturday and won all three! Warnock had his three wins inside the first week and we had another week off. We didn't train on a single Monday that season unless there was a game on the Tuesday. And that was on top of our day off on a Wednesday. The way he treated us players was first-class and the results spoke for themselves.

We felt invincible. Even when we played shit, which did happen occasionally, we would either draw or maybe nick a scruffy win. We didn't lose in the league that season until our 20th game. It was a similar dressing-room to the one at United – no nobheads, apart from maybe Adel on his day. The experienced lads I mentioned before were brilliant, as were the likes of Bradley Orr, Lee Cook, Peter Ramage and Tommy Smith. We knew we had to graft to win games, and that was fine by us. It was a snowball effect. Once we went on that run, we found it hard to believe we were ever going to lose. That was the culture we had at that time – and it came from the way Warnock treated us. It's not rocket science either, is it? Treat your people right in any walk of life and you will get more out of them.

QPR's chairman at the time was a bloke called Gianni Paladini, and what a character he was. He was born in Naples and somehow ended up settling in Solihull before getting involved in QPR. In 2005 seven men were charged with allegedly forcing him to resign from QPR at gun-point. But no-one could really say he didn't care about the club – he even broke away from his police interview later that day to celebrate a QPR goal. The seven men were eventually cleared and Gianni ended up as the club's chairman. I'll never forget the day Gianni invited me into his office and showed me his bulletproof vest.

We beat Barnsley 4-0 in our first game of the season, despite them absolutely battering us and hitting the post and bar, and Gianni came to the training ground. "Good clean sheet, Paddy!" he beamed at me. "You're not wrong, Gianni, but we were a bit lucky," I said. "It was a good job the post and bar were there!" He told me he didn't care, that all clean sheets are good clean sheets. "How many will you get us this season?" he asked.

I told him I planned for about 15 or 16, which should be enough to give us a chance of getting promoted. "Really?" he replied. "Okay then… If you get 16 clean sheets this season, I'll buy you a Rolex watch." He spat on his hand and we shook on it.

After 12 games, I had kept 10!

Gianni came back to the training ground and told me I was going to piss 16. I told him there was a fair chance. He offered me a gamble. "If you beat the club record for clean sheets," he said, "I'll buy you his and hers Rolexes." We spat again, and I told him he was on. I finished the season with 24 clean sheets from 44 games. But I never did see my Rolexes!

Gianni offered to bring them to the player-of-the-year do at the end of the season when I was planning to get absolutely trolled. "Don't do that!" I told him. I would have ended up losing them. I can't remember seeing him on the night anyway. So Gianni, if you're reading this, a deal's a deal where I come from – although, come to think of it, I can't remember spitting on my hand before shaking very often in Halifax!

18

PUSHED TO THE BRINK

We were in Embrace, a nightclub in the centre of Sheffield, when I first saw her. The ironic thing is that I hadn't even planned to go out that night. I was still at Sheffield United and we had just lost earlier that day to Scunthorpe, conceding the winner in the 90th minute. But a few of my mates were coming down from Halifax. If it had been an ordinary Saturday night, I wouldn't have gone out – it wouldn't have felt appropriate after we had lost. But the lads had made the effort to come down, so I thought: "Bugger it – I'll go out and just keep my head down." I got pissed, ended up in the nightclub and bumped into the woman I would later marry.

Louise was six years younger than me. I had enjoyed myself for nine months or so as a single man after what had happened with Karen, but there was something different about Louise. We got married in Las Vegas and had two beautiful daughters together, which wasn't a straightforward process. I'd had a vasectomy after my first two kids, Beth and Jonjo. I was still young when I had the snip at 27, but me and Karen were married and things were looking up for us. She didn't want any more kids and neither did I, so we made the decision. Then things changed. Louise moved in with me after about nine months, with her son from a previous relationship. Then she told me she wanted more kids. I was actually too young to have the snip in the first place and had to pull a few strings to get it done. A few years later I was back again to get it reversed.

It wasn't a pleasant experience. When I had it done in the first place, it was literally a 20-minute job and I paid an extra £78 to go to sleep through the whole thing. It was the best 78 quid I'll ever spend. When it came to reversing it, it was a four-hour operation. Not nice at all. Then came the heartbreaking news that it hadn't worked. There were that many antibodies around my sperm that we would never have got pregnant naturally. So we decided to go down the route of IVF, which was incredibly tough on Louise.

My part of it was easy, donating the sperm into a jar, but she went through what seemed like an endless cycle of needles and egg collections. It took about four cycles before it eventually worked with our first daughter, Kaelin, and then she had to go through the actual pregnancy. We froze some eggs and luckily the IVF worked first time with our second child together, Ashlin. Mentally and emotionally it was a tough thing to deal with and go through, but it was worth every second for our two beautiful girls.

The two births themselves could hardly have been more different. When Kaelin was born, I was at Leeds, playing in a Yorkshire derby at Huddersfield. I nearly went back home on the Friday night before the game because Louise was in a lot of pain, but I played in the game, which was an early kick-off, and had my car at the ground in case I had to shoot off quickly. To be fair to Huddersfield, they helped me out by organising a police escort so I could get through the traffic after the game and pick Louise up to go to the hospital. She was in labour for hours and hours and there were *a lot* of complications.

She ended up having to have an emergency caesarean and the midwife said to us later: "We left that a bit late. We only had 10 to 20 minutes to play with or we'd have lost Kaelin." *Wow.* She was also born with a heart murmur. I later found out that most babies are, but at the time I didn't know anything about it. I absolutely shit myself. We were told that she could grow out of it and thankfully she did. But at that moment I felt completely helpless.

Ashlin's birth couldn't have been more straightforward. The IVF worked first time and we were offered the option of another caesarean. It was just like going in to pick up a takeaway. We were booked in on December 21st and were given a time slot. It was a case of get in, get down to theatre, cut Ashlin out and get home. But the stress of the IVF and the pregnancy took its toll and, looking back now, I wonder if it all played a part in our relationship breaking down. There were other factors – which I explain later in the book – but me and Louise began to drift apart a bit after I retired as a player. Me moving down the M1 to QPR a few years earlier had not helped and we had tried to live half-and-half between mum in Sheffield and dad in London. It was tough on all of us and eventually, we called it a day and went our separate ways.

After me and Louise split up, I ended up not seeing Kaelin and Ashlin on my own for nine months after Rotherham social care got involved, and I don't mind admitting now that it made me suicidal. My kids are my life. Everything and anything I have done in my life and my career is so insignificant compared to my children.

I am a father first and a former footballer second and although there were a few issues between me and Louise at first, because of how our marriage had ended, she vouched for me as a good dad. So then social workers started questioning Louise's ability as a parent and suggesting *she* was putting the kids at risk. It was horrible and, when you read about some of the stuff that had gone on under their noses in Rotherham in the past, it makes me sick to think that they went to town on me – and almost cost me my children.

The Children and Family Court Advisory and Support Service – CAF-CASS for short – describe themselves as "a non-departmental public body in England set up to promote the welfare of children and families involved in family court." I certainly don't think they promoted the welfare of my kids during the time I was unfortunate enough to have to deal with them and even from my very first meeting with my social worker, I had a bad feeling. They were more bothered about little scrapes I'd had in my past, having daft fights on nights out as a 19-year-old in Halifax, than anything else. This was 20 years later and they were trying to make it out as if I was a monster.

The social worker asked if her team leader could sit in on our meeting for whatever reason, and I agreed. I had nothing to hide. But looking back, it strikes me that nothing was ever recorded in those meetings; it was all entirely down to how the social workers *interpret* what they see and hear. Once, they both disappeared to fetch a file, saying they would be back in a minute.

Half an hour later, I was still sat there. It was stupid of me, but I thought they were taking the piss so I got up and left. When I read the report later, the social worker said that both women had left at the same time because I had acted in an aggressive manner towards them and neither wanted to be left alone in the room with me. *What the fuck?* This is what I was up against.

On the rare occasions I did get to spend time with my daughters, it was every other weekend at a godawful place they call a "contact centre" in a rough area of Sheffield. It was the scruffiest place I have ever seen in my life and I had the indignity of paying about £65 to see my girls in there, for just two hours. If either of the girls wanted to go to the toilet, I took them and the bloke or woman who worked at the centre had to come with us and watch us.

I didn't dare ask what they thought was going to happen if they left me unattended with my own children and on at least two occasions that I can remember, I came out of there feeling suicidal. If it wasn't for my partner at the time, I don't know how I would have got through it. I crashed my car once because my head was all over the place and I wasn't concentrating on what was in front of me. I wasn't in a good place at all.

At one of my lowest points I confided in a cousin from Halifax, who had been through a similar situation a few years before, at my brother's funeral. "You've got to agree with everything they've got to say and lick their arses," he told me. "Just play the game." I took it on board, but when we went to my final court date, my barrister told me that it was a flip of a coin whether I would see the girls again or not. Even in that hearing, the woman from Rotherham social care still didn't want me to have access to them. But the judge overruled her, which I was told does not happen often, and there was light at the end of the tunnel at last.

The worst thing was knowing the effect it had on the kids. Fortunately, I suppose, Ashlin was too little to really understand what was going on, but Kaelin remembers it to this day. Every so often she will say to me, completely out of the blue: "I hated going to that house to see you, Daddy... It wasn't fair, was it?" She was five at the time and even she knew it was wrong, waiting to see her dad in the scruffiest place I have ever known, with 30 plates piled high in the sink and food dripping on the floor.

It breaks my heart every time she mentions it, but thankfully we're in a better place now. I know that I am a good dad to all my children and I would do anything to protect them. I have gone through quite a bit in my career, but the thought of losing them is the only thing, thank God, that has ever made me feel down enough to consider hurting myself. My head had gone after nine months of banging it against a brick wall until one day, I realised: *I can't keep doing this.*

At one point I was allowed to have the girls overnight for one night, as long as my mum and dad were also there. We took the girls to Blackpool as a treat and on a beautiful sunny day, we had a walk along the promenade. Life, for once in that period, felt okay. Then a family came past us, a mum and dad with four kids, and the stench of weed filled the air.

Without sounding disrespectful, they were as scruffy as anything and swore every other word, directly at their children. Instinctively I looked at my mum, who was already looking at me. "Wrong, it's wrong," she said, almost under her breath. And I knew exactly what she meant.

19

LONDON CALLING

When I arrived at QPR I had absolutely no idea who Alejandro Faurlín was, or the story of how he was supposedly signed for a club record fee a few years earlier. He was signed before my time and even before Warnock's, and it was only when QPR offered him a new deal that the truth came out; he was actually "owned" by a sports agency, an arrangement which broke the rules on third-party ownership. Those rules had ironically been tightened up after the Carlos Tevez affair, which cost both me and Warnock when United were relegated from the Premier League. My first season at QPR was the closest either of us had come to getting back there since – and now it looked like third-party ownership could cost us both top-flight football for a second time.

We had clinched automatic promotion from the Championship in late April 2011 with victory at Watford. And even though seven charges from the FA were hanging over QPR like a cloud, we as players were able to put it out of our minds for one evening at least and celebrate properly. The club's lawyers were confident of successfully defending the charges – although, remembering my QC's optimistic attitude towards my ban, I knew to take it with a pinch of salt – but there was always the possibility of a points deduction lingering over us. The nerves didn't go away when a story was printed in *The Sun* quoting an anonymous FA source and suggesting we were going to be docked 15 points.

That was *after* we had already clinched promotion and it would have been mayhem if it had happened. The FA had left it so late to hear the case and on the final day of the season we were five points clear of third. But 15 points taken off us would mean us just scraping into the play-offs in sixth place. That's a huge swing on the final day – we would either lift the trophy as champions or have the blow of having to prepare for the play-offs, after believing we were already promoted. The mood, understandably, was tense.

Personally I was thinking back to the Tevez saga and then my ban and thinking: "Surely I won't be screwed over again?" What else could go wrong? And as much as we tried to play it down, the points deduction was definitely in the back of the players' minds, especially the closer we got to promotion. It was crazy that the FA left it until the last day of the last game of the season to decide whatever punishment they were going to hand down. But for me, that just about sums them up.

Kick-off in the final game of the season was about an hour away when we heard the news. Gianni Paladini delivered it in his own eccentric way, sprinting down the corridor at Loftus Road and barging into the dressing room just behind me. "No points deduction!" he screamed at the top of his voice. "No fucking points deduction!" It had arrived at the 11th hour, but it was the decision we were all praying for. The club were fined almost a million quid, but for the players and Warnock it meant we could finally get our hands on that magnificent trophy – and look forward to getting back into the big time.

What a way to end an unbelievable season. We lost the final game of the season to Leeds and I missed that game, as well as the one that sealed promotion away at Watford. The injury didn't stop me getting involved in the celebrations, let me assure you, but happened in our third-to-last game of the season when incredibly, I came to catch a cross. My bungee cord snapped and I actually came off my line to try and claim something! I rolled over the Hull striker and landed vertically on my head and neck. I saw a photo of it later and it might have been a lot worse, to be fair. I did well to carry on for the rest of the game but in the build-up to the Watford match, it wasn't right.

I couldn't train so went to Champneys spa instead and sat in the cryotherapy chamber for a week. One day, I was in there with Frank Bruno. "Come on then, get down here on the floor," he said to me. For the whole three minutes we were in there – bearing in mind it was minus-150 degrees or something – he was down on the floor doing press-ups. "Come on, it's colder down here," he said to me. "It's better for you." I told him that I was all right, and left him to it!

I thought the chamber had done the trick but, when we were warming up before the Watford game, I couldn't lift my right arm quick enough to stop balls flying past me. I wasn't right and didn't want to risk it and let anyone down in a game that big, so I made the decision not to play. As it went, we won 2-0 and I wouldn't have had many saves to make anyway so I would have probably got away with it. But imagine if I had risked it and cost us a goal? If it meant we had the best chance of promotion, I would rather someone else play. Radek Cerny came in and kept a clean sheet and goals from Adel Taarabt and Tommy Smith meant we were over the line. Even with the FA charge hanging over us, we had some party that night.

We went to a club in London and Amit Bhatia, the son-in-law of our part-owner Lakshmi Mittal, spent nearly £100,000 on champagne for us; not even to drink, but just to spray around. These big, expensive, six-litre magnums were flying around everywhere. Personally I would have rather had the money, but Lakshmi and Amit could certainly afford it. When Amit married Lakshmi's daughter, the wedding lasted for six days and apparently cost $60m. Kylie Minogue performed at the reception and there were fireworks off the Eiffel Tower.

As far as I know, there were no celebrations in Paris for our promotion and we players had to make do with our bonus sheets. It was a decent figure, working out at about £3,000 per game you were involved in. I had played 44 games, missing the last two through injury. Radek, my understudy, had played those two games and had also been on the bench for the rest of the season, so he ended up with a higher bonus than I did – for playing two games! We had a good laugh about it and I didn't begrudge him a penny. He was a top lad and part of a good goalkeeping unit headed up by our coach, a bloke called Dave Rouse.

Dave's sessions were unbelievable. He had actually never played a professional game before he moved into coaching and eventually made his Football League debut at 30 years old, when Macclesfield had an injury crisis and he had to go in goal. His one and only professional game was a 1-0 defeat at Barnet, but he was a brilliant coach and he played a massive part in helping me to break the clean-sheet record that season – even if our chances to work together were limited. Warnock used to give us Mondays off unless we had a game in midweek and, if I had kept a clean sheet at the weekend, he told me there was no point in me coming in on Tuesday either. Wednesday was our rest day anyway and, considering that I kept 24 clean sheets that season, there were a fair few Tuesdays off. "See you Thursday," he would say to me. It was a godsend because it saved me trekking down to London from Sheffield and meant I could see more of my young family up north. But it did cost me a few batterings when I eventually turned up on Thursdays! "Oh look," my teammates used to say. "The golden boy's decided to show up at last..."

I don't think I fully appreciated at the time what an achievement it was to get QPR into the Premier League. Although our training pitches were good, the training ground wasn't the best; a lot of it was Portakabins all connected together. Although it only held about 18,000, I loved playing at Loftus Road. It reminded me of one of those old Subbuteo stadiums – a proper, traditional ground. It generated a great atmosphere even when it wasn't full, and I think it suited us because of the characters Warnock had assembled. We were old-school, proper professional players who weren't shy of rolling our sleeves up and having a scrap. Not many teams could compete with that throughout that season.

It helped that we also had Taarabt. Wow, what a player. When Adel was at it, he was actually unplayable and on his day he was too good, *way* too good, for QPR. I say that with the utmost respect to the club: when he turned it on, Adel's ability was frightening. But at the same time it was blatantly obvious why Tottenham had let Adel come to us, initially on loan. When he wasn't bothered, you would get nothing from him. He was a very all-or-nothing kind of kid, Adel.

His attitude could be terrible, but I don't think he was a bad lad deep down. He was young, coming from Spurs, and knew he was the best player in our team. He knew that, when we won, nine times out of 10 it was down to him. Maybe it was a case of too much, too young? Someone far more qualified than me would probably struggle to get to the bottom of Adel, but what I do know is that you have to be some player to be at clubs like Spurs, AC Milan and Benfica.

But he used to test all the lads, that's for sure. Solid pros like Shaun Derry and Clint Hill had to hold their tongues with him; it was a trade-off with Adel because we knew what he could do. He may have acted like a spoilt prick at times, but he could win us games on his own and he helped us all to become Premier League footballers, winning the Championship player-of-the-year award in the process. Warnock nailed it, to be fair. He called a meeting of the senior players early in the promotion season – lads like me, Clint, Shaun, Bradley Orr, Heidar Helguson. "Lads, you've got to bite your lip with him," he told us. "Please just put up with him… He'll get us promoted. It's as simple as that."

He was right, but it still wasn't easy. His attitude stank at times. In April we were nine points clear at the top of the Championship table and playing Scunthorpe, who were bottom. Adel refused to travel with us. Shit ground, he said. He wanted to go home for a few days. If that's how you feel, Warnock told him, then fuck off. So Adel did. We started all right without him, going 1-0 up after seven minutes, but ended up losing 4-1. We got absolutely battered in the second half and were lucky it wasn't more like eight.

That was on the Saturday and on the following Tuesday we were away again, at Barnsley. Warnock rang Adel and asked him to come back for the game. "We need you, we need a win… We need to get over the line." Adel agreed and Warnock told him to come back for training on the Monday. "No, I'll come on Tuesday and turn up for the game," Adel said. He played, scored in the first minute and we won 1-0!

That just summed him up. Another time Adel went AWOL from training for a couple of days but turned up on the day of the game against Sheffield United as if nothing had happened, assuming he would be in the team. I was just behind Adel as we got into the ground and Warnock pulled us both into his office. "Paddy," he said to me. "This cheeky twat wants to play today. We haven't seen him for two days and I've already got my team set up without him. I've told the lads the team and he's begging me to let him play. What would you do?"

For me it was simple. "Play him." I think it took Warnock by surprise a little. "What?" he asked. "Play him," I said again. "He'll win us the match, like you said. He'll get us promoted."

Adel was watching this, probably wondering what was going on. "Right," Warnock said. "I'm going to have to go and tell someone they're not playing then, aren't I?" I think Ákos Buzsáky was the unlucky lad to make way. "If he's shit today," Warnock told me as I left the room, "it's on your head."

Adel set up all three goals and we won 3-0. Warnock went into the changing-room before the game and said that I had told him to play Adel, but I'm not sure if I got any credit for that genius tactical decision afterwards! At the end of the day I didn't give a toss about anything else apart from winning the game. I knew he would help us to do that and he didn't let me down.

Adel finished the season with a ridiculous 19 goals and 21 assists, but he wasn't too happy at the end of season do when I won the supporters' player and players' player awards at the club. Adel stormed out of the awards night when my name was called out instead of his. He would have been a worthy player of the year, but Adel won the Championship award because people only saw what he did on the pitch on match days. The players see everyone all the way through the season, day in, day out, and that swung the players' player award for me. It meant a hell of a lot for me to win both awards in a year like that, and it was a great honour to cap a wonderful season.

We lifted the trophy four points clear of second-placed Norwich and eight ahead of Swansea in third. We might have sealed promotion even earlier, had we not drawn three games in a row towards the back end of the season. I know a few people were looking at us and thinking the bubble had burst, especially after we lost at Scunthorpe, but we responded in style by winning at Barnsley and our promotion felt pretty comfortable from there. To come back from a nine-month ban and be back in the Premier League a year later was pretty crazy and my only regret that season was seeing United relegated from the Championship. I'd had an amazing time there and, with the team they had, they should have never been anywhere near relegation, so I did feel more than a tinge of sadness for them. But now I was a QPR player – and I couldn't wait to see how we would cope with the challenges that were waiting for us in the Premier League.

20

IRISH EYES AREN'T SMILING

I f I had to choose a way for my international career with the Republic of Ireland to come to an end, it definitely wouldn't be on the back of a 5-2 defeat to a team 60 places below us in the world rankings. Cyprus were even ranked lower than teams like Benin, Malawi and Burkina Faso when we played them on that fateful night in October 2006, but they carved us open time after time on a night to forget for everyone concerned. The BBC called it "a nightmare night in Nicosia" and I wouldn't argue.

I hold my hands up fully and admit I was at fault for the second goal, coming off my line and getting nowhere near a ball into the box. But their first goal came from a shit header back from Andy O'Brien and the third was from the penalty spot after Andy had lunged in and wiped their lad out. The fourth was another defensive shambles and for the fifth, I made a decent point-blank save from their striker's header – only for the ball to rebound into his teammate's path for an easy tap-in.

Richard Dunne had equalised for us earlier, but then got sent off and John O'Shea didn't exactly cover himself in glory either for their first goal. But in the dressing-room afterwards the manager, Steve Staunton, came for me – and me only. As a goalkeeper, you know when you've had a bad game and at the same time it is possible to let a few goals in and not have really done too much wrong. This, I felt, was one of those nights – and said exactly that.

I stood my ground and told the manager that I felt he was coming for me because I was from little old Sheffield United. O'Brien was at Portsmouth and had been at Newcastle before, Dunne played for Manchester City and O'Shea was at the biggest club of them all, Manchester United. "I think you'll find it wasn't just me who fucked up today," I challenged

Staunton. He basically told me there and then that my Irish career was done and dusted, so I told him where he could stick it.

As I touched on earlier, I had actually come off the pitch in Cyprus with a little niggle and I believe that Staunton thought I had lost my bottle and was exaggerating how bad it was. I have never jumped a game in my life. I've lost count of the amount of times I have played through injuries. I had injections in the middle of the night so I could play for United against Arsenal and at Leeds I played for months with a damaged artery in my foot, which meant I couldn't feel my toes.

The idea that I would shirk a game, especially for my country, is unbelievable. I had one of those niggling injuries that can clean up with time and I was back fit for the following weekend, but there was no chance that I would have been ready for Ireland's game in midweek after the Cyprus debacle. Wayne Henderson played in goal instead as we earned a credible draw against the Czech Republic and, after I had returned home and everything blew up with Karen, I asked not to be considered for the next Ireland squad for personal reasons.

I simply needed a break to get my head around everything that was going off in my life. I had a lot to process and wanted some time to get my mind right, with the aim of coming back stronger. The call never came again, even when I got back in the Premier League after having the season I did with QPR. But I have no regrets about standing up for myself. I don't think Staunton appreciated me having a go back at him, but I was damned either way. If I had stayed on my line and the lad had a free header, people would ask why I didn't come for the cross. It's far easier to look from the stands and think: "He shouldn't have come for that." When you're in the moment, you have a split second to make the decision. Mine just proved to be the wrong one – both in terms of the match and my Ireland career as a whole.

But I had come a long way from the shy kid who didn't really know his place in the early days of being called up for Ireland. In one of my first games Kenny Cunningham gave me six backpasses on my weaker left foot before I eventually asked him if he was winding me up. He looked at me blankly and asked what I was on about. "Are you not left-footed?" he said. He didn't even know what foot I kicked with!

Gradually I grew in confidence and by the time I had played five games for Ireland, I still hadn't conceded a single goal. Someone picked up on that fact and decided to make a big deal out of it – with absolutely terrible timing. My next game was against the mighty Holland and we lost 4-0. Klaas-Jan Huntelaar scored from a free header at a corner, Arjen Robben made it two after we messed about with the ball and gave it to him in our own penalty area and Huntelaar dinked the ball over me when one-on-one for 3-0.

Robin van Persie made it four with an unbelievable finish and my clean-sheet record for Ireland went up in smoke. Holland's team that day was: Van der Sar, Heitinga, Ooijer, Mathijsen, Van der Vaart, Van Persie, Huntelaar, Robben, Janssen, Hesselink, De Jong. My next Ireland game was the Cyprus debacle. Very quickly no goals conceded in five games became nine in seven and I had very suddenly reached the end of the road.

It would have been nice to earn more caps for my country, but it simply wasn't meant to be. I still have some brilliant memories. I was away with Ireland when Liverpool played in that crazy Champions League final against AC Milan, when they came back from 3-0 down to win on penalties. Our man Steve Finnan started at right-back for Liverpool in Istanbul and Brian Kerr let us go out for a few beers after we had watched the game over dinner.

We were buzzing for Steve and I got a bit carried away when Dunne challenged me to a drinking contest with pints of Budweiser. I was giving it the big one – "I'll show you how it's done" and all that – but he absolutely wiped the floor with me. We went to a nightclub called Lillie's Bordello in Dublin and I was seeing about three or four of everyone. There were only about 10 people in the place, but to me it looked full!

The biggest compliment I can pay the Irish boys is that there were no big-timers, even though we had some big-name players at the time. We had lads like Robbie Keane and Damien Duff, while Shay Given was a legend of the Irish game. But there were absolutely no dickheads and the team spirit was spot-on. Duff had recently moved to Chelsea for big money and we had a bit of a joke at his expense because he never had any money.

Apparently his mum used to look after it for him. It was rumoured he was on £70,000 a week at Chelsea and his mum was in charge of it! We played cards in the hotel and, if Duff lost, he would ask someone from the FAI to cash his Ireland appearance cheque because he didn't want his mum to see that he had withdrawn money from the bank. Apparently she would kill him!

I remember Neil Warnock trying to push my case for an Ireland recall when we were at United together and again when we were flying at QPR, but in all honesty I wasn't too fussed that the call didn't come. I don't want that to sound disrespectful, but I felt as if my time had passed. I had been out of the picture for a while and, although I would have jumped at the chance to return if it had come up, I also wasn't too disappointed that it didn't. As I got older, I think I appreciated the rest more. I'd had trips away with Ireland before that had gone on for 10 or 11 days, stuck in the hotel room between training sessions or travelling here, there and everywhere. I think it's changed a little bit now in terms of international breaks, but back then it was pretty hectic. We would rush off after playing on a Saturday and United would want us back in training before our next club game, so me and Alan Quinn were getting the red-eye flights on Thursday morning to get back to training at 11am. The lads who played for Man United waved us off from the private plane their club used to send while me and Quinny slummed it on Ryanair!

Then we were back preparing for the game on Thursday and either trained or travelled on the Friday. It was so full-on that I didn't really have time to think about it when I was in the moment. It was only when I stepped out of it that I realised what actually went on. For me as well there was an added family aspect to it after what had happened with Karen when I was away in Cyprus. I didn't want to be away from my kids any longer than I had to be, so in a way it was a blessing in disguise that I wasn't called up again. Maybe Ireland agreed that I'd just had my time because there was never a call from anyone asking if I would be interested in coming back. By the time I went to QPR and was playing in the Premier League, I was older and much more experienced than I had been when Ireland first called me up and I am surprised that they never at least explored the possibility of a recall. Maybe by that point that ship had sailed.

I only received two actual physical Ireland caps, each with the number of games I had played in that season, and they are among my prized possessions. I have one at home and my mum and dad have the other. I could possibly have earned more, but Shay was the undisputed No. 1 and was an awesome 'keeper. He was loved in Ireland and, like me, just loved playing football. So it was always going to be difficult for me to get many games ahead of Shay. Maybe if he wasn't as good or didn't love playing as much, I could have earned more caps. Who knows? In truth I was still a novice goalkeeper during my time with Ireland and I did well to play as many times as I did.

I prefer to look at what I did achieve rather than what I didn't. Considering I was brought up in Halifax with an Irish background and supporting Ireland in big games, to be able to say that I pulled on that jersey at least once is unbelievable. I grew up watching Packie Bonner and Ray Houghton and Co. play in World Cups and to follow in their footsteps, even briefly, was like a dream. I was a full Irish international without ever having a full-time goalkeeping coach, basically dragging myself into the squad on the back of my own talent, character and natural ability. To think anyone now could become an international goalkeeper without any real coaching is mental.

And doing exactly that is probably my proudest footballing achievement of all.

21

AGUEROOO

It's finished at Sunderland... Manchester United have done all they can, a Rooney goal was enough for the three points. Manchester City are still alive here... Balotelliii... **Agueroooooooo**...! *I swear you'll never see anything like this ever again. So watch it, drink it in... Two goals in added time for Manchester City. To snatch the title away from Manchester United... it might just be the start of a dynasty. And I have to report that Queens Park Rangers, who may well have lost the game as Manchester City clinch the title, are* **safe**. *Bolton have failed to win at Stoke. So everyone's a winner!*
- Martin Tyler, Sky Sports, May 2012

Where were you when the most famous goal in football history was scored? Sergio Aguero for Manchester City on the last day of the 2011/12 season. The 95th minute of the game, to win a first Premier League title for City. To beat their oldest rivals, Manchester United, to the trophy on goal difference. City had been 2-1 down less than four minutes earlier and Aguero's winner, in a 3-2 victory, has been re-watched at least 20 million times since on YouTube. I will never forget where I was when Aguero smashed the ball home, the Etihad Stadium absolutely erupted and English football changed forever. I was right in the middle of it!

QPR went to City for the final game of the 2011/12 season, a possibly defining day for both clubs. City had to win the game to guarantee their first Premier League title and we had to win to guarantee our survival. The way the season ended was pure carnage and just as memorable as how it began for me. Still on the high of promotion from the Championship, I had gone to Dubai for the summer and was determined to make my second experience of the Premier League last longer than the first.

So, believe it or not, I was doing a bit of exercise in Dubai. I ran in the morning when the heat was just about tolerable and then noticed that I was pissing blood afterwards. One morning it was bright red. I texted the club doctor and the physio straightaway, and they promised to have a look a few weeks later when we went back for pre-season.

I just tried to keep my mind off it. *The doctor didn't seem too worried*, I reassured myself. But on the first day of pre-season I hadn't even dug my gloves out when the doctor had me pissing in a pot. My sample looked clear, but they dabbed it with something and there were traces of blood in there. After training they sent me for an ultrasound. It was exactly like the scan pregnant women have. I had the jelly on my belly and the scanner thing rubbing over it. *I always look pregnant in pre-season anyway*, I thought to myself, trying to lighten the mood. But the woman doing the scan wasn't laughing.

She had a weird look on her face as she moved over my stomach and, although she couldn't tell me anything there and then, I had a horrible sinking feeling inside. I was convinced it was bad news. I went back in training the next day, but I'd only been out for about 20 minutes when one of the physios came running out, grabbed me and Warnock and said: "You've got to come in now." We rushed in – me, Warnock, two physios and two club doctors – and one of them broke the news. "Your scan has come back. We think you've got two tumours on your kidney."

Fuck.

I was absolutely shitting myself. I was struggling to take it all in, but the club took over. They arranged for me to go to a clinic for an MRI scan to check my kidney out more thoroughly and then I was booked in to see a bladder specialist the following day. Ironically the best person in the country for bladders was based in Sheffield, so, after going for the MRI and having that horrid blue dye put through me, I got straight in the car and drove all the way back to Sheffield.

It was a route I obviously knew well and it felt almost exactly like the journey back from Wembley after I found out I had been banned. I was on autopilot – thinking about nothing, but at the same time thinking of everything. I was still a young man, supposedly in my prime, with children and looking forward to getting back into the Premier League. After I was banned, I was worrying about my career. This time, as I made my way up the M1 like a zombie, I was terrified that I could lose my life.

Unsurprisingly I had the worst night's sleep of my life and was straight up in the morning, calling and texting the club doctor to see if they'd had any results yet. No answer. Then an hour before I saw the specialist my phone rang. "Paddy, we've got some great news," the club doc said. "There are no tumours on your kidneys. You've got a horseshoe kidney."

I had no idea what a horseshoe kidney was, but I didn't care either. I was just over the moon that it wasn't a tumour. I found out later that it affects one in about 500 kids when the kidneys fuse together in the womb, creating a horseshoe shape. When I was dehydrated and exercised, it caused the blood in my urine. The relief was indescribable. I started crying uncontrollably in the car. I was going to be okay.

It wasn't all good news, though. The doc still wanted me to go and get my bladder checked while I was up in Sheffield, to rule everything else out. Not pleasant. They numbed the end of my cock and pushed a camera attached to a pipe straight up it. As my bladder filled with water, so did my eyes. It was probably the most uncomfortable situation of my life. What a way to celebrate the good news, I thought! But as far as the Sheffield specialist was concerned, everything was good. I was sent on my way to Cornwall for pre-season and the whole incident was barely spoken about again.

But it was the scariest 24 hours of my life. Thankfully, it just wasn't my time. Others I have played with have not been so lucky. Lenny Johnrose, my old Bury teammate, was later diagnosed with motor-neurone disease. Luton Shelton, who I played with at Sheffield United, also has it. Others have died of cancer, or committed suicide. Footballers are not immune to health problems, despite what some people seem to think, and sometimes it takes a scare like that to act as a wake-up call and make you thankful for everything you have in life that really matters.

At the same time, football is a cold-hearted business and I knew I couldn't afford to think too much about anything else. We had been joined in the Premier League by Norwich and Swansea and the bookies thought we were the most likely of the three promoted teams to stay up – apparently because we had more money to spend. If that was the case, I don't think anyone had told Warnock! The club's ownership was up in the air all summer and because of that no-one wanted to give him any cash.

Warnock remembers in his book that at the same time, Gianni Paladini and one of the owners, Flavio Briatore, were offering him the likes of Tal Ben Haim and Marco Materazzi, who were on £38,000 and £50,000 a week respectively. Materazzi had won the World Cup with Italy in 2006, so was clearly a player. The problem was that, by this point, he was 38. Warnock said he was quicker than Materazzi. Unsurprisingly he didn't sign.

Shit going off in the boardroom at QPR was nothing new and looking back now, I think we did an unbelievable job to get promoted despite everything else going on. There was always the feeling that Flavio and Bernie Ecclestone, his co-owner at QPR, didn't really want to be there and that they'd had enough. In the two years before Warnock took over, QPR had 10 managers and the madness was summed up pretty well in the documentary, *The Four Year Plan*. We drew a few games in the promotion season and Warnock was under pressure! Flavio was heard on camera calling Warnock "a joke" and saying he was "scared" to win games. As the record books show, we actually won 24 that season on our way to the club's first league title since 1983.

Later in *The Four Year Plan*, Flavio sent Gianni down to tell caretaker Gareth Ainsworth to make a sub – and Gavin Mahon ended up scoring after being thrown on. Flavio celebrated as if he was some kind of football genius! That all stopped under Warnock, though. When I joined, Warnock told me that he had warned the owners: "I pick the team and nobody else. The day you try telling me who to pick, I'm gone." That was a relief. The last thing you want at your club is others having influence over that kind of stuff. Otherwise what's the point in having a manager? You might as well not bother. But I'm not sure anyone dare say anything like that around Flavio, even jokingly. He would probably have ended up sacking another manager and taking charge himself!

The ownership saga finally ended in the middle of August 2011 when Tony Fernandes, a nice bloke who owned the AirAsia airline and had a few quid, bought out Bernie and Flavio and took a 66 per cent stake in QPR. Tony changed little things – the players didn't have to pay for their dinners any more, for one. We were paying about £400 a month to eat at the training ground and Tony put a stop to that. "You're coming to work for me, so I pay for your dinner," he said. He also stopped charging us for our match shirts. After our first five we used to have to pay for them every time we gave one away. Fans were asking for shirts from the lads and, although £50 a pop wasn't going to break the bank, it soon added up if you were giving away two after every game.

Tony certainly seemed more in tune with us as players than the previous regime, who were even late paying our promotion bonuses. One of the lads realised first that we hadn't got any of it and asked Warnock what was going on. We had just earned the club promotion to the richest league in the world, which guaranteed them more than £40m in TV payments alone, and were told: "We need to wait until we've got some revenue coming into the club." What the fuck? We knew we would get it eventually – there was no way Warnock wasn't going to get hold of his own bonus! – and it was written in our contracts in black and white. But it was just a strange time. I wondered why they had to hang on for so long?

In the end we got our bonuses and Warnock got his transfer budget, of about £10m. Still, most of his early signings were free transfers. We got Joey Barton, who'd had his fair share of controversies in his career, from Newcastle and I got on with him. I think he liked what we had done the previous season, winning promotion with a bunch of solid, senior pros, although it's probably no surprise to hear that he was a fiery bloke away from the pitch.

I would never want to get into an argument with him – you would be there all day because he would keep going until he came out on top – but he wanted to win. Simple as that. He was some player when he was at it, too, and he was a great signing for us. It was just… when he crossed the white line, absolutely anything could happen. We saw that later in the season on that fateful day at his old club City.

One of my fondest memories of Joey came in the tunnel before we played Wolves at Molineux. Joey scored the first goal after eight minutes, but had already got the better of Wolves midfielder Jamie O'Hara before a ball was even kicked. I don't know why, but Joey and O'Hara didn't seem to get on. We were lined up in the tunnel before the game and Joey asked O'Hara if he was all right. O'Hara didn't acknowledge him, so Joey changed his tune. "Hey, are you still with that missus of yours?" he asked. "I can name a starting 11 that's banged her."

Pretty juvenile stuff, I admit. We were all cringing in the tunnel, trying to stifle our laughter while O'Hara just stared straight ahead. Eventually the referee got involved. "Now, now, Joey, come on… Don't start," he said, trying to calm the situation down. Joey paused for a second before landing one last blow. "What are you on about?" he asked. "I could probably name seven subs as well." O'Hara had a stinker and we were 2-0 up inside 10 minutes, eventually battering them 3-0.

We left it late in the transfer window, but eventually strengthened with the signings of Shaun Wright-Phillips and Anton Ferdinand. Shaun was a great kid who once cost Chelsea £21m and Anton was a big signing as well, although me and him used to clash big time. We argued constantly and we were probably actually too similar as characters.

He was another player who came in from another Premier League club on big money: most of the signings that year were on at least quadruple the salary of the players who had got QPR into the top-flight. I say that without any bitterness or jealousy. When you're at a club that gets promoted, nine times out of 10 the players they bring in will already be in the Premier League and you've just got to accept what comes with that. As long as they weren't big-time or flash about it, it never bothered me.

Some I ended up feeling a little bit sorry for. Kieron Dyer was another big-name, big-money player who joined us on the way down in his career. He'd had problems of his own in the past although they were more to do with injuries than anything. Still, Warnock took a punt on him and, due to injuries elsewhere, had to play Kieron at right-back for our first game of the season, at home to Bolton. Kieron lasted seven minutes before he was stretchered off with a suspected broken foot. He later played a game for the reserves as he looked to get back to full fitness, damaged ligaments in his foot and missed the rest of the season.

It was a nightmare start for Kieron and for us as a team. We lost 4-0 on the opening day at home to Bolton, but, as mad as it sounds, we were all over them in the first half. Then Gary Cahill scored for them on the stroke of half-time and it knocked the stuffing out of us. Before we knew it, we were 4-0 down at home.

No disrespect to Bolton, but they weren't exactly one of the big teams in the league and I remember thinking: "Shit, here comes reality. God knows what's going to happen this season." We'd had a nightmare pre-season trip to Italy and I wondered if the hangover from that was going to affect us. Then we went away to Everton and beat them 1-0. We'd probably have taken winning three points from the two games, but thought they'd have come from beating Bolton and losing at Everton. It's a strange old game at times.

In early October we were dicked 6-0 away at Fulham – I gave away a penalty, again by fouling Andy Johnson – but showed our bollocks by bouncing back to take a point against Blackburn. Then, just over a week later we welcomed our local rivals Chelsea to Loftus Road. The game later hit the headlines because of the incident with John Terry and Anton, which ended up completely overshadowing the actual game itself. It was absolute chaos. We were 1-0 up from the 10th minute thanks to Heidar Helguson's penalty and Chelsea had two men sent off the first half. You may think that would make the game easier, but we were hanging on for dear life against nine men for the entire second half. We couldn't get hold of the ball and Petr Čech was basically playing centre-half. But we had a lead to protect, and somehow held on for a famous win against the onslaught of these world-class players. Chelsea's nine men finished up with almost 60 per cent of possession and Čech nearly got his head on a late cross after going forward, but we ended up with the points.

That was only the start of it. There were just over 18,000 fans inside Loftus Road for that game, but, as they roared us on, it sounded more like 80,000. Chelsea completely lost their heads and me and Terry had a few words late on, at around the 90-minute mark. I came out for the ball and Terry ran into me – he hardly touched me, to be honest, but it was enough to knock me down. I stayed down for a few moments and he dragged me up off the floor. He called me a fat cunt, I replied with something about his mum after she was arrested on suspicion of shoplifting flip-flops from a Tesco. After the game we both apologised and had a bit of a laugh about it, not knowing the storm that was already brewing.

After the game a video came out of Terry mouthing something in Anton's direction. I was obviously miles away from the incident at the time with a rowdy Loftus Road crowd behind me, so I have no idea what Terry said or to who. After it had become a story a few days later, I had to ask when in the game the incident was supposed to have happened. First half, second half – I had no idea. I do remember that Chelsea were not happy and were bad losers that day. They had lost a West London derby that they would have been expected to win and were really on one.

There were a few running arguments and battles as the players left the pitch at the end of the game and, as I walked down the corridor towards our dressing-room, I heard a massive commotion. I ran back to see what had gone on and saw that Branislav Ivanovic had two of our lads in a headlock, one under each arm. I briefly thought about getting involved and then remembered that Ivanovic was an absolute unit. No chance, I thought, and went back to the safety of our dressing-room. He was rag-dolling our lads all over. Someone braver than me must have rescued them!

After the game Terry had a word with Anton in their changing-room and they left on decent terms. Anton didn't know what had really gone off until his girlfriend showed him the video of the incident on her phone and Terry later made a statement effectively admitting what he had said to Anton, and attempting to explain why. A member of the public then reported Terry to the police and the whole episode completely blew up. Although Terry was cleared at Westminster Magistrates' Court, The FA found him guilty of racial abuse after their own inquiry and banned him for four games. In comparison Didier Drogba, his teammate, missed three matches for fouling Adel Taarabt against us and getting sent off.

Amongst the players, the incident and the fall-out were obviously spoken about afterwards. Anton was a teammate of ours and it was a huge deal at the time. Terry first lost the England captaincy over it and then retired from playing for England altogether. Fabio Capello quit the England job because of the scandal. Later in the season Anton was apparently sent a bullet in the post and had obviously become the villain in the whole story in the eyes of some people. That's football for you, I guess – it's so tribal. Some fans can't see past the colour of the shirt players wear, no matter the rights and wrongs of any situation.

Our 1-0 win is a memorable game that sticks out that season and not just because of what went on afterwards. The feeling immediately after the final whistle was like we had just won the league. It was a special day. When the fixtures came out, it was a game that we all looked for, but also one that we realistically knew we were going to get beaten in. If we had nicked a draw, we would have been happy. To take all three points? We were ecstatic, but quickly came back down to earth when the news broke and we found ourselves unwittingly in the middle of a media shitstorm.

Not long after I suffered one of the freakiest injuries I ever experienced in the game. We beat Stoke away in November and before our next game, against Norwich, I dived to save a shot in training as I had a million times before. This time, though, there was a massive shooting pain that seared through my hip. I had landed on one of those plastic toggles on the bottom of rain jackets to tighten the elastic. It had gone right into my hip and I had to come in from training. I couldn't walk properly and the scan showed I had damaged the bursa – it was like a rupture. That caused some damage down into my glute as well and I ended up missing four matches – because of a plastic toggle on my raincoat!

I was back on the bench in time for Manchester United to visit Loftus Road and luckily I was injury-free later in the season for the return game at Old Trafford. Man United v QPR was the first football game I ever attended, as a youngster standing with my brother Tony on the Stretford End, and I had been a Man United fan for as long as I could remember. It went back to junior school. Liverpool were the main team at the time, so we played Man. United v Liverpool fans in the playground at dinnertime. I had been pushed that way anyway by Tony, but playing "for" Man United in the playground seemed to reinforce the feeling I had for them. To be fair the Liverpool fans were far better than us, just like the team at the time, and it was like lifting the World Cup whenever we won the odd game!

So for that reason going back to Old Trafford and actually *playing* in that game, as a QPR man, was special. I sat next to Helguson on the coach and told him the story as we pulled into the stadium. My brother was still alive at that point and I couldn't help thinking how crazy it was that the short kid from Halifax, straining on the Stretford End to catch a glimpse of Man United v QPR, would end up playing in that same game nearly 30 years later. There wasn't too much time to reminisce when the whistle went, though – Man United had the likes of Wayne Rooney, Rio Ferdinand and Ryan Giggs on their teamsheet. Rooney scored an early penalty and Paul Scholes made it 2-0 in the second half, but it was a nice reminder that every one of these lads was once just like me – a young kid, stretching his neck and trying to catch a glimpse of his heroes.

By that point I had seen Warnock leave again, after he was sacked in early January. We hadn't won in 10 games, but strangely Warnock got the sack after we stopped the rot a little with a 1-0 win at home to MK Dons in an FA Cup replay. The run didn't look great, but it also didn't tell the full story. In one of the games we were beating West Brom until they equalised with less than 10 minutes left. We went to Anfield and lost 1-0 to Liverpool, which is certainly nothing out of the ordinary for a newly-promoted club, and conceded an 89th-minute goal in my first game back to lose at Sunderland.

We were cruising at 1-0 up against Norwich before Joey got sent off and cost us the game, which we lost in the 83rd minute. It might sound like making excuses, but it wasn't as if we were rock-bottom and being hammered every week. We were actually joint 16th with Wolves after 20 games of the season. Warnock came out in the Press and said his remit was to keep us out of the bottom three, which we were. But the owners still decided they want to change it. I can't lie; it was disappointing. I imagine Warnock found it difficult that he had worked so hard through a lot of shit to get the club into the Premier League and then – in my opinion – not be given a fair crack of the whip to keep them there. As a newly-promoted club in the Premier League, you have got to expect a few bad results, but our heads were very much above water when the axe fell on Warnock.

I had double the reason to be gutted when he left, too. I was on £18,000 a week at the time because of the lift that promotion had brought, but I was halfway through the three-year deal I had signed and we had more or less agreed a new contract, which would have doubled my money. My agent went in to the negotiations and pointed out the role I had played in promotion, keeping all those clean sheets and winning both player-of-the-year awards in my first season. "You need to sort Paddy out," he said. Warnock agreed, but wanted to get his players in first in January, so he had the budget left over. "We'll sort it out from then," he said. We had verbally agreed to double my money and then he got sacked! So it went quiet. Warnock had gone and so had my deal.

Talk about a double blow!

I was reluctant to talk about money in this book - I didn't want to sound like I was bragging, which is the last thing I would do - but I do think that my time came right in the middle of two different periods in the game – when top, top players earned fuck all in the old days, and more recently when average players earn stupid money because of all the cash flying around throughout football. Footballers and their wages are an easy target. A lot of people already knew that, but it really showed for me when the coronavirus pandemic hit in 2020 and all of a sudden Government ministers were calling out footballers in Press briefings to "play their part" and take a pay cut. I won't sit here and deny that footballers are well-paid, but I can also say that not every one is a millionaire either. I get it a lot when people find out that I used to be a footballer: "You must have earned millions!" they say. The £18,000 at QPR was the most I was ever on and that was taxed at 50 per cent – before things like a pension and national insurance took a chunk out of what was left over.

It's still a ridiculous amount of money. I know that. But in mitigation, you end up living to your means. You go on better holidays, flying to Dubai every year rather than going to Tenerife. You get a bigger car, or more cars, and a bigger house. The missus wants expensive shoes and handbags. I kept my house going in Sheffield and the one I had in London was costing me twice as much in rent as my mortgage up north. And I was there only two nights a week! That's life in London for you. There was no point in sulking about Warnock leaving and my deal going up in smoke: the professional in me took over, and the focus now was on keeping the club in the Premier League.

***

The club didn't waste any time in appointing Warnock's replacement. Mark Hughes was a legend of the game as a player, someone I had grown up watching as a Manchester United fan, but I found him to be a very strange man. He would walk past you in the corridor in the morning and, when you said: "Morning!" to him, he would just look at the floor. To be fair to him, training was very good. It was very detailed and the preparation for games was really thorough. But there were a few things he brought in that the lads didn't like. Little things, like wearing suits to away games. We wore them to home games anyway, but suddenly we were on a boiling hot coach to away games, sweating in the club suits.

Lads couldn't wait to get them off and get in their training kit before the game. Some would put their suits on to get from changing-room to bus and then change into their tracksuits. It was like a Sunday League team, getting changed on the coach. There were ties flying everywhere. Like with Bryan Robson at Sheffield United, we found out the team on the day of the game. Hughes also brought his own staff in and Kevin Hitchcock took over from Dave Rouse, who was superb with me but moved on to work with the U21s.

Different coach, different methods. Hitchcock wanted all the 'keepers in the gym for 45 minutes before training, doing pre-activation work like dips and squats and lunges and bike work. I went with it on the first day and trained like a twat. I felt shit and lethargic. I was 34 at the time and knew what my body was about. "I'm not doing that anymore," I told him. "I'll do it after training, but not before." When Hughes came in, we didn't have the best of starts and another change he had made was to install plaques in the car-park. His said: "Mark Hughes, OBE, Manager." One day he turned up to training and someone had written under the letters of OBE: "Out Before Easter." We never found out who the culprit was – my money was on Joey – and I don't think I was alone in finding his methods strange. It was difficult to be motivated by him and it was more his coaches Eddie Niedzwiecki and Mark Bowen who got the lads going.

Hughes' big name did work in our favour when it came to signing players, though, and on the last day of the January window we signed two new strikers, Bobby Zamora and Djibril Cissé. I'll never forget Cissé coming in and thinking: "Wow." He came to training in a different car every day – we reckoned he must have owned about 20 – but he wasn't big time with it. We had seen him score all those goals for Liverpool in the past and win the Champions League final against AC Milan in 2005. What a player and what a madman. He played eight games for QPR in his first season and either scored or was sent off in every single one. His record was: Goal, red card, goal, goal, red card, goal, goal, goal. Talk about making an impact at your new club!

He was an unbelievable character. He once offered to meet a QPR fan for a fight at the training ground after being insulted on Twitter and when he wasn't being sent off, he scored some incredibly vital goals for us. In our last 11 matches of the season, we lost all our six away games and won all five at home, beating Liverpool, Arsenal and Tottenham Hotspur along the way. At one point we looked as if we might be in trouble and it didn't bode well when we went to Chelsea and got battered 6-1. We did well to keep it to six. Of course Terry scored and we were level on points with Bolton in the final relegation place. The tension was starting to get to people. A fortnight earlier we had lost 1-0 at West Brom and Joey and Shaun Derry had had a massive scrap in the changing-room. They came off at half-time arguing, possibly about West Brom's goal, and it all went off in the middle of the room. For a brief second again I thought about getting involved. But I saw the two players who were scrapping and thought again: "Fuck that." Those two could handle themselves and I was glad to have no part of it.

We came from 2-0 down to beat Liverpool and that game kick-started a belief in us that we could pick up good results at Loftus Road. Dezza got one back and then two goals in four minutes, Djibril against his old club and a 90th-minute winner from Jamie Mackie, gave us hope again. We took nine points from three successive home games, keeping three clean sheets, but the decisive moment came when we beat Stoke in our penultimate game. We knew Bolton were winning and, as it stood, we were going to be in the bottom three with one game remaining. But then in the 89th minute Cissé turned the ball home after a bit of pinball in the box, which meant our fate was in our own hands going into the last game of the season.

***

It was just as well really, considering it was away at champions-elect City. Their record at the Etihad that season was frightening – of their 18 games at home before we went there, they had won 17 and drawn the other one, conceding only 10 goals. All City needed to do was to beat us and a first Premier League title was theirs. Cissé's goal against Stoke had changed everything for us. We were out of the bottom three and knew that Bolton had to win, ironically away at Stoke, to have a chance of overtaking us.

The build-up to the City game felt a bit like a play-off final, which is essentially what the game was. A huge, one-off fixture that would have huge implications for both sides. I personally couldn't believe that my two seasons in the Premier League had both gone down to the last 90 minutes and after being relegated on the final day before, with United, I had no desire whatsoever to experience that feeling again.

A few years earlier at United, we only had to draw at home to our relegation rivals Wigan to keep us up. Five years later QPR were going away to the best team in the country, who had dropped two points at home all season and needed to win to secure their first Premier League title. *We haven't got a fucking prayer*, I thought to myself.

Pressure can do funny things, though. It obviously wasn't the ideal game to decide our fate, but it wasn't the best for City either. They had the eyes of the world on them and were expected to turn over a relegation-threatened team, at home, pretty comfortably. So in a way, maybe it helped us. City were an unbelievable team, full of superstars, but I imagine it is a heavy weight to have on your shoulders when you're 90 minutes away from your first title in however many years with your biggest rivals breathing down your necks. For them it was now or never.

The noise at kick-off was unbelievable and we went in at half-time 1-0 down. We were desperate to know the Bolton score; they were 2-1 up at Stoke and, as it stood, we were down. That didn't help my mood at the break. I should have done better with City's goal, scored by Pablo Zabaleta of all people. I was set too low down and couldn't get back up quickly enough, so I ended up palming his shot into the air and into my net. Aside from that I made some other saves that I would have expected to make, but I wasn't being peppered.

Still, I felt completely drained at half-time. I had been constantly organising and shouting – even more so than usual because the stakes were so high – and that was sapping my energy even before I made any saves. Sometimes in my career I went through games in which I didn't make a save, but I came off the pitch absolutely knackered, with a headache, because of the concentration it takes for 90 minutes. There's no such thing as an easy game for a goalkeeper!

After a few minutes of the second half we were level. Joleon Lescott made a mistake and Djibril raced onto it, smashing the ball past Joe Hart and sending our fans behind that goal absolutely wild. I couldn't believe it. I thought: "Here we go... You never know, we might have a chance here." Then the onslaught came from City. It felt as if I must have made 20 saves in that second half alone. I was being peppered now. Looking back, I probably had one of the best games of my career in terms of the stops I was making and how important they were. I had no idea how Bolton were going on – I just tried to control what I could and keep that ball out of my net.

One of the best saves was actually from Aguero: I saved Carlos Tevez's shot and then Aguero followed up and I blocked it on the line. To be fair he should have scored and, if he had put the ball a yard either side of me, he would have. Instead it hit me on the elbow and I reacted quickly enough to snatch it on the line. I wondered if it might be our day after all.

Then Joey struck – literally. I didn't see the incident in real time because I was following the ball, but as replays showed, Joey elbowed Tevez after he looked for a one-two with David Silva. Joey claimed Tevez had aimed a sly punch at him out of sight of the officials, but somehow the linesman on the far side saw what Joey had done and Mike Dean showed him the red card on his return to City. Then all hell broke loose. Joey kicked out at Aguero, leaving him on the deck, and threw a sort-of head-butt at Vincent Kompany. The aim, I found out later, was to try and get a City player to retaliate and get sent off as well.

Micah Richards, Joey's old teammate, seemed to calm him down with an arm around the shoulder – until Mario Balotelli had a few words from the bench and Joey was off again. Kevin Hitchcock and Richards helped to shepherd him down the tunnel and we looked to adjust, to playing the final 35 minutes against City with 10 men. That was Joey all over, but, rather than make it easier for City, as you would assume, I think it actually hurt them more than it did us. The game was stopped for a while and their flow had gone completely. We had taken the sting out of City. And then we went ahead.

The most shocking part of it was probably me actually coming off my line for something. The cord snapped again and I claimed a cross. We had Armand Traoré playing at left-back for us that day, who had pace to burn, and I noticed he had loads of space in front of him to run into. Part of me wanted to throw the ball and another part of me wanted to keep hold of it for as long as I could – forever – and soak up the pressure. Then in an almost involuntary motion I threw the ball in front of Armand. "Why have you done that, you dickhead?" I asked myself. "Why aren't you slowing it down? If he loses it now and they score, I'm going to get hammered."

It turned out to be one of the most perfect throws I had ever made. It went exactly where he would have wanted it, on his outside, and Armand rode the challenge that came in and ran almost the length of the field. He crossed it with his left foot and Mackie met it perfectly to head it down past Hart and over Lescott on the line.

We were down to 10 men, away at a team who hadn't lost here all season and were going for the title, and were 2-1 up. As it stood, we were safe.

The only thing I could hear in the stadium were the QPR fans at the other side of the pitch. They were in absolute dreamland. For the City supporters, though, it must have been hell. They knew Man United were winning and their dreams of winning the title were slipping away by the second. You could feel the dejection in the stadium and I could see it on their faces. Then the noise rose again. But it wasn't the City fans celebrating – it was ours. We weren't stupid. We knew something must have happened in the Bolton game and it turned out Jonathan Walters had equalised for Stoke.

In the back of my mind I never thought Bolton would win away at Stoke. It was always a horrible place to go, no matter when, and we had done very well to beat them at our place the week before. But still there was no way we were leaving it to chance and, as the clock ticked over the 90-minute mark, I made a good save to keep out Balotelli's header from a corner after he had come off the bench. We were in injury time when City finally got a goal back, Edin Dzeko climbing highest at a corner and powering a header past me. All four sides of the ground went mental. Just before City's goal our fans and bench had heard the result from Stoke, a 2-2 draw, and were celebrating like mad. Bolton were down. We were safe. *Fuck me.*

We were absolutely buzzing our tits off and, after taking the kick-off, Jay Bothroyd smashed it straight out of play near the corner flag to waste some time. To this day I don't think we would have done that if we hadn't known the Stoke result. We would have knocked the ball back and across and then launched it. Everything might have happened completely differently then. But honestly we were safe and we didn't give a shit. It didn't matter. It's only when you look back now that you realise how big an impact it actually had. City kept coming and coming at us and eventually got another chance.

Aguero dropped short to get the ball off Nigel De Jong and fed Balotelli. Anton Ferdinand did just about enough to nudge him off the ball, but Aguero continued his run and Balotelli did brilliantly to keep his balance for long enough to scoop the ball into his path. Aguero took a touch to nudge it past Taye Taiwo, a lad we had on loan from AC Milan, and then absolutely smashed it past me and into the net.

Martin Tyler's commentary on Sky Sports – "Balotelliii… Aguerooooooo…!" – became iconic and the stadium absolutely exploded. There were 93 minutes and 20 seconds on the clock and City were champions in the most amazing fashion. Poor Clint Hill, our defender, thought the Aguero goal had relegated us. He hadn't heard our bench telling us that we were safe!

Even to this day I still have people saying to me: "Oh, you should never have got beaten there at your near post." I'm not having that for one minute. Aguero was about seven or eight yards out – and have you seen how hard he hit that ball? It was past me before I even had a chance. If it was five yards off the touchline, I would understand and, if I am being ultra-critical of myself, I probably could have taken another half-step to my left.

Even then I'm not saying I would have saved it! I would never have got down quick enough to get my hand to it. It would have been a foot, if anything. But then the most famous goal in football history wouldn't have been scored and I wouldn't see it on the television every so often! It was like a sliding-doors moment. Man United would have won the title that year, and who knows what would have happened to City?

Not that I was thinking about any of that at the time. I was raging to concede the goal. All our defenders were just lunging in at Balotelli and then Aguero like madmen. I actually thought someone was going to bring him down and I would have a penalty to face. Again, I think if we didn't know what had happened at Stoke, we wouldn't have lunged in and would have stood up instead, so Aguero might not have got a shot off. I jumped up as the ball hit the net to have a go at our defence, but couldn't get the words out. I was distracted by what was going off around me and allowed myself to take it in for a second. Wow.

The only shame was that we weren't able to celebrate with our own fans after the game because thousands of City supporters poured onto the pitch. For some reason one of them decided to celebrate his side winning the title by slapping me on the back of the head before someone else kicked me. I was absolutely fuming. We were told it was too dangerous to stay out on the pitch, so we celebrated in the dressing-room instead. Well, most of us did.

Anton wasn't too happy because his brother Rio hadn't won the league, but no-one else gave a shit about that. We ended up telling him to shut the fuck up and celebrate with us. In previous years I might have felt a similar way, given my loyalties as a kid, but I honestly could not have cared less. I think it was karma, because of what happened all those years before when Man United put out a weakened team and West Ham beat them to relegate Sheffield United. I had never forgotten reading a story a few days later when someone from Man United said something like: "You can't blame it on us, on the last day of the season, because you've had all those games in the season to stay up." Well, it turned on its head that day. They had all those games to win the league and couldn't do it.

Fuck them, I thought, as I sat in the away dressing-room at City and heard their biggest rivals celebrating through the walls. Man United had actually thought they had won the title and Sir Alex Ferguson was on Sky's camera when he heard about Aguero's winner. Maybe in that moment he felt a small bit of what we had felt at Bramall Lane a few years earlier. It was one of the most ridiculous endings to a season in history, we had stayed up, and I needed a beer. What I didn't know was that "the Aguero game" was to be my last for QPR. But at least I had signed out on a high.

22

BACK TO YORKSHIRE

Augufust 18th, 2012. On the back of a good 1-0 victory on my league debut for Leeds, and also a good few beers, I pulled my phone from my pocket and pressed call. Months of frustration had boiled over and I had so many things that I was dying to say to Mike Rigg. He'll never answer, I thought. *Hasn't got the bollocks.* Then I heard his voice and at first, all I could do was laugh hysterically at him down the line. Earlier that day QPR had been battered 5-0 at home to Swansea City. "It couldn't have happened to a nicer person," I told him, once I had stopped laughing. "I hope you don't win another game all season, just because of you. You prick."

My delight at QPR's scoreline was purely because of one man. It was not down to anyone else at a football club I have a lot of respect for, and certainly not the supporters who were brilliant with me. It also wasn't, as a few stories in the media later tried to make out, aimed at Rob Green, who had been signed to replace me in the summer. It was aimed squarely at Rigg because of the way I had been treated.

I was proud of everything I had achieved at QPR, including playing a part in our incredible survival bid. But once we stayed up, I sensed that Mark Hughes wanted a bigger-name goalkeeper in and his move for Rob made a lot of sense. He was coming on a free transfer from West Ham and had a lot of Premier League experience. He was also a former England No. 1, and I had no problem with the club wanting to get bigger and better players in. In fact, I was happy that at least they were being upfront and honest with me when they told me I was free to leave as soon as they signed a new 'keeper.

My time at QPR was relatively short, but it was very eventful. To win the title in my first season was incredible, but then to survive in the Premier League with the run we had towards the back end of the season was unbelievable. We were pretty much relegated until we won our last five home games – beating Liverpool, Arsenal and Spurs in that run – and went ahead against City on the final day before those mad five minutes that have gone down in football folklore.

In the lead up to this book's release I was *still* getting messages from people on Twitter accusing us of throwing the game against City to help them to win the title. They're mostly all from bitter Man United fans, but it makes me laugh that anyone could think that for a second. If we had gone to the Etihad, where City had won every single league game up to that point, and got spanked 4-0, no-one would have looked twice. Instead we played for 35 minutes with 10 men after Joey Barton had been sent off, were 2-1 up going into injury time and I had one of my best games in an QPR shirt. Put it this way – if you were going to throw a game, there would probably be easier ways to do it!

It was crazy after the game with everything that had gone off and we just wanted to get out of there as soon as we could. We celebrated properly the next day and had arranged via Blackberry Messenger to meet up at a pub in Chiswick and then go into London. I got the train down and used the time to think of everything we had achieved that season, letting it *really* sink in. I was the second one to get there, at 11 in the morning, and Joey had already put his card behind the bar. "The drinks are on me while we're in here because I let you all down yesterday," he said. No-one really discussed his moment of madness after the game because ultimately it didn't really matter, but we still took advantage of his generosity. I was so pissed, it was frightening and I slept the whole journey back on the train.

I have the shirt that I wore that day in a box somewhere and a few years later I asked Kyle Walker to get Aguero to sign it for me as another memory of the day. Not that I'd ever forget it! I will forever be connected to that goal. When my son was at college, lads would walk past him in the corridor and shout: "Aguerooooooo..." at him. On the field my time at QPR couldn't have ended in a better way, but my memories of how it was handled still leave a very sour taste in the mouth.

Rigg was Hughes' man and they worked together at Wales, Blackburn and City before linking up again at QPR when Hughes took over from Warnock. Rigg had been involved with some huge transfers at City when their mega-rich owners came in and I wonder if the idea of working with big names appealed more to him than someone like me. To be honest I had the feeling that Hughes and Co. weren't really having me from the moment they came in, so when Rob arrived it was time to put the wheels in motion and find a new club.

When Warnock heard I could go, he was straight on the phone. He had taken over at Leeds United about a month after being sacked by QPR and he made his first approach for me straightaway after I had sent him a text wishing him all the best at Elland Road. "I bet you'd love to come and play for Leeds," he replied. "Back home, right on your doorstep." I laughed it off and said: "You never know." Just a few months later, the move was on. The only real stumbling-block was my wages. Leeds could only offer £10,000 a week, which was a near-45 per cent wage cut on my QPR salary. Seeing your salary cut almost in half would affect most people in the world, and I was no different.

My QPR contract had a year left on it and, as far as I was concerned, it was them who wanted to sell me, rather than me wanting to leave. So I told them that we would have to come to some sort of arrangement on the shortfall. I have never been overly motivated by money, but at the same time I wasn't going to be taken advantage of either. After all it was QPR's decision to give me a three-year deal, rather than mine, and although I was never going to be a player who would sit in the reserves and pick up my money, I thought that it was reasonable that they met me halfway. Apart from the wage issue, everything else had been agreed with the move and I will never forget being on a beach in Marbella when Rigg called me. He told me I had to go, and go for nothing, otherwise I would be made to train with the under-18s side, three times a day.

If he was in front of me on that beach, I would have stuck one on him. "I'll tell you what, Mike," I said, calmly. "We're back for pre-season in two or three weeks, aren't we? Meet me at the training ground because I'm going to knock you out. Then you'll have to sack me, I'll feel a lot better and I'll go to Leeds anyway."

I couldn't quite believe what was going on. Me and QPR had been good for each other and after they signed me for £750,000, there was £500,000 on the table from Leeds. QPR would have saved almost £750,000 a year on my wages, even if they met me halfway, and none of what was going on really made much sense. Not long after I had put the phone down on

Rigg, Warnock called me. "What have you done?" he asked frantically. "What have you said? They said they're pulling out of the deal and they're not gonna let us buy you."

I explained what had gone off; what Rigg had threatened me with. Warnock understood, telling me I had done right, and I was by the pool the next day when my agent rang and told me that QPR were going to make me an offer after all. It still wasn't what I wanted, or what I was entitled to, but it was better than nothing and I was content to cut my losses. I didn't want to be at a club where I felt like I was being treated like shit. If I didn't take the offer, I would have gone back in pre-season and wanted to kill people. I think I ended up getting about £100,000 from QPR – a lot of money, but still less than half of what I wanted. And a lot less than I would have got if I had stayed and just picked up my wages.

What I think really sums up the pettiness of the whole experience is how I actually got that money. Rather than give the pay-off directly to me, QPR came up with a deal where they knocked £100,000 off the transfer fee and then Leeds were to give me that amount as a signing-on fee, meaning I got it over the length of my contract in three instalments. It had dragged on and on but with that obstacle out of the way, we wrapped up the deal with Leeds and I was back home in Yorkshire. When I came off the pitch after we had beaten Wolves on my league debut and saw QPR had been stuffed, I took great comfort in the thought of that hurting Rigg.

Then a few pints later, I decided to tell him.

What really disappointed me was the story that subsequently came out in the Press, saying that I had slagged off Rob. That didn't happen. I had played against Rob when he was at Norwich and he was someone I had, and still have, a great deal of respect for. I knew a couple of Norwich fans and he used to give me his shirt after games for them, that kind of thing. He was also a damn good 'keeper who had played in the Premier League for most of his career, and for England, so I would never have a pop at him for one minute. I blamed one man for the way my departure from QPR was handled – and it sure as hell wasn't the bloke they had signed to replace me in goal.

Looking back, I should have contacted Rob and explained that what had come out in the media was bollocks. I don't know if he believed it or not at the time, but I hope he didn't. I could easily have got his number off someone and given him a ring, to say: "Listen, not once did I ever slag you off" and I wish I had done. I wasn't one of those players who was bitter when someone took his place. It's part of the game and I know as well as any other goalkeeper that we are all in a difficult position. I have a lot of respect for anyone who pulls on the gloves, especially someone with the career that Rob had in the game.

I wasn't the only player Rigg had apparently pissed off in the past. Early in my Leeds career I played against a lad, who I won't name, who'd had a great career at the highest level, at one of English football's biggest clubs. Nothing tends to stay secret for too long in football, and news of my QPR exit had obviously spread. The player in question made a beeline for me after the game. "He's a fucking nob isn't he, that Mike Rigg?" was the first thing he said. I told him the full story, about threatening to knock Rigg out, and even a player of his experience in football couldn't fully believe it.

Despite all the fun and games, QPR's owner Tony Fernandes actually made a late attempt to get me to stay at Loftus Road. I don't know how much Hughes and Rigg knew about it, but Tony called me on my way to my Leeds medical and told me he didn't want me to leave. "I appreciate that, Tony, but the manager does and the staff do," I said. "No-one else wants me there." He offered to give me a new deal, but I told him my mind was made up. I didn't want to be anywhere I wasn't wanted and the chance of coming home, to a club the size of Leeds United, was a really exciting one.

Having grown up just down the road in Halifax, no-one had to tell me about Leeds and their history. When I was at Sheffield United and we beat them in both cups, they were still a Premier League team with big-name players like Lee Bowyer, Harry Kewell and Mark Viduka, but had fallen on hard times financially and dropped all the way down into League One at one stage. It just shows that it doesn't matter how big you are; if you aren't run properly from the top, there's only one way it's going to go.

But the potential was obvious and I thought that if Warnock could repeat what he had done at QPR, playing for Leeds could have been unbelievable. He knew it, too, and said the same when we met up. "Paddy, if we get this club on a roll, then it could do owt," he said, with that glint in his eye. "Absolutely owt." I didn't hesitate. It meant dropping back down into the Championship, but realistically I knew that was probably my level anyway. I wasn't stupid; the chance to play each week for a club the size of Leeds and at a level that I knew I was more suited to? Just tell me where to sign, I thought.

When I left QPR and the incorrect story about me slagging off Rob came out, I got a lot of messages from Rangers fans on Twitter and a lot of them crossed a line. A couple of people started abusing my young children, calling them fat and "ugly bastard kids" and some horrible other words that no-one should hear their kids being called, and I lost my head completely. I bit and called QPR a tin-pot club, which I didn't mean for one second. I was just angry at the horrible tweets I had received about my kids.

But once it was out there, it was there forever.

I have apologised since and say sorry again now. I should have risen above it, but I felt the abuse had gone too far and I actually ended up agreeing when one fan offered me a fight in Sheffield city centre. It obviously never happened, but the tweet made the 'papers and the lad who sent it revelled in his five minutes of fame.

The FA threatened to do me over it. Warnock pulled me into his office after training, where I told him my side of the story. He could see I was wound up and he understood, but he asked me a simple question. "Is it worth it, Paddy? Is it worth being on Twitter?" I got nothing but abuse and I thought: "Do you know what? You're spot-on."

It was taking over my life and at that time, 95 per cent of people on there were abusing me without a name or a face to their accounts. I went home that day and deactivated my account. Looking back, me and Twitter was never going to be a good mix while I was still a player because of my personality. If I saw someone on there giving me grief, then it was in my character and make up to give them some back. The best thing to do was take myself out of the situation.

I was one of 15 players brought in by Warnock that summer and, if in some ways I was the most predictable, there was no doubt over who was the most surprising. The year before, when me and Warnock were at QPR, he had called El-Hadji Diouf "a sewer rat" after Jamie Mackie broke his leg against Blackburn. Jamie was in obvious trouble, but Diouf accused him of exaggerating the injury. A couple of our lads followed him into the car-park after the game and his big, daft mirrored Jeep had its wing mirror booted off, with a nice dent left in the side for good measure.

After the game Warnock let rip in the Press. "I thought after in the tunnel you could see what a nasty piece of fish he is," he said of Diouf. "I called him a little sewer rat, but that might be a little bit harsh on the sewer rats. I can't abide people like that. For many years I have thought he was the gutter type... I think he is the lowest of the low. I think he will be the first to go [from Blackburn] and good riddance – I hope he goes abroad because I won't miss watching him. He is a nasty, little person."

Dioufy, who was twice African player of the year and signed for Liverpool after impressing at the 2002 World Cup, wasn't a big fan of Warnock either. "Who is Warnock?" he said after that game against QPR. "He's nothing to me. I know he doesn't like me, but it's the same for me, too – I don't like him."

Eighteen months later, Warnock signed him for Leeds.

I'd also had a few dos with Diouf earlier in my career although I got on really well with him at Leeds. When I was at Sheffield United, he was with Bolton and grabbed me by the bollocks when we were defending a corner. We cleared the ball before me and Diouf had a bit of an argument and, when he was talking, I could feel spit all over me. I remember thinking: "You dirty bastard." I wanted to rip his head off. He was actually a decent lad, but reminded me a lot of Joey Barton; when he crossed that white line, he became a totally different person.

It was a familiar situation at Leeds as Warnock again looked to surround himself with good, honest pros. Michael Brown was already there and another old Blades teammate of ours Michael Tonge joined us, along with the likes of Paul Green, Stephen Warnock and Lee Peltier. Brownie was at the back end of his career and I was getting on a bit, in my early 30s, but I thought we had a good squad at that level at the time. I think the fans took to me quite early at Leeds and I can remember them singing to me as early as my fourth game for the club. But every so often one moron would spoil it for the rest of the Leeds support.

I was at the other end of the pitch when the idiot ran on and whacked Chris Kirkland, who was in goal for Sheffield Wednesday at Hillsborough. It was absolutely disgusting; a horrible thing to see as a fellow player. It was an embarrassment to the club and the first incident like that I can remember. Why the game was ever allowed to be played on a Friday night, I will never know. The Leeds fan, who had been drinking all day, went to prison for a few months and I will never forget Kirkland barging into our changing-room after the game to confront Warnock.

He hadn't actually seen the lad run on and attack Kirkland, because we had just equalised. Someone told him that Kirkland had been hit by a fan, but had gone down easily. In his interview immediately after the game – still without seeing the incident – Warnock said that Kirkland had "gone down like a ton of bricks." Warnock's wife, Sharon, was watching at home and phoned straightaway to say he had made a mistake.

Warnock watched his first replay and planned to apologise to Kirkland after he'd had a shower. But before he had the chance, Kirkland came bursting through our dressing-room door, looking for the Gaffer. He had just got out of the shower and was half-naked as Kirkland tried to get hold of him and a few of our staff had to grab Kirkland and calm him down. Kirkland is a big guy and who knows what would have happened if he had got to Warnock? Kirkland also had Wednesday's No. 2 goalkeeper Stephen Bywater behind him, for good measure. Bywater always looked like a bit of a nutcase as well, but luckily it got calmed down before anything too serious went off.

Life at Leeds was never dull, and off the pitch things were just getting started. At one point we went a few months without any wages – "Wow," I thought. "We're playing for Leeds fucking United and we're not even getting paid!" – and it wasn't a good atmosphere at all. One thing I always found strange at Leeds was the crowds. We weren't on the best run at the time and Elland Road is more often than not full these days, but we got 24,000 through the door against Wednesday and then played Burnley at home three days later in front of 16,000.

Obviously Wednesday would have brought a few more fans, but an 8,000 drop is pretty noticeable, especially in a ground that holds 38,000. The atmosphere in there could be pretty horrible at times and my mum ended up having a go at a group of fans who were sat near her and slagging me off. Mum, who's not normally like that at all, had enough. "Listen," she said to them. "That's my son, that is. We're meeting him at the players' tunnel after the game to bring him home… If you've got anything to say, why don't you come with us and say it to his face?" My dad was trying to keep the peace, telling her to shut up!

A decent run in both cups, featuring wins over Premier League sides like Southampton, Everton and Spurs, papered over the cracks of our league form a little and Warnock was sacked on April Fools' Day, 2013, after a run of two wins in 13 games. After our top scorer Luciano Becchio was sold to Norwich, we scored 11 times in those 13 games and threw away so many points by conceding late goals.

With a bit more luck on our side Warnock may have stayed – and who knows where he could have taken Leeds? In the three years after Warnock went, *seven* managers took turns in the dug-out. And one of those seven, Neil Redfearn, had two goes at it. I spoke to Warnock after he went. "Keep doing what you're doing," he said. "I'm gutted it hasn't worked, Paddy.

"But that club is poison."

23

MARCHING UNTOGETHER

It was only later in my Leeds United career that I realised that Neil Warnock was absolutely spot-on. The club at that time *was* poisonous and I always had the sense, around Elland Road and the Thorp Arch training ground, that certain people were a hell of a lot happier on the Monday morning if the team had been beaten on the Saturday. If we'd had a good result at the weekend, they were miserable. But if we had been beaten, they walked around with springs in their step, laughing and joking.

After Warnock left, and following a spell with Neil Redfearn in caretaker charge, Brian McDermott came in and, to be honest, I found him to be too soft. I had obviously worked a lot under Warnock, who was a strong character and a good man-manager. Suddenly we had McDermott, who didn't like confrontation at all and didn't want lads arguing. McDermott was all right as a bloke, don't get me wrong, and I got on well with him until the back end of his time as manager. But I just found him so weird and couldn't understand his methods at all.

We weren't good enough as a team to play out from the back, but he was insistent that we try it. We went to Derby early in the season and had more of the ball, but got beaten 3-1. We were stringing 25 passes together, but Derby were just standing off us and watching it happen, waiting for a chance to nick it off us and score. We barely got over the halfway line. On Monday McDermott had a board up in the meeting-room. At the top of the board was the score – Derby 3, Leeds 1 – and below it, all the stats from the game were up for us to see. McDermott pointed at the "passes completed" stat with his fancy pen and we had something like 250 more than Derby.

"Lads, look," he told us. "It's not as bad as you think. We've got to keep at it. Look how many more passes we had." I was looking at him and thinking: "Is this guy for real?" Stephen Warnock was sitting next to me and nudged me with his arm. "Paddy, there's only one fucking stat on that screen that counts," he said. "That's the top one." He was spot-on.

In pre-season we went to Slovenia and McDermott didn't let us have a single drink. We were gagging for a bit of freedom, more than anything else, so a few of us ended up sneaking out. We had played our last game of the three-match tour and it was the night before we came back home, so me, Jamie Ashdown, Stephen and Michael Brown – the older lads in the squad – found the only bar anywhere near our hotel.

We didn't make any attempt to hide, and probably had four drinks maximum. McDermott and his staff magically found us after deciding to go for a walk when they couldn't see us around the hotel. We were all over 30 years old, on the final night of pre-season, and he got the face on with us because we had gone out for a beer before we flew home.

I think McDermott felt a little bit threatened by me because I was a vocal character and not scared to make it clear how I was feeling. We had an away game at Reading, one of his old clubs, and it took us an hour-and-a-half to travel the two miles from our hotel to the ground. The traffic was unbelievable and I plugged my phone into the coach's sound system, playing "Entrance of the Gladiators" – better known as the circus theme tune – throughout the bus. McDermott went mental and raced to the back of the bus until he saw it was me with the phone in my hand. He shit himself and walked off, back to his seat.

We finished 15th in the Championship that season, which was nowhere near good enough for a club the size of Leeds, and the low point was undoubtedly a 6-0 hammering we took at Hillsborough against Sheffield Wednesday. It was tough for us all, but you can imagine the stick I took, going there as an old United player and shipping six goals. Before the game though, I was absolutely buzzing. I used to love getting all that grief, which people think is strange. I used it as motivation to prove them wrong and tried to use it as a positive.

At half-time, we were 2-0 down.

I was in front of the Kop end for the second half and things didn't get much better when Matt Smith came on as a half-time sub and lasted 45 seconds before being sent off. From then on we got peppered and it felt as if every shot they had found a way in. I'm sure any Wednesday fan reading this will take pleasure in me saying that it was absolutely horrible! I still get grief about it to this day, but it was just one of those games as a goalkeeper that you have to try and forget.

But of all the places to let six goals in, Hillsborough is one of the worst for me. I have a lot of Wednesday fans as mates, so they were buzzing their tits off, and I have taken a lot of shit about that game ever since. Don't worry, though – I have given them plenty back, too! I've lost count of how many times I have got the better of them, with United and Leeds and even later in my career with Rotherham. The Millers went there, we beat them 1-0 and from my place on the bench I was getting absolute pelters. I will always have that connection as an ex-Blade, but in my eyes they can give me all the abuse they want. At the time this book was written, they hadn't seen Premier League football for 20 years... in which time I was promoted there twice!

That whole period at Leeds was one that I really didn't enjoy. I had played injured for a while and, although as a footballer you are never 100 per cent fit, I was probably closer to 50. The injury happened in a game away at Nottingham Forest when a Lithuanian lad we had called Marius Žaliūkas sold me short with a backpass directly from the kick-off. I kicked the ball clear and followed through with my foot, straight onto the studs of Greg Halford. How I got through the game, I will never know. I was struggling to walk and definitely couldn't kick, but McDermott begged me to play in an FA Cup tie against Rochdale a few days later.

"Listen," he said to me in his office. "I need Paddy Kenny on my teamsheet. I need you to play even if you don't kick. I'll get someone else to take your goal-kicks or just throw it out." I hated doing that – it had been ingrained in me from years under Warnock – but I always wanted to play, so I did. We got battered and lost 2-0, but I somehow had a decent game. I should never have played and, when I actually got the issue looked at, it turned out that one of the two arteries going into my foot had been squashed by the impact of Halford's studs. There was basically no blood going through to my foot from that artery, which made a lot of sense to me. I was wondering why I couldn't feel my toes and was having to put Deep Heat on them at half-time to get some kind of sensation back.

I played for two months with that injury and it was a huge mistake. I couldn't even train properly and some of the goals I conceded in that time were embarrassing because I was nowhere near as sharp as I should have been. I got beaten at my near post against Wednesday, which was one of the worst goals I had conceded in my career, and David McGoldrick managed to score past me from about 40 yards for Ipswich. Two months earlier I would have thrown my cap on the shot but instead the ball bounced up just before me, hit my shoulder and went in.

It was a vicious cycle. Fans were on my back then because I was letting soft goals in, but no-one from the club ever attempted to explain that I was training for one day a week and should have been nowhere near the pitch on the Saturday. Stupidly, I agreed to play when McDermott begged me to. I did myself, and the team, no justice and, looking back now, I think that not only finished off my career at Leeds, but my career in football full stop. But that side of football, playing through the pain barrier for the good of the team, is one that people on the outside often don't see.

I had done it before. At Sheffield United I had a little lump on my leg and the club doctor decided to cut it out and stitch it up. He just did it at the training ground, a five-minute job. The lump came back six months later, so he sent me to a specialist, who told me it needed to come out in surgery. I told him the doctor had just taken it out at the training ground and he couldn't believe it. I went straight into surgery where he cut it out and stitched it. Then he told me I had to rest it for a week. *What?*

"I've got a game Saturday," I told him. "Couldn't you have told me this before? I would have waited until the end of the season if I knew!" He was adamant that I had to leave it for a week to heal, but I had a game to prepare for. I went into training on Thursday and within five minutes there was blood pissing down my legs. The stitches had ripped open and the skin around the wound had torn, too. There was nothing left to stitch. I ended up playing for two months with a bandage covering a gaping hole in my leg until it scabbed over. I have another beauty of a scar to remind me of it to this day.

One of the games I played injured for Leeds was away at Yeovil, live on Sky. Yeovil's pitch is on a slope and in the first half I was kicking up it, playing in the most horrible conditions I can remember. Our opening goal came when Marek Stech's kick out of his hands blew back to the edge of his own box and Ross McCormack curled a beauty in, and we won the game when Stephen Warnock's free-kick from miles out was caught by the wind and carried into the Yeovil goal. Jimmy Kebe, our midfielder who became a professional poker player when he retired, was twisting and turning in midfield before playing the ball all the way back to me.

The wind was swirling, I was kicking uphill and he knew I couldn't feel anything in my kicking foot, so I ended up side-footing the ball straight out of play. At half-time I ripped into him. Looking back now, it was a bit unfair, but, if that had been me on the other end, I would have had a go back and told "me" to fuck off. Instead Jimmy started sliding down in his seat. I ended up having to apologise to him when I calmed down and because we won the game, nothing else was said between us.

On the Thursday before training McDermott pulled me in the car-park. "Right, Paddy... I'm pissed off at you for the way you spoke in the dressing-room last Saturday. You were out of order... You don't win any-thing by shouting at players like that."

"I'm not having that," I said to him. "I've been in dressing-rooms where players have had each other by the throat and been scrapping. It's a reac-tion... it's passion."

But McDermott wasn't interested. "I don't have that," he said. "I didn't have it at Reading and I'm not having it here." As far as he was concerned, he said, I wouldn't play for him again that season, and he was bringing Jack Butland in on loan. I reminded him that I had played with an injury for two months and asked him if this was his excuse to leave me out of the team. "Yeah, you're on the bench," he said. Fuck that, I thought, and it was the only time in my career I refused to report for duty.

"I'm not sitting on the bench," I told him. "I've been injured for two months now and played through it, for you. Not once have you come out and told anyone, so I'm getting my foot right and I won't be available until I am fit again." Butland came in on loan from Stoke – at that point managed by Mark Hughes – and my Leeds career was effectively over.

Only then did I get a scan on my foot, when the artery problem was spotted. Every time I played or trained, it made the problem worse and I was told that eventually blood would force its way through and open the artery back up. While it did, Jack played for the rest of the season in goal. He didn't have the best of times and after about six weeks or so I was fit enough to return to training with him.

I was volleying balls at him one day and he wanted every one straight down his throat. I volleyed one slightly off path and he smashed the ball down the training ground. He was a kid at the time, on loan from the Premier League, and I tried to bring him down a peg or two. "What the fuck are you doing?"

"What are *you* doing?" he countered. "It's supposed to be at my face."

"It doesn't always come at your face in a game, does it?"

Every ball after that, I absolutely lashed at him. He got them out of the net and punched them away. You could sense the tension between us and it was the closest I ever got in my career to having a do with a fellow 'keeper in training. Andy Leaning ended up stopping the session, which was probably for the best. We had both gone a bit.

Despite McDermott's faults I did feel a bit of sympathy when he was sacked as manager in January 2014 by a bloke who didn't even own the club. Massimo Cellino was determined to gain control of Leeds, but was initially prevented from doing so by the Football League because of some issues about non-payment of income tax on a boat. McDermott remembers being sacked by a phone call from Cellino's lawyer on a Friday night, before we beat Huddersfield 5-1 on the Saturday under his assistant Nigel Gibbs and McDermott was reinstated on the Monday when the people who actually owned Leeds at the time got wind of what had happened. I'm not sure any of us players knew what was going on.

A couple of months later Cellino got the ownership decision overturned, and things began to change. He spoke to my agent and said that he was bringing in an Italian 'keeper. "So if you can get Paddy out," he said, "then get him out." Again, I had no issues with that and actually felt grateful to know the situation. I left my future in my agent's hands that summer and went to Cyprus with my missus and four kids, before all the players got a message saying we they had to report back to Elland Road for a meeting a few days later. Apparently in our contracts there was a clause that said Cellino was allowed to do that after we had been on holiday for so long. The Professional Footballers' Association told us that, if we didn't report back, he had grounds to sack us.

I left my family in Cyprus, while a few other lads had flown back early from Las Vegas and other parts of America and we sat in a room at the ground for four hours before Cellino even turned up. When he eventually arrived, we were summoned to the other side of Elland Road for one-to-one chats about our future. They were supposed to last about five minutes each, but mine wasn't even that long.

"I'm bringing an Italian goalkeeper in," Cellino told me, "and you're free to leave." I took a breath before I replied. "I know that... You told my agent that a few weeks ago. I haven't got a problem with that." That was the end of the meeting and I had another three weeks off before the start of pre-season. He was just flexing his muscles and showing who was in charge, but it was only the start of the fun and games.

24

'MAD' MASS

The increasingly bizarre world of Leeds United has taken another turn for the strange after it emerged that Massimo Cellino, their maverick new owner, has such a dislike of the number 17 it has turned him against one of the club's key players who was born on that date. Cellino is so suspicious of the number 17 that he had the seats at his former club, Cagliari, taken out and replaced with 16B. Now he has instructed the new Leeds head coach, Dave Hockaday, not to select Paddy Kenny after discovering that the goalkeeper's birthday is on 17 May and concluding that he is bad luck for the Championship club. Kenny, the second-highest earner at Leeds on £10,000 a week, has been left at home while the other players embark on a pre-season trip to Italy and he will not play for the club again.
- Daniel Taylor, The Guardian, July 2014

I bet you have seen the photo. It's on the first page of Google Images if you search for "Paddy Kenny Leeds" and has followed me around ever since, held up as an example of me apparently coming back to pre-season training miles overweight and basically taking the piss. It's a still shot from a video – I haven't ever seen the actual footage anywhere – showing me in a Leeds United training kit and looking, let's say, in less than tip-top condition.

If you have seen that picture, I bet you haven't seen the other of me taken on that same day, walking out for the first day of pre-season with a smile on my face, boots in hand. I post them side by side on social media whenever someone inevitably sends me the snap that did the rounds at the time and the funny thing about it is that I actually went back to training that summer lighter than I had ever been in my career. I look at the actual photograph and think I looked fucking fit, for me at least. And I have always honestly felt that the still of the video was an inside job, by someone, and had been edited in some way in an attempt to force me out of the club quicker.

It just wouldn't add up otherwise. I had been told at the beginning of the summer that I could leave, so I worked extra hard over the break to make sure I came back in better shape than ever in time to move to a new club. And if anyone at Leeds thought the picture would get me out quicker, they weren't very bright. If you were a manager looking for a new goalkeeper and saw that, would you have rushed to sign me? I bet a few thought: "Jesus, I'm not touching him!"

It might seem a little paranoid to suspect that someone had deliberately edited the photo, but things at the club had become so bizarre that it was difficult to rule anything out. I was left out of the squad for a preseason trip to Santa Cristina, Italy, in the summer of 2014 and had the indignity of not even being given a squad number. So I improvised with a roll of masking tape and made my own for my training gear. N/A. That was me at the time – non-applicable.

Being honest, I don't know if the owner, Massimo Cellino, *actually* wanted to get rid of me because I was born on the 17th, or for some other reason. But nothing would surprise me where he is concerned. As well as changing all the number 17 seats at Cagliari, he altered the Leeds programme for a game against Nottingham Forest to issue 16b rather than 17. He walked out of a Press conference with the media halfway through to go outside for a fag, and drained the pool at the training ground to save money. Billy Sharp remembers playing five-a-side in the empty pool and washing his own training kit. Cellino sacked all the cleaning staff at Thorp Arch and made the under-18s do the job instead. But his biggest moment of madness was probably appointing David Hockaday.

Hockaday was apparently highly-rated as a coach, but had most recently been in charge of Forest Green Rovers in the National League. That was the first managerial job of his career, and suddenly he was in charge of a club like Leeds United. I don't think Hockaday himself could quite believe it and with every decision, Cellino appeared to be turning the club into a fucking joke. I had grown up knowing all about the history of Leeds – the great Don Revie team, Billy Bremner and Co. – and I can only imagine how much it hurt the supporters to see how Cellino behaved while he was in charge of their huge and proud club.

Until May 2017, [Leeds United] were owned and run by a madman. Massimo Cellino took control of Leeds when the club was in utter financial disarray. Fans hoped he would be their saviour but, by the end of his three-year reign between 2014 and 2017, Leeds had become a laughing stock.
- Amitai Winehouse, Daily Mail, March 2019

I don't blame Hockaday personally because working under those conditions must have been a nightmare, to say the least, but from where I was standing at least it seemed like he was basically a puppet for the owner. Hockaday remembers Cellino signing certain players, rather than him, although he was at least allowed to appoint a coach in Junior Lewis. If anyone thinks my record with Warnock is amazing, Junior's with Peter Taylor was something else. Taylor signed him SIX times as a player, and he worked with him twice more as a coach!

One article about him arriving at Leeds summed it up for me, though: "The appointment was met largely with surprise by the fans of Leeds United, as Lewis had previously been with eighth-tier Hendon." It reminded me a little of the film Mike Bassett: England Manager when Ron Benson and Tony Hedges get a call-up to the England squad despite playing in the Third Division with York and Plymouth, and one of them being 46. But playing for that club should have been no joke.

My only real dealing with Lewis was after I had been given a rare day off and I took the family to a caravan we had in Blackpool. It was in the school holidays so they were going to stay up there when I went back to training, but at 10pm on the first night I got a call from Graham Bean. He was a former copper who was employed by Cellino as some kind of consultant. "Paddy, change of plan," he said down the phone. "You're travelling to Northern Ireland with the under-23s."

It felt like the club were trying to grind me down, but I dug my heels in and decided to see how far it would go. It became a bit of cat and mouse as they tried to get to me, but I played the game and left my family to report for the flight over. For the previous four or five years I had roomed on my own because I liked my own company. I could walk around the room naked if I wanted, go to sleep and get up when I wanted and do whatever else blokes do on their own in hotels when I wanted. On this trip I was put in with one of the young lads and I told him respectfully that he could have the room to himself. I paid £75 out of my own pocket for my own space and Junior, who was in charge of the under-23s on the trip, came to find me to tell me he was pissed off.

"What's it got to do with you, Junior?" I asked him.

"I've spoken to the manager," he said, "and you don't have to play in the game tonight." I asked him if he was taking the piss. "You've dragged me all the way over here and now you're telling me I'm not playing? You can fuck off. I'm playing."

He asked me if I wanted to play 45 minutes and then 75. "No, I'm playing the whole game," I told him. "And if you try and sub me, I won't come off." It actually turned out to be a decent game and I made a few saves in a 3-0 win. After the match we got back to the hotel, had something to eat and then all the young lads went to bed. Big Matt Smith was the only other pro with me on the trip, so Matt and the second-team kitman had a drink with me at the bar. It was ice-cold Peroni fresh out of the freezer, the dog's bollocks, and it was going down nicely when I felt a tap on my shoulder. I turned round to see Junior standing there. "No drinking, Paddy."

"Fuck off, Junior," I said. "You've pissed me off on this trip already."

"Paddy, no drinking," he repeated. "It's not a good look for the young lads."

I looked around the bar. "Junior, there's not one young lad here. They've all gone to bed. Now please fuck off." He called me a disgrace and sat at a table behind me. I ended up having seven or eight beers, mainly just to spite him, and sent him over a coffee every time I bought a pint. He was just trying to be a twat for the sake of it and I wasn't having him trying to treat me like a kid.

***

It was Hockaday's first meeting with the players as Leeds manager and basically set the tone for what was to follow under Cellino. He gathered the entire squad into this room and we were expecting some big, rousing speech about what it meant to play for Leeds.

"Right," Hockaday began. "Cellino's not providing food for us any more, so you're going to have to start bringing your own dinners in. Also he's refusing to buy you socks for training, so we've looked into it and, if every player puts in 20 quid, we can get seven pairs of Macron socks each. We'll chuck them all into a basket and use them throughout the season."

I sat there open-mouthed and wondered if I was dreaming. Hockaday noticed me shaking my head and asked what my problem was. "What's my problem?" I asked. "I've got to pay for training socks?"

"It's only 20 quid," Hockaday replied.

"That's not the point! I play for Leeds United, we all play for Leeds fucking United. It's not about 20 quid, it's about bringing in our own dinners and having to buy our own socks. It's embarrassing. We're Leeds United here, in the Championship. It's an absolute joke." The whole room went quiet. Surely, I thought, I can't be the only one who thinks this is madness? No-one was rushing to back me up, until Stephen Warnock piped up. "I agree with Paddy," he said. "It is a fucking joke."

It did no good, but I felt like I had to say something. I couldn't believe what I was hearing. I just don't think Cellino could get his head around the finances of an English club. He had experience of football back in Italy, but things apparently worked differently over there. If he had a player on 10 grand a week at Leeds, I think he thought that the player would cost him £520,000 a year and no more. But that same player might be on bonuses; a grand a game, a grand a goal, a grand for man of the match or whatever. And I don't think he could understand that it worked that way in England. I wonder how much he actually ended up saving on the trainer socks?

Hockaday and Lewis lasted 70 days at Leeds – Hockaday's next job was apparently back in non-league with Swindon Supermarine – and I felt a determination that I would follow them out of the exit door. I was told, by letter, that I had to report for training six days a week, for a minimum of three hours. On some of the days there was no-one else at the training ground - no physios or any staff, and no teammates who were enjoying a day off. I was in there all alone, with my N/A training gear on, and one day I took a picture of the empty changing-room, captioning it something like: "Having a right laugh with the lads today." The photo went down well with the rest of the squad, but it wasn't really a laughing matter.

My agent at the time went to the PFA and the FA to let them know how I was being treated and there was apparently a rule that there had to be so many staff present if a player was made to come in and train. I made sure every day that I was there for three hours, even though no-one would have known any differently if I wasn't. I obviously couldn't do any actual training because there was no-one else around, so I just ended up sitting on an exercise bike and playing on my phone. I was determined that I wouldn't be broken.

After the FA got in touch with Leeds, a coach was suddenly brought in to work with me and some of the younger goalkeepers. His name was Rudi Coleano, who went out with an actress who played one of the Dingle girls in *Emmerdale* and was a superb coach. One day he was late arriving, so me and the young lads went out to wait for him, doing a bit of two-touch and a few kick-ups. Rudi never came out, so I wandered over to Redfearn who was coaching the other young lads on the next pitch along.

I asked him where Rudi was. "I don't know," he replied dismissively. I reminded him of what the FA said, that I needed proper coaching, and he tried to fob me off by saying that the warm-up game I was playing with the younger lads *was* goalkeeping training. His whole demeanour started to wind me up, so I walked in before I ended up losing my cool with him. Inside, I bumped into someone who worked at the club and asked if she knew what was going on. "Mary, what about this deal we had with the club? I'm supposed to have actual goalkeeping coaching rather than sitting about doing nothing."

"Paddy, I can't do owt if Rudi's ill," she said.

"Oh, right," I replied. "Why didn't anyone think to tell me he wouldn't be coming in?"

"I told Neil Redfearn to tell you."

If I was annoyed before, I was well and truly raging now and looking back, I could easily have ended up getting sacked for doing something rash. I thought he was a shithouse anyway but the thing that really tipped me over the edge with Redfearn was an interview he did in 2016, with a journalist called Simon Austin. That was the year that Redfearn was sacked as Rotherham United manager after winning five of his 21 games, leaving them third bottom of the Championship, and my name was shoe-horned into the conversation when he was talking about working under Cellino.

"He [Cellino] drained all the water out of the pool," Redfearn said.

"The pressure of the water had kept the tiles in place and they started buckling. It cost £25k a year to heat and treat and he said: 'We're not having that.' He made the cleaners redundant, getting the apprentices to do it. That's when the bug went round. Spores from the swimming pool area caused a sickness bug. He got rid of security. On a night when we had hundreds of kids in, anyone could walk in. He was getting rid of people on £12k a year and still paying Paddy Kenny, who couldn't stop a pig in a passage, £20k a week."

The only surprise to me is that he managed to stop talking about himself long enough to mention anyone else. I read most of the article as an attempt to big up himself and his missus, who also worked at Leeds; how he reckons they kept the club going and all that. I couldn't believe it when someone showed me the article, so I asked one of the lads for his number. I sent him a screenshot of the bit about me and told him that, one day, we are going to cross paths again.

Redfearn wasn't top of my Christmas card list anyway, but I felt that his comments were completely unwarranted and disrespectful. It was nothing whatsoever to do with me that Cellino was sacking people, and Redfearn decided to double my salary to make it a better story. I was on 10 grand a week and, for reasons only he knows, he decided to make that 20. I haven't seen him since that interview and, if I ever do, I would be very interested to see what he has to say about his comments about me. If we had bumped into each other within a few weeks of them being published, I would not have been as calm.

Perhaps I got too involved in the cat-and-mouse game with Leeds, but I passed up the opportunity to move to Doncaster Rovers. Again it was a case of pride and asking the club to meet me halfway on the wages I was owed; Donny were offering me five grand a week, so I proposed that Leeds paid me £2,500 a week during the last year of my contract. They got rid of a player they didn't want and paid a quarter of what they should have; I would have got out of the circus and would only have taken a 25 per cent pay cut this time. It seemed a win/win scenario to me. But Leeds said no, the deal collapsed, and I went back to training with Rudi and the kids.

Then, one day, Bean asked for a word out of the blue. My agent had got wind that an offer was on its way for me and Leeds to part ways and when I sat down with Bean, in a room as far away from the first-team changing-room as possible at the training ground, I was offered 70 per cent of my wage to leave. A month earlier, when a move to another club was on the table, they had turned down my request for 25 per cent. "No," I said. "I'm not taking it."

Bean urged me to reconsider, telling me that Cellino was determined to get me out. I wish I had recorded the conversation and it left me torn, umming and ahhing about what to do. My agent had been in my ear, re-minding me how I had been treated and telling me that I shouldn't accept a penny less than I was owed. But eventually I decided to take the deal and cut my losses, even though the season was a few weeks old by this point and most clubs were already fixed up with the players they needed. I was absolutely kicking myself that I didn't sign for Donny because, hand on heart, the chance of playing meant more to me than the money.

But once again it had become a game of brinkmanship between me and the club and, although I could forgive anyone reading this for won-dering if I was some kind of bad influence, I can honestly say that I was not. Whether it *was* because of my date of birth, or that he just didn't like the look of me, I don't know. But Cellino made it pretty clear to me that he wanted me out of Leeds from very early on. His biggest mistake was probably thinking I would just lie down and take it.

Cellino sold his stake in Leeds a few years later, and it's probably no coincidence that they were back in the Premier League not long after. In my view, which is probably shared by a lot of Leeds fans, the club deserved far better. At least now they seem to be Marching on Together once more.

BEGINNING OF THE END

I f I thought things couldn't possibly get much stranger after leaving the madness of Leeds United, I was wrong. One of the final acts of my 20-year professional football career was to grab hold of my manager in the dressing-room at half-time and attempt to fight him. To be fair, my agent warned me that I wouldn't get on with Lee Johnson and tried to persuade me not to join Oldham Athletic, on loan from Bolton Wanderers. But I hadn't played a minute since joining Bolton and the chance was there to go and get some games. "I'll give it a week before Johnson tells you he was on 10 grand a week at Bristol City," my agent said. It actually took him about two hours.

"Yeah, but wasn't your dad the manager?" I asked Johnson in reply. He didn't like that at all. From the first time we met, I just took a bit of a dislike to him because he really loved himself. He has gone on to do well for himself in management and I don't know what he is like to play under now he's a bit older. But in my experience of him, he was a cock. There were a few times when I wanted to rip his head off and then, in the away dressing-room at Milton Keynes Dons, I almost did.

It's a lovely ground, Stadium MK, but also a weird place to play football – it holds 30,000, but there were just under 8,000 in that day. We were being pummelled from kick-off and MK finished the game with 27 shots. They had Dele Alli playing for them and I felt as if I was making save after save. But somehow, five minutes before half-time, we were only 1-0 down. We got a free-kick about five yards outside my box and I cleared everyone upfield. Johnson wanted me to play it short to my fullback, but I thought: "Fuck that, I'm putting it in the corner. If we go in at half-time only one down, that would be a right result... We can regroup at half-time."

So I kicked it long and heard, as clear as day, from the touchline: "You fucking cunt." It was Johnson. The atmosphere at MK isn't the loudest anyway and we ended up having a bit of back-and-forth, with about 50 yards between us. "You what?" I asked him. He repeated what he had said.

"We'll sort this at half-time," I shouted over to him. As it happened, we conceded again two minutes before the whistle to go in 2-0 down – but by the time I reached the dressing-room, I had calmed down a little and pulled Johnson to one side. "Gaffer, do me a favour," I said to him. "Show me some respect. I don't think I've done anything wrong. There was no need to shout that on once, let alone twice. I made a decision I thought was right at the time... Don't ever call me that again."

The rest of our team had arrived in the dressing-room by that point and thought something was kicking off, so a few of the bigger lads put themselves between me and Johnson, telling me to calm down. I felt perfectly calm until Johnson leant around big George Elokobi. "You're still a fucking cunt," he said. Within a few seconds I had barged George and a few other lads aside and had Johnson pinned against the wall. I had asked him to treat me with a bit more respect and then he spoke to me like that? I wasn't having it. The lads managed to get in between us again before I had the chance to crack him. And I would have. In that moment, I didn't give a shit.

Johnson's only about two foot tall anyway, but thought he could play the big man when he had a few players between us. It goes without saying that I shouldn't have gone for him. He was the manager! But that wouldn't have stopped me punching his face in if I had the chance in the moment. It's probably not surprising that the game ended up being my last for Oldham. And to cap it all, we ended up losing 7-0.

My agent was spot-on about Johnson and I should have listened to him and Neil Lennon, who was in charge of Bolton. He didn't want me to leave, either. But the lure of playing games and maybe putting myself in the shop window proved too good to turn down. I had only signed a short-term deal at Bolton anyway after Adam Bogdan had got injured, and I was 36 years old by that point.

My agent knew Dougie Freedman, who was in charge of Bolton and looking for a 'keeper. Freedman had seen that picture of me in training at Leeds and, like I suspect many managers were, was initially put off. But my agent told him it was bollocks, I had a couple of days in training so Freedman could see for himself, and I was back in the game.

Unfortunately it took an injury to Bogdan to give me that opportunity, but that's the life of a goalkeeper. I was basically training by myself, waiting for someone else's luck to turn because of injury, suspension or just a lack of form. Fortunately I didn't find training alone as challenging as some players do – I think my ban helped a little in that respect – but it was still a relief when the call eventually came, especially from a club like Bolton. They had been in the Premier League for a long time – ironically, we sent them down when I was at QPR and we survived on the last day of the season at Manchester City – and, although they had cut their cloth financially after relegation, the set-up was still brilliant.

We had everything laid out for us in the morning and the training ground was unbelievable. There was a cryotherapy room – although I never saw Frank Bruno in there, doing press-ups on the floor – and the pitches had undersoil heating, so were always in brilliant condition. Everything was done the right way and it made a huge difference, even if results perhaps didn't show it. Andy Lonergan was first choice in Bogdan's absence and I watched from the bench as we lost four games on the bounce immediately after I had joined. Freedman left two weeks after signing me and we lost the next match, at home to 10-man Bournemouth, for good measure.

The fact Andy was our best player throughout that period said a lot about how we were playing and when Freedman was replaced with Lennon, I could tell straightaway that he was going to be my sort of manager. He took no shit and, although he could have a laugh on the training ground, when it was the time to do things right, he made sure they were. Straightaway he banned hats and gloves and got in everyone's faces. Fitness levels went up with players suddenly running their bollocks off and we started to turn it around.

I saw him lose it big-time in the dressing-room on more than one occasion, but even before then you could just tell from his aura that he was a hard man. Until recently I had never seen the video of Alan Shearer kicking Lennon in the face when he was playing for Leicester against Shearer's Newcastle. I was only surprised that Lennon didn't bounce straight back up and knock Shearer out! I loved his management style and he had only been in the job a few days when he pulled me to one side at training. "Hang in there and keep training as well as you have been," he told me. "I've got to give Lonners a chance because, looking back at the videos, he's been our best player." I told him he was spot-on there. "But if things deteriorate with his performance, you'll be straight in. And then the shirt is yours to lose."

I couldn't ask for more and to be fair to Andy his levels remained high all the way through. Once Lennon got to grips with us, we didn't lose for eight games. I knew that Andy wasn't coming out of the team any time soon and my deal at Bolton was up in January anyway, so the chance came up to move to Oldham and I took it with both hands, despite my agent's reservations about Johnson. I had no problem at all about dropping down into League One, but it was a bit of an eye-opener compared to what we had been used to at Bolton.

Every day in training it was a complete free-for-all when it came to grabbing whatever training kit you could find from a big basket in the middle of the changing-room. If you were one of the last in, you'd get the shit with holes in or that didn't fit properly. A couple of times I ended up with a T-shirt so small that it looked like a sports bra on me. We would get changed at the stadium and then drive up to the training ground, which was an absolute bog. So after throwing myself around in training for a few hours, it was a case of getting stripped at the side of the car and driving back for a shower, soaking wet through. Proper old school!

It took me back 15 years to my days at Bury when we used to have a similar set-up and in some ways, I had gone from one extreme to the other – from Leeds, an unbelievable training ground, to Bolton's, which was probably even better. Then to Oldham, where it was ip-dip-do for kit and we had to drive to train on basically a park pitch. It was just how it was. They were not as financially secure as other clubs and that was the only way they could do it. Some of the lads knew no different, but, when you've come down the pyramid, it can be a little difficult to adjust. When I was at Bury, I thought everyone was in the same boat. The higher up you go, the more you realise that that's not the case.

My time at Oldham got off to a decent start when we beat our neighbours Rochdale 3-0 at their place and my second game was in the FA Cup against Doncaster Rovers. If things had worked out differently, I could have been in goal for Donny that day, but instead they had Sam Johnstone on loan from Man United.

He was brilliant and made four or five unbelievable saves before Elokobi scored an unlucky own goal in the 86th minute and we lost 1-0. Anyone who knew anything about football knew that we would have won that game on any other day, but Johnson had the face on with us players.

Apparently if we had a decent run in the FA Cup, he would have got more money to spend on players in January and he took it out on us by having us in for training on Sunday morning at eight o'clock. A week earlier we had battered our local rivals to go into the play-offs and we had been very unfortunate to lose to Donny, but Johnson wasn't having it.

On Monday he made us come in again and stay until the evening to watch the FA Cup draw and see who we could have played in the next round if we had beaten Donny. I remember warning him: "You're going to lose the lads. We got an unbelievable win against Rochdale and the way you're treating them is disgusting. We're in the play-offs!" He told me that he was the manager and it was his decision, which was fair enough. The following weekend we played Yeovil at home and got stuffed 4-0. It was 100 per cent a knock-on effect from the way he had treated the players the week before.

Losing the dressing-room is one of the biggest clichés in football, but here I could see it happening in front of my eyes. I was trying to do him a favour by telling him he needed to apologise to the lads for dragging them in on Sunday and then keeping them back to watch the FA Cup draw because we had lost a game 1-0. There was absolutely no need for it and the players were honestly raging. They didn't want to come in to training. And this was a team in the play-offs!

It all came to a head at MK Dons. We got torn to shreds in the second half and we were probably lucky they didn't score 10. The lads had gone completely and what had gone off at half-time between me and Johnson probably didn't help either. He sat us down after the game and asked us: "What's gone wrong? We were flying and in our last two games we've lost 4-0 and 7-0." Elokobi spoke up first. Johnson had absolutely torn into him after the Donny game, going mental in his face. George is a big lad, but he took it at the time.

At MK Dons, he was the first to break the silence. "It's your own fault because of how you've been treating the lads," he said. "How you've been today with Paddy and how you were with me at Doncaster. You were lucky I didn't rip your head off last week because you were way over the top."

I went back to Bolton, Johnson moved to Barnsley and Oldham dropped out of the play-offs, finishing 15th in League One. I was no stranger to half-time fall-outs during my career, but the one with Johnson was the worst. He crossed a line by making it personal. I have wondered since if he wanted to have a go at me to make some kind of statement. I was an experienced player – I was actually older than him – and it's something other managers have done in the past. I didn't take it with Kevin Blackwell and many years later I wasn't taking it from Johnson either.

As I expected, my short time at Bolton came to an end in January and I soon ended up back in the Championship under Mick McCarthy at Ipswich Town after Dean Gerken got injured, and they needed back-up for Bartosz Bialkowski. Ipswich ended up reaching the play-offs that season, losing to their rivals Norwich in the semis, but I can claim absolutely no credit. Gerken recovered towards the back end of the season and I dropped to No. 3 goalkeeper – a position which, to be fair, Mick had explained when I signed. He was another old-school manager I enjoyed working under. He took no shit, with his Barnsley accent, but he was also brilliant with the lads while they were doing the business for him on the pitch.

Again, though, I didn't have a sniff of playing and I started to get a little disillusioned with everything. The final straw came when I was called into training after being given the day off. I drove down from Sheffield to find that none of the first team were training, so I did 30 minutes with a coach and a 16-year-old kid before being told I had the next day off. "If you want to go back to Sheffield," I was told, "go back up." I had spent seven hours in the car for half-an-hour's training and at 36 it wasn't exactly what I needed. So, when that season came to an end and I was a free man again, I honestly felt a little relieved. I had no idea that the next time my phone rang, it would bring an offer to go back to where it all began.

BACK TO MY ROOTS

It was during my time at Bolton that I first started to feel it. I would drag myself off the immaculate training pitches there with a sensation I hadn't really felt before; at least not like this. Pain. My knees were starting to hurt every day and I felt the same in my hips. Training became a slog physically and sometimes I used to find it hard to even get through the session. The mileage on my clock, so to speak, was starting to take its toll; I was something of a late starter to professional football, but I had certainly made up for it by playing a *lot* of games. Apart from the season I was banned and a couple of injuries, I had played pretty much week in, week out between coming through at Bury in 1999 and leaving Leeds United in 2014.

Still I wasn't ready to give in just yet. I loved being a footballer and, even when I wasn't playing at Bolton, I was clinging to the idea that I might get back out there and get another game if someone got injured or was playing badly. I had the hunger back that had left me a little as I travelled back along those horrible A-roads from Ipswich and, being honest, I also had bills to pay. I had started up a building company, which I was putting money into, and I had kids and a family. I still had outgoings, so I had to earn, but the phone wasn't ringing. I was 37 and wondering if the end was nigh when the chance came to return to Bury.

David Flitcroft was in charge then. I had played with his brother Garry at Sheffield United and another injury to a goalkeeper had given me another chance. I was absolutely buzzing to go back to my roots and I watched from the bench as we battered Wigan 4-0 in my first game. "Bloody hell," I remember thinking. "These are decent, these!" I had signed a short-term contract and, although a lot of faces at the club had not changed, the training ground certainly had. Bury had moved into

Manchester City's old place at Carrington and, as you can probably imagine, it was a far cry from what I can remember in my first spell!

Back then we trained down the road from the stadium at a place called Goshen and it was one of my jobs to clear all the dog shit off the training pitch with a cone. It was just a free-for-all, a normal park where people walked their dogs and let them shit all over. I would get covered in mud and whatever else from diving about, so the lads wouldn't let me back into their cars to drive back to the stadium.

I had to jog or walk through a graveyard to get back to Gigg Lane and have a shower. Sometimes the senior players had to carry the goals back to the stadium as well. The YTS lads would carry them there, but they would often bugger off early and we'd have to carry them back. That was us, as professional footballers playing in the equivalent of League One and preparing for a game at the weekend while clearing dog shit from the training ground and carrying goalposts through a graveyard!

There was none of that in my second spell after the move to Carrington and it was brilliant to be involved again. At the time Bury were paying out serious money to players – there weren't many lads on £400 a week like I had been the first time around, if any. Lads like Leon Clarke and Tom Pope were there on top money, especially for that level. And for a team who only got 3,000 or 4,000 through the door, it was probably only going to go one way. Clarke and Pope both scored in that 4-0 win over Wigan and our 'keeper at the time was Daniel Bachmann, an Austrian lad on loan from Stoke. He was called up for international duty a week after I had signed and I was told I would be playing against Gillingham – who, ironically, I had made my Bury debut against the first time around, 16 years before. I had trained for about five days maximum and had no pre-season to speak about. Welcome back, Patrick!

I never ended up playing the game. Two days before, I jumped to catch a routine cross in training and felt my calf pop. I couldn't put any weight on that leg whatsoever and I just knew that I had torn my calf. I went for a scan and was told that it would take six to eight weeks to heal. I had only signed for 12 weeks, so I did what I thought was the decent thing and rang Flicker, offering to cancel my contract.

He tried to persuade me to see it out, to stay and get fit, but I didn't want to take the money off them. "Whatever you were paying me, use it to get someone else in on loan," I told him. "It just doesn't feel fair." I didn't have to do that, but Bury was a club close to my heart and it just felt the right thing to do. Flicker tried to talk me out of it again, reminding me that I had got injured while training with them, but my mind was made up and we parted on good terms.

The decision got some good publicity, but that wasn't the reason behind it. I would have made the same decision at any club, but the fact it was Bury certainly made it easier. If I had a contract for the entire season, I would probably have thought differently. I would have backed myself to get fit and contribute later in the year. But I was only there for four months anyway and spending the majority of that time on the treatment table was not something I was willing to do.

So much for greedy footballers, eh? There are players out there who would have taken the cash, which I would have been entitled to do. But, as with anything, a minority give the majority of us a bad name and shit tends to stick in football a little better than anywhere else. My homecoming had proved a short one, but a chat with Flicker a few days after I had signed suddenly made me look at things a little differently. "Have you thought about what you're going to do after you retire?" he asked me. "It would be criminal for you not to be involved with your experience." He suggested I start taking my coaching badges and pointed to Ian Wilcox as an example.

When I was at Bury the first time, Wilco was a masseur, but took his badges and ended up working under Flicker as a goalkeeping coach. "He's decent," Flicker said of Wilco, "and he's working at professional level. He's never played the game. He's never been in your position. Think of the advantage that will give you." I thought: "He's spot-on. I need to start looking into that." Typically I didn't. And as it turned out, my playing career wasn't quite over yet anyway.

***

I can still remember hearing the news, around the summer of 2019, that Bury had been kicked out of the EFL. The club didn't play a single game in the 2019/20 season and the pitch at Gigg Lane may never host another game of football again even though the long-serving groundsman there has kept it in pristine condition for months afterwards, just in case. The whole situation is a tragedy, for football as a whole as well as Bury. People like Jill Neville had been involved with the club for 30 years and all of a sudden it went pop. Jill's husband Neville had worked there for decades as well before he sadly died and, when I went back the second time, there were still so many old faces that I remembered from 12 or 13 years earlier.

Those people are the lifeblood of any football club and it's a similar story at Sheffield United – when I go back now and see people like Kevin Cookson, Johnny Garrett and Pete Stone, who were there when I arrived as a player. For the fans to see their club just disappear under the weight of financial problems must be heartbreaking. It was so good to see supporters of other clubs rallying round with busloads of fans travelling to Bury to drink in the local pubs near the ground and keep them going. But ultimately there is a huge void left – and I don't mind admitting that it brought a tear to my eye when the news was officially confirmed.

I had kept a close eye on the story all the way through and although I didn't know the full ins and outs, I thought that a club in this day and age would never go under. That someone would *surely* step in and save them. But it wasn't to be and it just proves that, if you don't have the right people in charge of a club and they don't look after it in the way that they perhaps should, anything can happen. Now surely something needs to happen to ensure that it doesn't happen again. Somehow the lower-league clubs need to be looked after and the money needs to be filtered down a lot better. How can players in the Premier League be earning 300 to 400 grand a week when clubs like Bury go bust owing a few million? It's utter madness.

I'm not saying that footballers should be expected to save football clubs, but, when a top player's wages for two months or so is enough to keep a club in business, something has gone wrong at some point, hasn't it? Maybe the coronavirus pandemic will help to focus a few minds in football. Anyone reading this in a few years will have the benefit of hindsight to say whether it did or not, but I must admit I'm not holding my breath. A lot of clubs will no doubt struggle in the aftermath of the pandemic and I don't think football can afford more teams to go to the wall. For as long as I have followed football, the pyramid in England has had 92 teams and seeing that go to 91 without Bury is tragic enough, without it dropping any lower.

27

THE GAFFER

He has always been that to me. I called him Gaffer even when he wasn't actually my manager and even to this day, years after I called time on my professional career, his number is still stored under "Gaffer" in my phone contacts. It was inevitable that he would feature heavily in the story of my life and career because Neil Warnock has done so much for me in both. We have been through so much together, good and bad, and I don't think it's overstating it to say that he has looked after me as if I was one of his own children.

He's certainly been a father figure to me over the years and, as he kindly wrote in his foreword for this book, he knows that deep down, I am just a big softie. When I have had to stand my ground and go toe-to-toe with someone, I have not been afraid to do that. But when I have had to let my emotions out – and there have been many of those times, too – I'm not afraid of that, either.

Warnock has seen me at my highest and my lowest and, when all is said and done, he knows that I am not a dickhead. I have seen players toss it off and not care one bit, but that was never me and I like to think that's something he admired. He knew what he was going to get from me, as a player and a person, which is why I think he kept signing me. We worked together at five different clubs and, but for a few things, that number could have been six or seven. He first took me to Bury in 1998 and it was another 16 years before a manager other than Warnock signed me!

On the day Warnock got the Cardiff job in 2016, Google searches for my name went through the roof. People saw us as a package and wondered what I was up to and when Warnock would sign me. I don't think it ever got out that he actually tried to bring me to Cardiff before that plan was scuppered. It's not as if I missed out on much... They only went up to the Premier League in his second season there!

That was his eighth promotion as a manager, a run stretching back to 1987 when he took Scarborough out of the Conference and into the Fourth Division, and no-one has won more in the history of English football. But for me, the job he did at Rotherham United, keeping them in the Championship in 2015/16, is right up there with his biggest achievements in the game. It was absolutely phenomenal. The football we played that year wouldn't have won many beauty contests, but it was damn effective because the club was on its arse when he came in. They were only three points away from safety, but the players were knackered and the mood around the place was horrendous. The way he turned it around showed what kind of bloke he is.

Warnock got the job when my old pal Neil Redfearn was sacked and became the shortest-serving manager in the club's long history. Redfearn lasted just four months and, when he got the boot, Rotherham had lost eight of their last 12 league matches. I saw Warnock had been appointed, but honestly never expected him to come for me. I hadn't played a game since that 7-0 loss on loan at Oldham and I had cancelled my contract with Bury early after getting injured in training. I was only a few months shy of my 38th birthday and was out running on the streets of Dinnington in the evening when my phone rang. "Gaffer" flashed up on the screen.

"Hey up, Paddy," he said. "What are you doing?"

"I'm just out running, Gaffer," I told him. He burst out laughing.

"Fuck off!" he said. "Listen, I've got the Rotherham job. We're struggling and I've got work to do. Are you fit?"

"I'm *Paddy fit*," I told him.

"That'll do for me, son. Come down next week and we'll talk through the details. See you Monday." With that he put the phone down and I was a Rotherham United player! He wanted someone purely to put a bit of pressure on his No. 1 goalkeeper Lee Camp and basically bring a bit more character around the place. To be fair, there was plenty of that in there already. The lads were just completely shot. Confidence was rock-bottom and they had been flogged to death in training as well. Warnock steadied the ship a little bit with a draw at home to Birmingham in his first game – although two of our lads, Richard Wood and Joe Mattock, did manage to get sent off – and I watched from the bench as we lost back-to-back games after that, away at Burnley and Reading.

With 13 games of the season left we were now six points from safety and Warnock went back-to-basics with his football. He told his defenders to head and kick the ball rather than messing about with it at the back, and get it into the opposition half. We got up and running with a 2-1 win over a good Brentford side at the New York Stadium and Warnock rewarded the lads with days off. It was the oldest trick in his book and I had seen it all before, but the results afterwards speak for themselves. An 11-match unbeaten run, including six wins, saw the Millers survive comfortably in the Championship for another year.

Along the way we beat Leeds at home – Marco Silvestri, the goalkeeper Massimo Cellino signed to replace me, was sent off – and won 1-0 at Sheffield Wednesday before battering MK Dons 4-0 at Stadium MK to virtually guarantee survival. The scenes in the away dressing-room were very different from my last visit there, I can tell you! But it wasn't half as sweet as winning away at Wednesday. Matt Derbyshire scored the winner in the first half and it was the first time I had ever sat on the bench at Hillsborough, so I was getting absolute pelters from behind me. I just kept laughing at them as they got more and more irate at little old Rotherham beating them on their own patch.

The weird design of Wednesday's main stand means that coaches can't fit underneath it, so visiting teams have to get off the bus and walk the gauntlet to the players' entrance a couple of hundred yards away. That isn't a major problem for most players, but it leaves the likes of me and Warnock completely exposed to all sorts of abuse from the waiting Wednesday fans. To be fair I didn't mind most of it because I loved having banter with their supporters at Hillsborough, but I hated one song I used to hear. *"Die, die, piggy, piggy, die."* United and Wednesday fans both call each other 'pigs' but that wasn't the part of the song I had a problem with. I was a human being with children and in my view, that chant crossed a line.

Not that it particularly bothered Warnock! He used to wait until the very last minute to get off the bus and wind them up even more, waving to them with a big smile on his face while they chanted about him dying. He absolutely revelled in it. There was once talk about him taking over at Wednesday when his old pal Milan Mandaric was chairman. But a few fans protested and they decided it was best to just leave it. With his record, who knows what Warnock could have done with Wednesday? Thinking about it, it's probably a good job he didn't go there!

The Wednesday win was undoubtedly the sweetest, but the most memorable game of that run was actually one we only drew, 3-3 at home to Derby County. They were absolutely all over us and went 3-0 up with three goals in 10 minutes in the second half. Warnock turned around to us on the bench. "I'd take 3-0 now, you know," he said. He took off Derbyshire and Paul Green at three down and they sat at the side of me as we scored three times in the last seven minutes to draw 3-3. Leon Best equalised in the 91st minute and everyone was going absolutely mental. Then Derbs and Green sat back down on the bench. "I don't know what you two are cheering for," I said to them. "We were 3-0 down when you came off!"

We eventually finished nine points clear of the bottom three, which was a phenomenal achievement considering where the club had been when Warnock was appointed, and I was gutted that he didn't carry on for a second season. It was a great club and I would have loved to stay there for another year – it was right on my doorstep and I still go and watch them now sometimes. I guess it just wasn't to be.

I think one of the reasons he didn't stay was the training ground. It was basically made up of Portakabins, and he hated it. We had two separate dressing-rooms there for the first team and, if any of the other lot had the showers turned on, there would be no water on our side. The owner, Tony Stewart, used to point at the New York Stadium and say: "We've got an amazing ground."

He was right. But as Warnock reminded him, we were at the stadium once a fortnight, but worked every day at the training ground. Without meaning to sound disrespectful, it was difficult for Rotherham to attract players anyway and the state of the training ground didn't make it any easier. I think Warnock wanted something more than another relegation battle, so he and Tony ended up shaking hands and going their separate ways.

For me, one of Warnock's biggest strengths is that he doesn't complicate the game. He told his defenders to defend and, if his wingers got a chance to put the ball in the box, they were told to put it in the box. Any winger who checked back and tried to beat his full-back two or three times never lasted under Warnock. He signed Keith Gillespie for Sheffield United on the back of Bestie putting in 14 crosses in the second half of a friendly against Scarborough and he used to tell poor Nick Montgomery to tackle his man, win the ball and then pass it to someone who knew how to use it!

The game has changed now; defenders try and play out from the back and you see so many errors – even from the top players. When I was at Northampton as goalkeeping coach under Rob Page, we played Swindon and they had a free-kick on the edge of the centre circle in their own half. We lined up five yards outside our box for the long punt forward, but instead they knocked it back to their 'keeper. We squeezed up the pitch and they must have put together 30 passes, but didn't get over the halfway line. We nicked it off them and scored and I could almost imagine Warnock going absolutely mental. "Put it in their box and make them defend. It's not rocket science!"

He is the master of man-management. When he signed me for QPR from United after my ban, we went to Italy for pre-season and I was one of about 10 new players. He had been out there for a few days with Sharon and the kids before us players flew out, and called a meeting when we arrived. "Every night around here is like Saturday night," he told us. "It's unbelievable. There are a lot of new lads here and, if I say there is no drinking on this trip, you're going to break it. I'm not stupid. You'll sneak out and we'll fall out, which I don't want, so I'll cut you a deal. You can go out every night, with no curfew, when we haven't got a game the next day. The rest of the time, go out and get as pissed as you want, as long as you're up for training the next morning. But if one of you doesn't turn up, you'll all be fined."

There were lads sitting there with their mouths hanging wide open in total shock. Some of the new players wondered if it was a test. There are managers who wouldn't dream of letting their players have a beer in pre-season, but a squad of 25 lads who are living in each other's pockets for a week or 10 days will always need a little release. He gave us that bit of freedom, treated us like grown men instead of babies, and got the entire squad on board with a click of his fingers. In the end, we had two nights out on the whole trip, and they were only because the lads were sick of hotel food and went for a wander for something different to eat and a few beers. That year, we ended up winning the Championship title and getting into the Premier League – and for me it all started on the first day of pre-season, inside that meeting-room in the hotel.

Chris Morgan, who played under him when we were at United, reckons Warnock has split personalities – a laid-back family man and a born-winner football manager, who would do whatever he felt he needed to do to win a game. Warnock had a great knack of knowing how to take the pressure off his players when he could sense it building up, and I can see where Morgs is coming from. The two of them going at it after a game against Wolves was one of the highlights of the Warnock documentary that aired a few years back after the cameras followed us around.

Morgs had made a decision to swap the player he was marking with Phil Jagielka as we defended a corner, and Morgs' man ended up scoring. Warnock was absolutely spitting in the dressing-room after the game and the two of them had a bit of a barney, with Jags getting involved as well. I felt for Morgs a little bit. If he hadn't swapped men with Jags and we'd have conceded as a result, he would have got it in the neck anyway!

I had it myself with Warnock; that sense of: "I can't win here." I was beaten once by Nicky Shorey at Reading, who stuck a free-kick right into the top corner with that left foot of his, and Warnock had it in his head that we had to have a man on the post. I told him that it wouldn't work, because the other side would just crowd the box in front of me and I wouldn't be able to see a thing. But he wouldn't budge. A few months later we played West Ham and were 3-2 up in the 85th minute when Teddy Sheringham lined up a free-kick just outside the box.

We did what Warnock wanted and put a man on the post and, as I thought they would, West Ham dropped a load of bodies on top of me. I could barely see a thing, but the free-kick was coming straight at me until Jags stuck his knee out and deflected it into the corner. "Fucking hell, Paddy," Warnock shouted at me after the game. "Why did you have someone on the post?"

I can laugh about it now but we had a big argument about it at the time. We had a few over the years, actually, but they were all forgotten about immediately and that was the difference between us and someone like Kevin Blackwell, who would hold a grudge and let the whole thing fester. Me and Warnock had our good times, but we also clashed a lot and argued like cat and dog because we both just wanted to win so badly and deep down, I think a part of him also liked it when his players stood up for themselves and had a go back. He knew that he would certainly get that from me.

I would always lose the barney – because he was still the manager at the end of the day – but that wouldn't stop me having a damn good go at it! Other times he would just drop a few grenades in the dressing-room and get the lads to argue among themselves, sort stuff out and get a re-action. Without getting involved himself, he had sorted out problems before the players even knew they existed. He is tagged as a certain kind of manager, but the intelligence that went into it should never be under-estimated.

Warnock was a lot calmer later in his career when we worked to-gether at QPR, Leeds and Rotherham, but at Bury and United I saw him lose it completely at his players after games. At United he also developed this unnerving habit of getting undressed while he was shouting at us. He would be standing there naked, still going, and then he would get a towel and go into the shower. We could hear him shouting at us from the shower and then he'd come out and dry himself down. He would reach into his bag and pull out some pile cream before cocking his leg up on the bench and wiping this cream on his arse.

Throughout all this he was still grilling us and sometimes it went on for half-an-hour after the game. We would still be sitting there in our full kit, looking anywhere other than at him wiping cream on his arse until he told us to get out of his sight and get a shower.

In some ways I think Warnock's rants helped to sort out the players who would succeed for him and those who wouldn't. I used to use it as extra motivation when he had a pop at me and lads like Morgs and Alan Quinn loved it, too. But it didn't work with everyone. Warnock signed Danny Cullip for £250,000 from Brighton and sold him again after he'd played 15 games. I got on all right with Cullip, but he had a big argument with the Gaffer about a free-kick and suddenly he was gone.

Warnock just didn't think he fitted in with the rest of the lads and he wasn't afraid of getting rid of players if he didn't feel they were up to it. The do with Cullip was the last straw as far as his United career was con-cerned and he was gone almost as quickly as he had arrived. Mind you, I had far worse arguments with Warnock than Cullip did, so it probably helped that he liked me!

For whatever reason Warnock seems to have a reputation in the game for taking money off players and I seem to get asked quite often how much it cost me to play under him for all those years. For the record it never cost me a penny and, in the decade or so I spent playing under the man, I never saw anything like that going on. It baffles me to think people believe that: A) he would have been able to win eight promotions picking teams based on who gave him money and B) that behaviour like that wouldn't be found out. He used to say the odd thing as a throwaway comment, but I have never known it actually happen and I have been with him more than any other player.

I know from first-hand experience how things can get twisted in football. Every time a story is told, something is added on to make it sound better. Then it spreads and spreads and suddenly Warnock is apparently charging lads to play a game! What utter bollocks. But mud sticks and, when people hear something a few times, they usually just assume that it is true. I have had conversations in the past with people who have been *adamant* that Warnock only kept signing me because I was giving him backhanders. "Why else would he sign you?" they would ask. Because I did a good job for him, I say. I can't deny that Warnock was good for me and my career. But I like to think that I did all right for him as well.

I remember asking him, just after I had gone to Leeds, why the hell he wanted to sign me again. "Paddy, it's easy," he said. "I don't have to worry about you. If you're shit, it's because you've just been shit – it won't be because you've tossed it off. But when you're good, you're very good and I know exactly what I'm going to get from you. I can trust you to get on with your work." I was a good character around the place, but, when it came to a game, I was serious about my business.

Warnock loved his good, reliable senior players, but also showed how good he was with how he handled Adel Taarabt at QPR. So many managers would have given up on Adel because of how difficult he was, but Warnock knew he would give us something no-one else could if we indulged all the other shit that came with it. He even made Adel captain and was repaid a million times over when he lifted the Championship trophy on the last day of that season.

He knew the value of treating players as individuals, each with different needs and motivations. I've told the story before of our old fitness coach at United, a lad called Tony Daley, who decided I needed to lose some weight. I was always partial to the odd cake and a bit of chocolate, so I used to go out running in the evenings to try and keep my weight down on top of training all week and playing on Saturday. My best playing weight was 15 stone and, after Tony put me on a fitness plan, I lost 12 pounds. But I played horrendously for about a month to six weeks afterwards. I just didn't feel right and it was showing in my performances, so Warnock told me to get the weight back on. "You're meant to be your size," he told me. "Stop off at McDonald's on your way back home." I wasn't going to protest about that - and I still had a grin on my face a few hours later as I pulled into the drive-through!

28

A NEW LIFE

All good things come to an end. I can't say that I would have chosen a 7-0 defeat as the ideal farewell to professional football, but not many of us get to choose our goodbyes, do we? After almost 20 years and more than 600 appearances in the professional game, I couldn't be too disappointed with my lot – even if my career might have been extended further with another spell under Warnock.

He tried to get me in with him at Cardiff when he went there, but that plan was foiled when he tried to send Ben Amos back from his loan and Bolton refused. Amos had played for Bolton and Cardiff that year already, so Bolton wouldn't be able to send him out on loan anywhere else. Cardiff were also paying about eight grand of his wages, so Bolton understandably said no – and that scuppered the chances of me working with Warnock for a sixth time.

There was also a chance of him taking me to Blackburn. I was on my stag do in Benidorm that summer after leaving Rotherham United when he told me he might have got the Blackburn job, and asked if I'd go with him. Too right, I said. I was buzzing, thinking I might get another year yet. But by the time I got home, Warnock had changed his mind. The club had moved the goalposts with a few things and he had decided against it. I was gutted, but it just wasn't to be.

What's that saying about one door closing and another one opening? Soon after I got a call from Rob Page, my old Bramall Lane teammate. He had just been appointed as Northampton Town's new boss and wanted me to go in with him as player-goalkeeping coach. Warnock told me to hang fire when I mentioned it to him because he knew he would get a job eventually and take me with him, but I knew that this was a good chance to get my foot in the door with coaching. So I made the decision to take Pagey's offer.

Northampton were fresh into League One after promotion, which actually worked against us. Town had won the League Two title with 99 points under Chris Wilder before he went to Sheffield United, and it was quite a rare thing to take over a club that is on such a high. Usually managers go into a club that is struggling and someone has been sacked, but this was totally different. With the wage budget we had, just keeping the club in the division would have been an amazing achievement. But after the job Wilder had done, that was never going to be enough for the club and the fans.

I was registered as a player when I signed, but on that side of things I didn't do very much. I trained maybe two or three times if we were short, but, when I took coaching sessions, I volleyed more balls than I had ever done in my life. I ended up doing my cartilage in the knee that I had injured as a kid when nicking balls from the golf course! I hadn't had any trouble from that in nearly 20 years as a player and it went within two or three weeks of becoming a coach. Talk about good timing!

One of our 'keepers was Adam Smith, a lad who was at Leicester City before he was sacked for his part in an orgy with some Thai birds on a pre-season tour. A video of him, these girls and two of his Leicester teammates ended up on the internet and Leicester sacked all three of them – including the manager's son, James Pearson. Smithy was apologetic about the whole thing later, but with footballers there's always that risk of something getting out and the player ending up in real trouble. This case was a bit different – the players filmed it themselves and sent it to their mates back home – but nowadays there is always someone lurking with a phone if footballers let their guard down for a second.

Smith had a bit of an up-and-down time of it while me and Pagey were at Northampton and I remember the chairman coming into the office and asking what we had done with him. "What's gone off? Chris Wilder said he was the best 'keeper outside the Premier League." At the time United were desperate for a new goalkeeper. "Has Chris put a bid in for Smithy?" I asked the chairman. It turned out that he hadn't. "Well," I said, "he can't think he's that good then, can he?"

Knee troubles aside, I enjoyed coaching and, after playing so many games in my career and working with so many coaches, I had an idea what I was doing on the training ground. I knew how to put a session on and also took bits of what I liked from different coaches. I went into it with the attitude that every player is different and at first I really relished the opportunity.

But after a while it began to grind me down. I don't know if it was the travelling. I used to share the journey with Paul Wilkinson, who was Pagey's assistant manager and had been in charge of Bury when they were kicked out of the league. We would be up and away at 6am and getting in at half-11 at night, setting the alarm for the early hours to do it all again the following morning. I soon realised that I wasn't getting the same buzz from coaching that I had got from playing. I think you have to love coaching to be successful at it and I just didn't have that in me.

It probably didn't help that things weren't going our way out on the field and that had a knock-on effect with everything else. The fans there were used to winning after Wilder's time and it didn't take long for them to turn when we began to struggle a little bit. We knew the writing was on the wall when we lost 5-0 to Bristol Rovers – we were 4-0 down inside 25 minutes and one lad scored four goals, including a seven-minute hat-trick – and the call soon came that Pagey had been sacked. The coaches were asked if we would take the team between us in our next game, which we were unlucky to lose quite late on. But soon after we followed Pagey out of the exit door.

Being honest, it was a relief. I wasn't in a good place at all in the last few weeks of my time there and, when the call came, I rallied a few lads and went out on the piss to celebrate. I thought about all the time I could spend with my two young kids, Ashlin and Kaelin, rather than being on the motorway or at an under-23s game. I thought about maybe getting something closer to home. But most of all – and this might sound strange for someone who played professional football for nearly 20 years – I thought about how much I was looking forward to getting my weekends back.

Northampton also proved the final nail in the coffin of my second marriage. Me and Louise just drifted apart. I was sleeping in the spare room because of the time I was getting up and coming home, and then I bumped into an old flame, completely by chance. I had first met her some years earlier when I was still playing. She knew a mate of mine, Steve Greaves, and by chance they started chatting after she passed the bar he was standing at. When they eventually said their goodbyes and he walked over to my table, I had one question on my lips.

Who the fuck is that?

"Don't you bother her," Steve smiled. "She's way out of your league." I gave it a go anyway and we had about three months together before she fucked me off. Her reason? She didn't want to go out with a footballer.

I saw her once in the next 10 years, just a brief: "Hello, you all right?" at her baby shower, and that was it. Then, just as things reached rock-bottom in my marriage to Louise, we saw each other five times in a single week. At the supermarket, at the nursery, in a pub at a 30th birthday we were both at. She was there with her husband at the time and I was meant to be going with Louise, but she couldn't be arsed and told me to go with my mates. I bumped into my ex at the bar and we ended up talking about our lives.

She had heard that I was happily married and I told her I had been sleeping in the spare bedroom for months. She hadn't been happy with her fella for two years and one thing led to another. We ended up messaging each other and had a six-week affair, which only ended when she gave me an ultimatum: "I can't do this any longer. It's either you or him." It was another tough decision in my life, but deep down I knew what was right. I left Louise and we decided to go for it.

But it wasn't a straightforward time. I was married with two kids and you've got to have a pair of bollocks about you to make a decision like that, leaving your wife and young family. But at the same time you can't stay with someone just for the children. I firmly believe that. I would have just been lying to myself about everything and no-one knows the harm that that might have caused further down the line.

That wasn't enough to stop the feelings of guilt, though, and I remember confiding in a few of my mates and telling them that I felt horrible over what I had done. "Fair play to you," one of them said. "People stay in relationships for the wrong reasons, then they get to 50 or 60 years old and they're thinking: 'I don't even love this twat.' They've spent the last however many years miserable, and for what?" He was spot-on.

Leaving football gave me a sense of freedom that I never realised I was missing until I tasted it again and it dawned on me that, for about 10 months of the year, for 20 years, my life was dictated by the game. I dread to think how much of my kids' lives I missed because I had been away with work and that is time that I will never get back as they grow older. People ask me now if I miss football and I tell them I don't, not one bit.

In a weird way I have more structure now to my life. Footballers are rewarded very well at the top levels, but they are also basically the property of the clubs in return. Now I am my own boss with a car transporting company I set up, after falling into that line of work almost completely by accident.

I didn't do anything for about six months after Northampton apart from play golf, drink and take the dog for walks. That was my life. I was sleeping in the afternoons just to break up the boredom and some days I felt so down that I didn't see the point in getting out of bed at all. My life had changed completely and, although I love it now, I had absolutely no idea where it was going at the time. Another defining moment began with a simple phone call.

This time it was from a mate who had just started his own transport company. "Do you fancy coming to work a few days a week for me?" he asked. "You need a purpose to get up every morning." I knew he was right, so I took it. Immediately I told him I wanted to work a full week. All or nothing. I love driving anyway and I love my own company, so I began a new life on the road – picking up cars and dropping them off.

Looking back, my mate did me a big favour but we fell out when a copper pulled me over, just as I was coming out of Southampton. Legally I was only allowed to carry so much weight on the back of the truck and, when it was weighed, I was found to be overweight. Insert your own joke here! I had to take the car off the back of the truck immediately and someone else had to come and pick it up. The copper pulled me to one side and gave me some advice. "Listen, if you kill someone on your way home because you're overweight, it won't be your boss who will do time. It'll be you."

I rang my mate and told him what had happened. He just laughed. "Well, no-one's died, have they?" he said. I got back, parked the truck up and dropped the keys straight off at his house. "Stick your job up your arse," I told him. "I'm going on my own."

I set things up a couple of days later and haven't looked back since.

I was grateful to get that little kick up the arse to give me a purpose in my life again, but I do feel that it should have come from someone inside football – maybe the Professional Footballers' Association. I have never to this day had as much as a call or a message from them to see how I was coping with life after football and if my head was all right. Because at times, it wasn't. I once told Louise in a video that I was going to kill myself.

I had no intention of doing it – it was a cry for help completely. But so many footballers do go through things like that when they retire and I can understand why some do struggle mentally after they hang up their boots. You go from training day in, day out with your teammates and picking up a healthy wage, playing in front of thousands of people every week... and then it's gone. Suddenly you're old, too old to work, and no-one wants you. That's how it feels. No-one cares any more. Imagine how many players have felt those same things and not had the help that they needed to get through it. It's frightening.

I also count myself fortunate to be in a decent place financially, which is not something all ex-footballers can say. I'm not a millionaire, and I would have been a lot better off financially if I had stayed with my first wife. Two divorces, it turns out, can cost you a few quid! At one point I was paying Karen five grand a month plus her mortgage of £1,000 a month and £500 for her car. I was too soft with her and it was a fair chunk of money that I could have saved instead. But still I am comfortable. I own my business outright and I have got a few things tied up elsewhere. But I have seen and heard some absolute horror stories about people preying on footballers and pretending to be looking after their finances, while absolutely stitching them up. I always tried to be really careful with who I trusted and making my own decisions when it came to my money. Not that that always made me better off!

One of my ideas for retirement was to build some houses with a mate of mine, Gav Hirst. We bought some land at Greasbrough in Rotherham and built four houses on it. That was our first mistake – we should have built three-bed semis instead. Then we found out that there was a strip of land going right through the plot that someone else owned and our solicitor decided not to tell us about it. That cost us another £20,000 and, although we eventually built the houses and sold them, we did well to break even on the whole venture. For the stress and everything else that came with it, it wasn't worth it at all.

My next plan was to buy houses that actually already existed and rent them out. I couldn't see anything going wrong, until it did. The family who were in the house in Halifax hadn't paid November's rent. I knew they had two young kids, so I told them not to worry about paying it, or December's either. It was Christmas and I knew what it was like for a family in Halifax with two kids, trying to make ends meet. I was trying to do the right thing, but it was thrown back in my face. I didn't see another penny. In the end, I got some people a friend of mine knew to go and have a quiet word and get the family out. But they ended up getting back in and I had to go through the proper channels to evict them for good. It took a good 11 months before anything happened. When we finally got the keys back, they had absolutely *wrecked* the place. In doing it back up again, court fees, bailiffs and loss of rent, the whole thing probably cost me 10 grand. As soon as the house was habitable again, I sold it on and cut my losses.

***

In hindsight I probably should have done the same with my football career before I was tempted out of retirement to dust off the gloves again. Out of the blue one day a mate of mine rang me to ask if I fancied playing for his team in the Toolstation Northern Counties East League's Premier Division. It's officially the ninth tier of English football and I politely declined the offer. "Do you know what?" I told my mate. "I haven't played for two or three years now and I don't know if I can be arsed."

Then I got another call. "Will you come and play for Maltby?" It was another good pal of mine, Scott Mason, who had become Maltby Main's joint manager. I played a lot of golf with Scott at Sitwell Golf Club and we used to go out drinking in Wickersley. "Come on, for me," he pleaded. "Go on then," I said. "I'll give it a crack, since it's you."

It was a few quid in my pocket, a bit of spending money, and I thought: *why not?* I thought I had kept myself relatively fit – *Paddy fit,* anyway – and my first game for Maltby was away at Worksop Town on August 12th, 2017. There were nearly 400 fans there and I was getting stick from behind my goal. It was like the good old days. I lasted 10 minutes.

I went to kick the ball clear and my hamstring went straightaway. Six weeks later I made my big comeback in an FA Vase match at Ashton Athletic. While I was out injured, I had tried to build my legs up and strengthen them because they were weak as piss, but it didn't look particularly promising for my afternoon when I was beaten for the opening goal after 20 seconds of the game. We went 2-0 down in the second half before I dropped the ball again just outside my box and pinged it downfield. My thigh went this time. I came straight off, walked into the changing-rooms and threw my boots and gloves straight in the bin. That was me, done and dusted.

I was probably daft to think I could do myself justice. I could still catch the ball and make saves, but it was all the other little bits and bobs that went with being a goalkeeper. My legs had gone, for a start, and my timing was all wrong. I fucked up for one of the goals against Ashton because I couldn't make my mind up whether to come or stay. In my prime I would have instinctively known what to do, but my decision-making was shot. And then the couple of injuries came and I knew I was done.

I had played at Wembley in front of 80,000 and at Ashton's Brocstedes Park with 64 watching on and I still got the buzz when that first whistle sounded – even if I was struggling to breathe in the shirt I had been given. Maltby's chief executive reckons he had to buy an XXXL shirt when I arrived, but I am convinced it was more like a medium! Either way it is now signed and hangs on his office wall as a memento of my short but eventful time there.

After hobbling off, I watched the rest of the Ashton game from the bar, having a beer with a Maltby fan called Jack Trueman. He also supported Wednesday and absolutely hated me at first. He refused to speak to me on the team bus. But we bonded over a pint in the bar, went out that night when we got back and became really good mates.

Isn't that what football is *really* about? I thought it was quite fitting that my career ended pretty much as it had started a few decades earlier; playing at the lower levels, hard but fair, and having a pint in the bar afterwards. In-between there were some really good times and some incredibly low points as well. But as I look back now, I wouldn't change a minute of it for the world.

29

EXTRA TIME

You fat bastard!
- Football fans, everywhere

How many times do you think I have heard that aimed at me, in my career and my life? I honestly would not even know where to start if I had to guess. I played more than 600 games for nine clubs in my professional career of 20 years and must have heard it in every single one. Having thousands of people standing behind me and chanting personal stuff like that? I loved every minute of it. Honestly. It sounds weird, doesn't it? But the truth is that I could look people who were shouting abuse at me straight in the eye and laugh because deep down I knew that they would give up almost anything to be playing on the pitch that I was on.

I can still picture some of them now, screaming stuff at me like, 'You fat wanker, I've shagged your wife." Some of them were about 25 stone and I used to ask them where they got their mirrors from, because I wanted one! I once played away at Rotherham and was offered a pork pie from behind the goal. I would like to say I declined, but I ended up playing with heartburn throughout the entire second half.

If anything the abuse actually inspired me. These people who were shouting all sorts had actually *paid* to watch me play football and it gave me even more motivation to perform. But in respect of having the mental strength to be able to rise above it, I was lucky. A lot of lads I played with would have wilted under that strain but honestly, not once did it affect me during my playing career. I am not saying that I was perfect or superior to anyone else in any way. Far from it. Playing football made me quite a defensive person and I do believe that being a goalkeeper played a part in that. I was out there on my own and got the blame for a lot of things, so it was important that I developed the ability and confidence to stand up for myself. If someone had a dig at me and I felt it wasn't my fault, then the lot would go off and I wouldn't hold back. Even after I finished football, I had a lot of road rage and pent-up anger. When Ian Wright went into the jungle on *I'm a Celebrity...* and talked about his anger issues, I could relate to that a lot.

It was something I had to work on earlier in my career. I came from a council-estate environment, where I had to look after myself, and I believe that upbringing instilled something in me – a mental toughness and resilience that stood me in good stead later in my life. I had far worse chucked at me than a few words about my weight. I suffered heartbreak and rejection at a young age at Halifax and further down the line I was beaten up, bitten and betrayed.

I saw everything I had worked for since I played on parks pitches in Halifax almost snatched away from me because of an innocent mistake and among all that I played for my country and in the Premier League. I can't imagine that there are many footballers who have gone through such a range of ups and downs. But everyone has their own problems and issues on and off the pitch and I was no different. A lot of people may have gone under, but I took things on the chin, apologised when I needed to and tried to move forward with my life.

I also count myself incredibly fortunate that I haven't suffered mentally to the same extent as some of my former teammates. I was in a dark place during the nine months I wasn't able to see my kids but I can't imagine what someone like Gary Speed, who I played with at Sheffield United, went through. Speedo was someone I looked up to over the years, even before I got the chance to play alongside him, and I would have said that he was one of the strongest people I had ever met, character-wise.

It was a massive shock when I found out that he had taken his own life in 2011. On the surface he had everything. He had an unbelievable career and was doing well in management, too – in charge of his national team. He had a family and was always talking about his kids, but something drove him to that dark place that no-one who hasn't been there could possibly begin to imagine.

I spoke to another former United teammate, David Cotterill, just after he had completed a year sober. Cotts had his troubles with drinking and tried to end his life three times, but he came out of the other side and has helped me a couple of times. Footballers have their own stresses and struggles and are in no way immune to issues, either mental or physical. Christian Nade, who I played with at United in the Premier League and scored an iconic winner against Arsenal, tried to drown himself in a river a few years ago.

No amount of money or success can make up for what goes off in the brain, any more than it could prevent any physical issue. Ugo Ehiogu, who I also played with at United, died at Spurs' training ground after suffering a heart attack. Liam Miller, my old Irish teammate, passed away from cancer at 36 years old. It's a cliché, but it's true – it's so important to enjoy life while you can before it is taken away.

A few years back we lost Tony, my brother from my dad's first marriage. He had taken lots of drugs and stuff like that over the years and eventually it just took its toll. For the last three or four years of his life my mum and dad had to look after him and for the last six months he was in a home. He died on New Year's Eve, not long past his 50th birthday, and I will never forget the day of the funeral. It pissed it down with rain and my dad just stood there, shaking. I prefer to remember Tony as the person who took me to my first ever football game, rather than how he was towards the end of his life.

I am close to my dad and still speak to my mum about four or five times every day. They both had kids in previous marriages, so we have quite a big family. Sean, my brother, is a schoolteacher and has adopted a two-year-old lad with his husband, Paul. I couldn't be any prouder of him and what he has achieved. I stayed close with Sean, but drifted apart from my other siblings, Paul, Marie and another Tony, over the last 10 years. Recently we have made an effort to meet up more. When everything else is stripped away, family is all we really have, isn't it?

Football has given me so much, but I am a father of four children firstly and a former goalkeeper second. I was lucky enough to make a living from playing catch for two decades, but anything I achieved in the game is completely insignificant compared with Beth, Jonjo, Ashlin and Kaelin. I live a comfortable life and, although I don't get 30 grand into my bank every month any more, I am happy.

I no longer have people hanging on to me because I am a footballer; when I was playing and earning a few quid, I couldn't get them off the phone. Now my career is all over, I don't hear from half of them any more. I am happy with that, but life isn't all plain sailing. I still take propranolol tablets to calm me down as an after-effect of the battle to be able to see my children, and I do get anxious sometimes in everyday life. It happens sometimes when I'm in a crowded place or when I can't deal with something that's winding me up.

Last Christmas I was in a shop and I couldn't cope with the queues building up behind me and how slow the staff were at the tills. I had to leave the stuff and get out of there. I have got it largely under control, but I have been told that it might affect me for the rest of my life. I may come across to some people as a tough cookie because of what I dealt with on the pitch, but away from that I am just a human being like everyone else.

Still, I would not change anything that has happened to me. All the shit times I have been through have made me a stronger person and I do firmly believe that everything happens for a reason. I don't have a single regret. Sure, there are things that I would have handled differently in my past if I had the chance, but I don't look back and *regret* anything. I wish that my private life had been private rather than being plastered all over the newspapers, but I am also glad to have had the chance to put the record straight about a few things that have happened throughout my career.

The people who were hammering me for being a greedy bastard when I left United for QPR were very quiet when I cancelled my contract at Bury because I didn't want to take their money and toss it off. The way I was treated at a couple of clubs in my time was disgusting and it was only towards the back end of my career that I realised the beautiful game can sometimes have a very ugly side to it. That doesn't make me any less proud of what I achieved and I think that anyone who becomes a professional footballer should feel that same pride, however he or she gets there.

I personally believe I massively over-achieved in my career considering my ability levels and a lot of that was because of my own self-determination. I still find it staggering that I did not have a full-time goalkeeping coach until I was 25 years old, by which time I had almost reached the Premier League and was on the verge of playing for my country.

How might my career have gone if I'd had that coaching earlier? Who knows? It would be easy to sit back and be bitter about it, wondering:

"What if?" But the truth is that I'll never know. It just as easily could have gone the other way. I prefer to look at what I did. Going from parks pitches to Premier League, playing for my country and being involved in probably the most famous goal in English football history isn't a bad lot, and I am incredibly proud of every minute.

Not bad, I guess, for a fat bastard from Halifax...

ACKNOWLEDGEMENTS

My life has always been up and down, a very rollercoaster experience, and I wanted to do this book to clear up a few things that have been written about me over the years and put my side of the story across. Going back over my life has made me realise how well I did in my career, considering the cards I was dealt and I must thank my family, and primarily Mum and Dad, for being by my side throughout the ups and the downs. I hope I did you proud.

To my kids, Beth, Jonjo, Kaelin and Ashlin. My greatest achievements in life. I love you all more than you could ever know and I am so lucky to have four amazing children. Thank you to every club that I have ever played for and to every supporter who cheered me on over the years. And thanks to the ones who chanted abuse at me, too, for helping to spur me on.

I am hugely grateful to every goalkeeping coach I ever worked with during my career, but especially to Andy Leaning. I hope it comes across in this book how much he has helped me over the years, on and off the pitch. The same with The Gaffer, Neil Warnock. We had some real lows together, but also some unbelievable highs and I will always be grateful for him taking a chance on the chubby 'keeper playing for Bradford Park Avenue. I don't think either of us thought at the time we would later get to the Premier League, twice. Thank you for everything.

And, last but not least, thanks to Danny Hall and Vertical Editions for helping to write and then publish this book. I didn't realise what a big project it would be and I think he did a fantastic job. I hope you had as much fun reading it as we did putting it together.

- Paddy Kenny, 2020

When the chance came to work with Paddy on this book, in late 2019, I knew it was an opportunity I couldn't pass up. But it was only after sitting down with him that I realised how incredible his life story has been. We come from similar working-class backgrounds and for him to have reached the Premier League and play for his country is an unbelievable achievement – and one that I know he is rightly very proud of.

I would like to acknowledge the support that my partner Natalie has once again offered me throughout the book-writing process and also thank my editor at The Star, Nancy Fielder, for allowing me to work on it. Thanks, too, to Janice Stretton, Liam Collins and Nicky Boella North for their help with transcription; to everyone who took the time to read the book before it was printed and offer help, advice or a review; to Richard Markham for the front-cover image and to David Bond for his invaluable proofreading work. Rob Hollingworth and Andrew Bell provided helpful and much-appreciated legal advice, while Frank Orrell, Marisa Cashill, Kevin Cookson, Sam Todd and Darrell Johnson, Nick Dunhill, David Watts and Wilf Race either provided or helped to source photographs. Thanks to you all.

I should also acknowledge Paddy's commitment and honesty during the many, many hours, weeks and months we worked together on this project. As someone who used to watch him from the Bramall Lane terraces, it has at times been a strange experience to work with him to document his story – but also a very rewarding one. I only hope to have done it some justice.

- Danny Hall, 2020

The Ecstasy: Saving a penalty for the Blades at Bramall Lane against Barnsley. Photo: Martyn Harrison